Transformative Leadership in Education

In the volatile, uncertain, complex, and ambiguous world of education today, leaders need to take an engaged, activist, and courageous approach to help build optimistic futures for all students. *Transformative Leadership in Education* presents an alternative approach to leadership for deep and equitable change. Using vignettes, stories, research, and drawing on scholarship from a range of disciplines, noted scholar Carolyn M. Shields explores the concept of transformative leadership and its potential to create learning environments that are just and inclusive. Drawing on examples from transformative school leaders, Shields demonstrates that this leadership can promote academic achievement, family and community empowerment, democratic engagement, and global citizenship.

Special features include:

- End-of-chapter guiding questions to help readers reflect on their own practice and to apply the concepts in their own contexts.
- Vignettes and stories from students, teachers, and community members to illustrate how transformative leadership can promote academic achievement and democratic engagement.
- A robust companion website with extra resources, video and audio clips, and an author blog to further understanding and lead to sustained action toward the goals of transformative leadership. Please visit www.routledge.com/cw/shields

This exciting text will appeal to all aspiring and practicing leaders who want to prepare students to be successful, caring, and engaged citizens of the global community.

Carolyn M. Shields is Dean of the College of Education at Wayne State University, Detroit, USA.

Transformative Leadership in Education

Equitable Change in an Uncertain and Complex World

Carolyn M. Shields

 Routledge
Taylor & Francis Group

NEW YORK AND LONDON

Please visit the companion website at www.routledge.com/cw/shields

First published 2013
by Routledge
711 Third Avenue, New York, NY 10017

Simultaneously published in the UK
by Routledge
2 Park Square, Milton Park, Abingdon, Oxon OX14 4RN

Routledge is an imprint of the Taylor & Francis Group, an informa business

Library of Congress Cataloging in Publication Data
Shields, Carolyn M.
Transformative leadership in education : equitable change in an uncertain
and complex world / Carolyn M. Shields.
p. cm.
Includes bibliographical references and index.
1. Educational leadership. I. Title.
LB2806.S356 2012
371.2'07—dc23
2012001593

ISBN: 978-0-415-89253-7 (hbk)
ISBN: 978-0-415-89254-4 (pbk)
ISBN: 978-0-203-81440-6 (ebk)

Typeset in Sabon
by RefineCatch Limited, Bungay, Suffolk, UK

Table of Contents

Preface

Change is the order of the day. From the time Heraclitus said in the 6th century BCE that the only constant is change itself, educators have been wrestling with how to deal with change—changing fiscal environments, increased demands for accountability, changing demographics, new policies, difficult personnel issues and so forth. This book is an attempt to help leaders think about addressing the complex questions, issues, and dilemmas that constitute change. It is not intended to be an objective (dry) scholarly treatise on education, but instead an impassioned, yet reasoned plea for educational leaders to think and act differently, to conceptualize their roles and their work for the 21st century rather than for the past, and to acknowledge the changing qualities of the world in which they exercise leadership. I do not, will not, and cannot offer definitive answers, prescriptions, steps to follow—for those belong to the previous world of scientific management. Instead, I offer reflections on values, approaches, concepts, and theories that offer hope and promise for education today.

To do so, I will first attempt to demonstrate the need for change, arguing that as Maxine Greene stated (1998), we live in a "world of unfulfilled promises," and that, as educational leaders, we have a role to play in their fulfillment. I will introduce readers to two relevant concepts that will act as a kind of refrain throughout the book. The first emphasizes the complex and rapidly changing nature of our world and of institutions and organizations that are trying to survive, indeed thrive, within it. Here, my argument is that understanding the educational *context* in which we exercise leadership is critically important. The second is the concept of *transformative leadership*—an approach to leadership that is clearly critical and adaptive rather than technical or mechanistic, one that focuses on both intellectual achievement and social justice (broadly conceptualized).

Overview of the Book

Each concept will be developed using current research, examples from transformative school leaders, stories, narratives, and data to help school leaders understand how transformative leadership can promote academic achievement, family and community empowerment, democratic engagement, and global citizenship.

In Chapter 1, I elaborate the current *context* of educational leadership, perhaps best represented by the concept of a VUCA world (a world dominated by volatility, uncertainty, complexity, and ambiguity). Here I show how VUCA helps to explain some of the current challenges and opportunities facing educational leaders. Chapter 2 discusses the confusing multiplicity of leadership theories and argues that *transformative leadership* differs from other current leadership concepts and theories and offers considerable promise for organizational change in today's context. In Chapter 3, I argue that the changes needed are deep and equitable and that their achievement requires both the deconstruction and reconstruction of dominant knowledge frameworks. In other words, we need to change the way we think. Chapter 4 emphasizes that, despite the multiple demands and pressures on school leaders, they must determine how to use their power morally and equitably. Then, the chapter offers examples of both negative and positive uses of power. In Chapter 5, we focus on a discussion of the dual and sometimes competing goals of education—the notion of both private and public good and how education can, and should, contribute to each. Chapter 6 acknowledges that the reach of transformative leadership extends to global awareness and includes recognition of inequity and disparity, not only at home but throughout the world. Here the discussion focuses on identity and interconnectedness in a global community and on the need to foster a concept I call global citizenship. In Chapter 7 I return to the key concepts of optimism, hope, promise, and moral courage—key tenets of transformative leadership. In this chapter, I draw extensively on the experiences of practicing school leaders to pull together the concepts from the book and to further demonstrate some of the potential and possibilities of transformative leadership. Chapter 8 ties these concepts together and summarizes, again, the benefits of transformative leadership to more adequately address the complex challenges of providing excellent and equitable education for all students. Then, following the Conclusion, the Appendix presents a case (with some suggested responses) that might form the basis for further consideration of the issues raised here and how to implement them in a school site.

Following each chapter, I have included a series of questions intended to promote further reflection and hopefully action on the part of concerned and engaged educators and educational leaders. The questions are intended not only for individual consideration, but could also form the basis for discussion by book study groups or school staffs as a whole.

Overall, this book explores how transformative leaders can not only offer a critique of the current system but, through an engaged, activist, and courageous approach, how they can also create learning environments that promote both academic excellence and civil society, private and public good, and a more optimistic and hopeful future. Thus, it shows how transformative leadership holds the potential for the significant transformation of schools in this complex and uncertain world of the 21st century.

Related Website

In each chapter, readers will find vignettes of schools and stories of school leaders. Sometimes, there will also be stories from students, teachers, or community members. Further information, audio passages, video clips, and supporting articles for further reading will be available on a dedicated website and available to those who purchase this book. To ensure readers find these additional materials on the website, you will notice an icon ⓣ indicating a direct connection to additional material. There you will find elaborated transcripts, a few pictures, and additional and related stories as well as links to supplemental readings, original texts, and related websites. Readers will also be able to participate in a blog of questions and comments from readers, and responses by the author. The symbol ⓢ throughout the book will suggest some possible topics for beginning the discussion. They are not restrictive, but only suggestive of possible issues that readers might want to explore in the safety of anonymity and with others concerned about the issues. This is your chance to ask a question, comment, agree or disagree with the author, further consider the material presented and so forth. This symbol is intended as a signal that it may be useful here to stop, reflect, and engage in some dialogue about the topic under discussion. It is my hope that the website will further our understanding of the nature of a critical and ongoing, dialogic reflection and lead to more sustained action toward the goals of transformative leadership.

Underlying Assumptions

As with my other books, I write assuming that *educational leaders* are not just those in formal positions of authority, but that the term includes teachers and other educators whose goal is simply to "make a difference." I assume that these educators want to do the best job they can, that they are dedicated to the success of their schools, their students, and committed to their communities. At the same time, my assumption is that, too often, educators do not necessarily know how to lead in a VUCA world of relentless change and so fall back on past practice, on mantras such as "best practice," or commonly accepted and widely adopted interventions such as "professional learning communities" or "Effective Behavior Systems"—sometimes without reflecting on the underlying assumptions and hidden messages contained therein. It is for these reasons I propose a form of leadership that explicitly addresses assumptions, goals, and values, leadership that is critically conscious of itself, and reflective of its impact on the various groups that comprise any school community.

As in previous books, I also write with the conviction that schools are more diverse than many of us recognize, that diversity of ability, interests, and ideologies co-exists with diversity of ethnicity, language, religion, or sexual orientation. For that reason, many of the dominant Eurocentric perspectives and assumptions that have guided and undergirded western education during the past decades need to be explicitly revisited to determine the extent to which they are still appropriate norms and/or the ways in which they have become hegemonic—marginalizing and disadvantaging some and advantaging and privileging others.

Unlike in my other books, I emphasize here a more global perspective, in the firm conviction that more global awareness is necessary for several reasons. Helping educators become more aware of multiple realities will provide the impetus for creating learning environments in which more students feel welcome and valued and in which they find space for the recognition of their unique lived experiences. This includes both connecting domestic students to students in other cultures and contexts as well as ensuring that all educators are better equipped to address the needs of the many students who, in growing numbers, come from those cultures.

This does *not* require, as is often stated, that educators know enough about the cultures and backgrounds of each student in their class to teach *about* them. Indeed, attempting to do so not only places undue pressure on educators, it results in superficial and essentializing treatment of differences. At the same time, I firmly believe that all educators—administrators and teachers alike—must learn to create spaces in which students can bring the reality of their varying experiences and perspectives into the classroom learning situations in order to enhance and make sense of the formal curriculum. This is consistent with curriculum theorists who define curriculum not as formal texts, standards, or lesson plans, but as "complicated conversation" (Pinar, 2004) or as the "conversation that makes sense of things" (Grumet, 1995). Taking the tenets of this book and of transformative leadership seriously will, first, result in more engaging, more challenging, and more equitable learning environments. Second, it will suggest that a clear vision of individual and collective learning should replace the current emphasis on test-taking and Adequate Yearly Progress and refocus the institution on intellectual development, respect for and understanding of differences, global curiosity and responsibility, individual excellence and global citizenship.

It thus becomes clear that my goal is twofold: a reorganization of schools so that society as a whole benefits from transformative leadership, and a reconceptualization of learning and pedagogy that engages students in intellectual inquiry and that (re) connects them to the challenges, inequities, beauties, and wonders of the marvelously diverse and complex world in which we live.

Acknowledgments

This book owes its existence to many people, but especially to the students, teachers, and school leaders with whom I have had the opportunity to explore these challenges, to discuss these topics, and to work to introduce positive change. Without the stories that form the fabric of this work, that provide the impetus, the inspiration, and the validation for our work, this book and its accompanying website would be an empty shell. My heartfelt thanks go to all who will recognize themselves in these pages. Most importantly, I am sustained by the ongoing enthusiasm of the transformative leaders I have had the privilege to know (many of them my former students), who strive every day to make a difference in the lives of children and who continue to assure me that these ideas are useful and relevant. This book is dedicated to all of you.

Chapter 1

Living in a World of Unfulfilled Promises

Examining the Context for Educational Leadership

Why am I known as the "Asian freak?" Why are my eyes slanty and why do people think it's funny? Why does everyone think I eat fried rice or chop suey? . . . Why do people tell me to go back where I came from and make me feel like I don't belong? Why am I like this? Why can't I fit in? I can't fit in because I'm Asian.

(Amy, fourth grade)

I came to these shores as a refugee, kicked out of Uganda during Idi Amin's expulsion. We used to have servants and a huge house, but when we arrived here, we had nothing. I did not know how to skate, I wore hand-me-down clothes. And when I tried to make friends, they said my house stank of curry. At school, I was the token Indian, always asked about my culture and my religion.

(Satish, now a PhD consultant)

I live with my father and younger brother in a shelter. Life is difficult and school makes it even more so. I can't go to the craft stores to buy figures for those projects the teacher is always assigning. When we had to do a project on states, mine was Florida. We were supposed to bring food for the class that represented the state. I thought perhaps I could afford orange juice, but she said that wasn't food.

(Danny, fifth grade)

The above vignettes, while dramatic and shocking, represent the real stories of real children who suffer indignities, marginalization, prejudice, and exclusion on a daily basis. They have names; they have faces. They have hopes and dreams; but too often they dry up like a "raisin in the sun" (Hughes, 1951). They often suffer in silence, fearful that speaking up or speaking out will draw more unwanted attention to themselves and their families. They are only a few of the thousands of children for whom, on a daily basis, schools fail to provide hope and the promise of a better future. The first two struggled to succeed. Their families made sacrifices for the possibility of a better future for their children, but the chips were still stacked against them. The third will likely drop out of school before tenth grade, becoming another statistic in an international crisis of school failure, believing (all too correctly) that school is not really for the likes of him. Another 100 million children worldwide are unlikely ever to be able to attend school at all.

Many of us are too willing to ignore these realities, perhaps forgetting, perhaps unwilling to openly admit that, for some, the Great American Dream is a myth. We are reluctant to acknowledge that not everyone who works hard enough and who subscribes to "traditional American values" can climb the ladder of success. The disproportionate incarceration or arrest rates of African Americans or Hispanic Americans attest to this, as do the ongoing academic achievement gaps between White students and their non-White classmates. Additionally, immigrants by the thousand come to North America on an annual basis seeking opportunities for themselves and their families, only to find their credentials are not valued, their ways are mocked or, worse, feared, and their opportunities are often limited by societal norms and legislative barriers to success. In 1988, Maxine Green addressed this issue, saying that we need to raise the critical consciousness of students so as to facilitate collective action against injustice, and urging that we teach

> to the end of arousing a consciousness of membership, active and participant membership in a society of unfulfilled promises—teaching for what Paulo Freire used to call "conscientization" (1970), heightened social consciousness, a wide-awakeness that might make injustice unendurable.
>
> (p. xxx)

A "society of unfulfilled promises" is a phrase that dramatically expresses some of the beliefs underlying this book, yet is one with which not everyone can identify. At a recent academic conference, when one of my doctoral students introduced our joint paper with the above quotation, a member of the audience interrupted asking, "What do you mean by unfulfilled promise?" We were surprised but glad the person had asked for clarification. Our intent was to build upon what we had believed to be quite obvious—the fact that some people, by virtue of an accident of birth (poverty or privilege, skin color, location) have more or fewer opportunities than others. Some groups of people in our society are more likely to be incarcerated, to fail to graduate from high school or to attend college, and some are less likely to be hired and so forth. The promise of equal opportunity for everyone has yet to be realized—and we were certain this was something everyone recognized and cared about. The fact that this was and is not the case provides additional support for the need for this book.

A Changing Global Context

In the last few years, the world has seen many changes that obviously were not welcome:

- A global fiscal crisis has increased the debt of almost every nation and brought untold hardship, starvation, and death to millions of people worldwide.
- The Deepwater Horizon oil spill that began on April 20, 2010, killed 11 men, and resulted in millions of gallons of crude oil being leaked into the Gulf of Mexico.
- The March 2011, 9.0-magnitude earthquake and a subsequent devastating tsunami hit Japan, killing over 12,000 people. The human scope of this disaster, however, was eclipsed by international fear related to the resulting failure of some of Japan's nuclear reactors.

In other words, although change is the order of the day, often we must endure change we do not want, change we cannot predict, change we definitely cannot control, and change to which we often lack an appropriate response. Often the magnitude of uncontrollable change and the images with which we are bombarded on every side—crime, earthquakes, oil spills, tsunamis, death, disaster—frighten us. At other times, change frustrates us. At still other times, it angers us and even brings us into confrontation with others who hold different perspectives on the challenges and what should be done. Sometimes it leaves us feeling impotent and in despair.

What is clear is that we can never predict, command, and control all the forces that impinge on the successful operation of our organizations. Engineers promised that safeguards were in place to prevent oil spills in offshore waters. Scientists believed they had instituted sufficient safeguards to prevent a nuclear leak in Japan. Managers of large manufacturing corporations, energy producers, high-tech communications corporations, and global money markets all proceeded under the illusion that huge profits and unbridled expansion could continue—until the global economic downturn of the 21st century caused turmoil, bankruptcy, collapse, and economic crises.

At the same time, there is much that is within our control—and many changes we can influence, initiate, and support. Because most people are quite willing to acknowledge that the world has changed, we can now argue the relevance of educational assumptions, policies, and practices that take global changes into account. The world in which many educators grew up—communities in which almost everyone looked like them, spoke the same language, and even went to the same church, and in which the school population was, on the surface, similarly homogeneous, is no longer today's reality.

We are well aware that in most developed countries, the rich are still getting richer and the poor poorer; Whoriskey (2011) reported that

> the median net worth of a white family now stands at 20 times that of a black family and 18 times that of a Hispanic family—roughly twice the gap that existed before the recession and the biggest gap since data began being collected in 1984.
>
> (¶4)

Statistics demonstrate that, in the United States alone, 1.3 million children are homeless and that members of visible minority groups are still disproportionately represented on welfare rolls and in prisons. Those with lower incomes are not only struggling for survival, but suffer more severe and chronic illness than their more advantaged neighbors. Add to these facts the knowledge that one billion people worldwide have no access at all to clean water; that three billion have no access to proper sanitation; and over 300,000 children in Rwanda alone live in child-headed households. Now add to these human issues, considerations of the degradation of our oceans, the destruction of rainforests, the rapid decline in the world's glaciers, and the impending extinction of many plant and animal species. It is certainly not an exaggeration to say that something is seriously wrong. Indeed, our planet is in crisis.

Education is not immune. As the stakes rise in terms of desired outcomes on standardized tests and student demographics change rapidly, calls for vouchers, for political takeovers of large urban school districts, for increasing the number of charter schools, for restructuring existing systems and increased accountability abound. Teachers across the country are under attack. In March 2011, 22,000 teachers in California were given "pink slips" with many not expected to be recalled. The future of teachers' unions and collective bargaining are in question in Minnesota, Michigan, and elsewhere. Half of Detroit's public schools are likely to close in the next few years, and many of those that survive will become charter schools; class sizes are predicted to rise to 60 students per class.

Educators in the United States and other developed countries are increasingly pressured by legislators and members of the general public to address the perpetual "achievement gap" related to ethnicity, social class, home language, and other cultural differences. Globally, despite the United Nation's goal of free, universal education, over 100 million primary-school-age children do not attend school. Educational leaders are confronted by demands for accountability, for meeting standards for Adequate Yearly Progress (AYP), for restructuring, being taken over, made into charter schools and so forth. The list of problems seems endless and our ability to remediate them seems negligible.

The military have an acronym that provides a compelling description of our current reality. VUCA (see Table 1.1)—*volatile, uncertain, complex,* and *ambiguous*—is a term that first came to prominence in the late 1990s, and has more recently come to refer to the need for strategic leadership in many fields, including education.[1] It reminds us that approaches that may have worked when we (incorrectly) saw the world as a giant clock—predominantly clear, certain, stable, and predictable, will absolutely not be effective in the rapidly changing world of the 21st century. And yet, too often, education is still conceptualized in rational, technical, or prescriptive terms. Too often, it is seen as a series of prescriptive interventions or steps that deskill teachers and rob students of any possible emotional connection to the subject matter being taught or to the world around them. Too often, educational leaders seem to be caught in the middle, wanting to empower and support their teachers, but pressed from above for increased accountability and higher test scores.

In an interesting and informative presentation about the VUCA world, creator Denise Caron says that "We are moving from a world of problems, which demand speed, analysis and elimination of uncertainty to solve—to a world of dilemmas, which demand patience, sense-making and an engagement with uncertainty." Further, such dilemmas are complex, messy, threatening, confusing, and fundamentally unsolvable. This does not mean we cannot or should not act—only that there are no good-for-all contexts, easy or "right" solutions. Instead, each time we attempt to address or resolve a complex dilemma, we raise new questions and new challenges that

Table 1.1

Characteristic	Description
V = Volatility	The nature and dynamics of change and the nature and speed of change forces and change catalysts.
U = Uncertainty	The lack of predictability, the prospects for surprise and the sense of awareness and understanding of issues and events.
C = Complexity	The multiplex of forces, the confounding of issues and the chaos and confusion that surround an organization.
A = Ambiguity	The haziness of reality, the potential for misreads, and the mixed meanings of conditions; cause-and-effect confusion.

Source: adapted from Wikipedia, http://en.wikipedia.org/wiki/Volatility,_uncertainty,_complexity_and_ambiguity.

require ongoing reflection, dialogue, and action. Caron goes on to suggest the need to "turn the VUCA world on its head" and to emphasize, not the volatility, uncertainty, complexity, and ambiguity that are givens, but the need for *vision, understanding, clarity,* and *agility* through "foresight, insight, and action."

An Educational Response

In the face of all of these challenges, it is incumbent on us to ask: what is the role of education? Specifically, what is the role of educational leaders? What would it take for us to successfully accommodate the volatility, uncertainty, complexity, and ambiguity of our world? What are the implications for our educational practice when we realize that, of the world's estimated 191 million immigrants, many seeking solace from social or economic devastation in their home countries, approximately 38 million live in the United States, making up over 13% of its population (Shah, 2008). Do we know who these students are and what prior knowledge and experiences they bring to our classrooms? Can we identify which of our students have been born here and which are recent refugees, never having experienced formal schooling until arriving at our doors? Do we have any idea of how the conditions under which we live compare to those of other countries and what difference this knowledge might make? For example, what difference does it make that 20% of the world's population have 82.7% of the world's "wealth" or that, at the other end, 20% of the population survive by sharing 1.4% of the world's wealth and resources (Elert, n.d.); or that according to a 2005 report, in sub-Saharan Africa, 46.5% of the population live on the equivalent of less than $1.00 a day, while 78% live on less than $2.00 (World Bank, 2005). Can we, in North America, continue to be oblivious to such statistics, failing to educate our students about global issues? Could such widespread disparity contribute to unrest and even violence on the part of those who are falling farther and farther behind?

It is not an exaggeration to suggest that educational leaders are complicit (often unintentionally) in the perpetuation of today's educational shortcomings. North American educators, despite legitimate concerns about working in systems of high accountability, with disparate resources and funding, and with little public support for the profession, have a responsibility to our students, to the future of our country, and to the world. We have a responsibility to ensure that students are adequately prepared— not simply to pass the mandated standardized tests, but to take their places as well-informed, caring, and engaged citizens. To accomplish this, we cannot simply do more of the same—protesting loudly the need for more money, greater accountability, more parental involvement, and so on. We cannot continue to turn to solutions that have not worked in the past—increased centralization or decentralization, new prescriptive programs, new sets of textbooks, tighter standards, more tests, and so forth.

It is for this reason that, in this book, I am positing *transformative leadership* as a way of taking into account the material realities, disparities, and unfulfilled promises of the world in which our students live, and of working to ensure more equitable and inclusive opportunities for all. We need to do things differently if we are to implement changes that will rectify these inequities and create a more level and more optimistic playing field.

Above, we noted the increased gap between rich and poor in most ethnic groups in society. Indeed, the wealthiest members of the population continue to thrive and to dominate policy-making arenas, maintaining the American income tax at its lowest rates in almost a century, and resisting or rejecting policies that would provide additional food, health care, or social supports to those who need them most in our society. And as the wealthy maintain their assets and privilege, the wealthiest 10% of the population also increases its hold on its share of national assets (from 49% to 56% between 2005 and 2009, Whoriskey, 2011); and hence, their hold on the power and influence they wield.

In schools, as numbers of impoverished children increase, often from immigrant families who speak limited English, there are repeated demands to address the achievement gaps. Sometimes, these calls take the form of demands for increasing remedial services—more after-school, noon-hour or Saturday programs for failing children. Sometimes, there are fervent attempts to create policies purported to offer solutions (English-only instruction, less time in second language support)—all responses that have been shown not to be successful in the education of minoritized students. The solution is not more of the same or a reintroduction of policies and practices that have political currency but that have been proven ineffective. The solutions lie in reforms related to changing hearts and minds—to ensuring that all children are provided with high quality instruction, engaging learning opportunities, and are held to similar high expectations. This does not mean expecting students to do the impossible (as some states have done when they require English language learners to take standardized tests in English). It does not mean expecting all students to perform well in exactly the same ways. It does mean implementing educational approaches whose goals are specifically and explicitly designed to promote both equity and excellence.

What we have been doing for almost two centuries has not been working. We do not need more of the same. If we want significant, equitable, and meaningful change, we must stop shouting louder, talking slower, trying harder—and turn our attention to thinking and acting differently. When times change, society changes, contexts change, and we too, as educators and educational leaders, must change as well, demonstrating the new VUCA strengths of *vision*, *understanding*, *clarity*, and *agility*.

Oakes and Rogers (2006) advocate the same thing. They maintain that

> the persistence of racial inequality in the face of equity reforms is consistent with the contradictory role of schools in our capitalist democracy. Despite our prized cultural legacy of the common public school as a "great equalizer," American schools also serve the mission of preparing students for their "rightful" places in an unequal labor market and society.
>
> (p. 21)

To rectify the situation, they advocate developing and implementing "equity reforms"—reforms aimed at more inclusive and socially just education. Such reforms, they argue, are of a different nature from other reforms and require different, non-technical strategies, because "technical reforms, even in the hands of committed and skillful professional 'change agents' or backed by court orders, are too weak to interrupt the intergenerational transmission of racial inequality" (pp. 21–22). Instead, they call for reform strategies that disrupt the social inequality of today's schools— exactly the same kinds of strategies advocated by transformative educational leaders.

Given the reality of the VUCA aspects of today's world, educators must adopt non-technical approaches. We can no longer assign a single textbook as a resource for a course, and teach its material in a linear fashion, having students dutifully read page after page to complete the exercises at the end of each chapter. Instead, with the new, rapid, and widely accessible forms of communication, students must be taught how to understand the facts and follies of the constant barrage of information. How do we teach our students to discern fact from fiction when the number of people present to protest a speech by former vice-president Gore is reported to be twice as large as the crowd attending the presentation itself (Santana, 2009)? How do we interpret the fact that the percentage of Americans who believe that global warming is factual declined from 71% in 2008 to 57% in 2009 (Cappiello, 2009) when there is general consensus in the scientific community of the reality and dangers of global warming? How do we separate fact from fiction when a large proportion of the American electorate believed, even after his election, that President Obama was not really born in the United States?

During the summer of 2009, when the debate raged in the United States over the introduction of more universal health care, I was first amused, then appalled, and subsequently somewhat frightened by the number of times I heard comments like, "Look at Canada. They have death panels that decide whether the elderly should have care or be euthanized" (Paul, 2009). As I thought about the widespread acceptance of this obvious untruth, I often wondered aloud whether it somehow exemplified a failure of our education system. Most frequently, my friends and colleagues (many themselves educators) responded, "Don't you think you are over-reacting?"

I did not, and still do not, think so. I am convinced that in this complex and volatile world, it is critically important to help our students to make sense of the myriad of information that bombards their senses on a daily basis. Teachers must be able to think differently about information and communication and recognize that the world of our students, with Tweets, Facebook, cloud computing, iPads, iPhones, and iPods, is one of constant factoids, entertainment, images, and text. What is particularly noteworthy is the proliferation of conflicting messages and the almost universal lack of teaching to help our children understand that their world is not comprised of true or false statements, multiple-choice options, or the kinds of short answers required to be successful on so many of today's accountability measures or identified as learning standards in many states. It is, therefore, important for school leaders to ensure that all teachers reflect on how the rapidly changing world of communication can enhance and/or inhibit meaningful learning.

To do so, educational leaders must think differently about their roles, the ways they communicate with others, the topics of communication, and to address the misconceptions, myths, and deliberate misconstructions that so often appear in news media today and that inhibit equitable and meaningful learning for all students.

I am calling for all critically reflective educators to help students understand that their world is made up of multiple and often conflicting perspectives, of numerous historic and cultural interpretations, of shades of gray, and of contextually determined truths. The volatility of our social, economic, and political systems should no longer be in question after the global economic meltdown of the first decade of the 21st century or the sudden and unpredicted "Arab spring" of the first half of 2011. Demonstrations in Syria, Libya, Bahrain, Egypt, Yemen and beyond were not only unexpected, they raised questions about the stability of the world oil supply, as well as the geo-political stability of many countries. Yet most students cannot even identify parts of their own country on a world map, let alone these other nation states. And if they fail to even know how to locate them, we can be sure they are unaware that the US Navy's fifth fleet is headquartered in Bahrain. When they hear various talk-show hosts and commentators gleefully reporting on catastrophes in Arabic states or Japan (even describing them as a kind of "just retribution" for unknown wrongdoing), how can we expect today's young people to react appropriately and knowledgeably?

Needed: A New Approach

Instead of being prepared to address such significant issues, educational leaders and their preparation programs are still frequently and too narrowly focused on principles of scientific management, reacting to forces that too often overwhelm them rather than being proactive in terms of prompting reflection and creating understanding. Hierarchical command and control, prescriptive programs, narrow accountability measures, or rigid statewide scrutiny of school improvement or restructuring plans still dominate both the discourse and the preparation of educational leaders. No manager or leader today would likely dare voice the words of Frederick Taylor (father of scientific management) who believed that organizations should run like baseball teams in which "every man [*sic*] on the team obeys the signals or orders of the coach and obeys them at once when the coach gives those orders" (1912/1990, p. 207). Indeed, Taylor's philosophy of scientific management was grounded in his philosophy of pig-iron handling in which

> the man who is fit to handle pig-iron as his daily work cannot possibly understand that science; the man who is physically able to handle pig-iron and is sufficiently phlegmatic and stupid to choose this for his occupation is rarely able to comprehend the science of handling pig-iron.

The rest of this statement contains the fundamental principle of scientific management— one that, unfortunately, is still prevalent today. He summarizes:

> I assert, without the slightest hesitation, that the high-class mechanic has a far smaller chance of ever thoroughly understanding the science of his work than the pig-iron handler has of understanding the science of his work . . . the man who is fit to work at any particular trade is unable to understand the science of that trade without the kindly help and cooperation of men of a totally different type of education.
>
> (p. 209)

In educational organizations, this disdain for workers, for those who are less formally educated, even for those who are in some ways different (due to socio-economic or cultural characteristics) is still pervasive. We send newsletters and information *to* parents (assuming that those who do not attend our meetings according to our timelines don't really care about their children); we develop "*teacher-proof curricula*," assuming that teachers do not have the expertise to truly engage with or teach all of their students; we emphasize the need for *data-informed decisions* without asking, "decisions for or about what?"; we call for *professional learning communities* without stopping to ask what we want to learn or why; and we dismiss students who are homeless, or economically disadvantaged, or who speak a home language other than English, and so forth as having less ability, less motivation, and less potential for success than mainstream children from middle-class families. Further, we *prove* their lack of ability by citing standardized test scores, failing to acknowledge the importance of teacher attitudes and expectations, of pedagogy, indeed, the critical role of school leadership, in offering a just, equitable, and democratic education to all children.

For numerous reasons, including, but not simply because of, the ongoing and widening achievement gaps between groups of children, it is clear that education, as it is generally "delivered" in schools, is neither the custodian of the American Dream, the "great equalizer" envisioned by Horace Mann, nor a catalyst for global peace, prosperity, or sustainability. School reform efforts have done little to disrupt the inequities that inhibit our efforts to equalize the playing field for all students. Thus, the question for educational leaders is how to fulfill our responsibility to truly educate all students for individual intellectual excellence and for global citizenship, how to help them reflect on and act on critically important issues of our times, and how to sort out truth from fiction. In other words, we need to ask both "What is our responsibility as educational leaders?" and "How do we fulfill it?"

Margaret Wheatley,[2] a leadership scholar who studies the lessons leaders can learn from what she calls the new sciences (chaos theory, quantum mechanics, field theory, and the new physics) argues that too many of us work in organizations that are still deeply rooted in the 17th century, influenced by Newton's view of the world as a giant clock. This mechanistic metaphor is too simple a concept to capture today's complexity. Organizations are not composed of static, interchangeable parts of a machine. People cannot be expected to perform their duties like cogs in a machine and students should certainly not be treated like fungible widgets. For almost three centuries, leaders have viewed their work as predicting, commanding, and controlling the forces that impinge on their organization's ability to be successful—an impossible task, she maintains, because it misunderstands and misrepresents the true nature of organizations. Instead, her argument is that scientists increasingly acknowledge that order emerges from chaos and that understanding patterns and their pressure points is far more productive than attempting to control them. (We may not be able to predict where each card in a house of cards will fall, but we can certainly know how to exert pressure to make the whole house collapse.) She argues that information informs and forms us; it is the fuel that drives organizational change. Moreover, because scientists cannot study particles that exist in isolation, she claims that relationships are the new building blocks of the organization. Finally, Wheatley argues that we expend much unproductive time and energy trying to reform organizations from the outside in, rather than working from the inside out. To do this requires a clear sense of the core vision of the organization, trust in colleagues, and room for messiness around the edges. (See also Wheatley, 2000.)

Some may ask what this means for organizational life and whether it is truly possible to change our hierarchical control systems for more fluid, flexible, and creative systems. Does this mean starting with the teachers or with the students? From whom do we seek information and to whom do we provide it? Very recently I interviewed a school principal whose description of her approach to educational change is helpful here.

Vital High School is located in a Midwestern university town with a dominant white, middle-class population. Nevertheless, in the last two years, the school has become what is popularly known as a "majority-minority school." Its population of approximately 1100 students is comprised of 46% White, 35% Black, 8% Hispanic, and 11% mixed race or other ethnic groups, 60% of whom are from low-income families. If one goes to the school's website, one now finds a new mission statement borrowed from Chaucer's *Canterbury tales*: "Gladly would we learn and gladly teach," indication of two recent national awards (one placing the school on the College Board's 2011 AP® Achievement List for opening AP classroom doors to a significantly broader pool of students, while maintaining a high academic standard; the other a bronze medal from the U.S. News & World Report), and a social justice video produced by a committee of students and teachers. The principal, Leslie Thomas, reports that the school has changed significantly from a place of mistrust and hierarchical leadership to one of collaboration, energy, and communication. She describes how half of her staff members are active on one of many leadership teams and how she uses the team meetings and professional learning community strategies to involve everyone in a core focus on learning. She says: "But it is learning from each other, and that is part of what we're about. We are a collaborative school. We are working with each other and learning from each other."

An example shows this very clearly. Leslie Thomas described how, as happens in many high schools, teachers were concerned about students wearing caps in school. Some ignored it; others desperately wanted a policy to end caps. A few years ago, staff held a series of conversations in which they probed the question of whether wearing caps was a "learning issue" and ultimately decided that, because it was not, students would be permitted to wear caps in class. Although the issue seemed resolved, something nagged at Leslie. For several months she discussed her unresolved ideas with faculty and groups of students. In part, she was reflecting on Giroux's (1998) concept that "how others see us becomes in part how we see ourselves" (p. 15). She recognized that when the average citizen saw students either individually or in groups, faces hidden in the shadow of their peaked cap, it affected their perception of the students. She worried that if these students were then thought of as "losers," "rabble," perhaps even "gang members," their self-images as learners would be less positive and their academic achievement would follow suit. So, last year, at the opening school assemblies (she meets with all students at least twice a year in small groups), Leslie engaged in a similar conversation with students: "What do you think of when you see students standing around in groups wearing caps and baggy clothes?" When students' replies mentioned gangs and losers, as she anticipated, she asked how they wanted to be seen by others. As the conversation progressed, it became clear that wearing caps actually was a learning issue, and the policy changed once more.

In a VUCA world, there are no prescriptions and no right answers (good for all times and places)—simply an engaged messiness, a determination to solve dilemmas, to continue to share information and reflect on it, consistent with the core vision (in this case: a focus on learning). In Vital High School, teachers who used to blame students for their lack of motivation or achievement are now often "in tears" worrying that they have not yet figured out how to reach certain students. The responsibility is shared although the paths to fulfill the goal are as varied as the staff members themselves. This is leadership for a VUCA world. It is leadership that is creative, collaborative, innovative, and messy. It is leadership that requires *vision, understanding, clarity*, and *agility*. It is not about adopting the newest program (although one may, as Leslie did with the professional learning community literature, take some components of it and adapt them to local conditions). It is not about simply improving current leadership practice but, instead, it requires a totally different and alternative approach to previous technical and mechanical approaches to leadership.

Wherever we look, the challenges of VUCA surround us. This is not to say that there are no useful responses, no promising approaches, and no good answers. It is, however, to suggest that the answers do not lie in more of the same, in greater control, better prediction, resistance, retrenchment, or in renouncing of responsibility or power to the whims of fate. We do not need more new programs, more accurate diagnostic tools and more powerful prescriptions, more rigorous teacher testing, educational incentives, or more uniform standards. Instead, I argue here that what is needed is a new and more comprehensive approach to educational leadership, one that requires leaders to take a stand, embrace the chaos and ambiguity, focus on information sharing and relationships, and develop a strong sense of the core organizational vision. It requires that we identify our "non-negotiables"—those aspects of education that will not be sacrificed to the current pressures of accountability, or standards, or testing.

Overall, a VUCA world argues for a form of leadership known increasingly as *transformative leadership* because its focus is not "business as usual." *Transformative leadership* (not to be confused with transformational leadership) is a critical approach to leadership grounded in Freire's (1970) fourfold call for critical awareness or *conscientization*, followed by critical reflection, critical analysis, and finally for activism or critical action against the injustices of which one has become aware. Hence, it begins with awareness—of the strengths, weaknesses, and challenges of our society and of our school system. It requires critical reflection of for whom the system is working and for whom it is failing, of who is advantaged, privileged, and always included, and who is marginalized and excluded. Once problem areas of inequity are identified, transformative leadership calls for critical analysis of beliefs, values, practices, and policies that need to be changed in order to promote equity. Finally, transformative leadership calls for action—action to redress wrongs and to ensure that every child who enters into an educational institution has an equal opportunity to participate fully, to be treated with respect, and to develop his or her capabilities.

In the next chapter, we will develop this concept of *transformative leadership* and explore some of its guiding principles and useful approaches to leading more equitably and more creatively to address the challenges of our VUCA world.

For Further Reflection and Action

1. In what ways is ours a "society of unfulfilled promises"? For whom is the system working and for whom is it failing? Who is advantaged, privileged, and always included, and who is marginalized and excluded? How can you raise the critical consciousness of students to understand inequity and to facilitate collective action against injustice?

2. Is addressing the achievement gap the primary task of educators or is the gap a result of deeper and more pervasive systemic inequities?

3. Stop to consider your responses to questions posed throughout the chapter, such as: what is the role of educational leaders? What is our responsibility as educational leaders? How do we fulfill it? What would it take for us to successfully accommodate the volatility, uncertainty, complexity, and ambiguity of our world? What might be the long-term implications of failing to address global inequities?

4. Identify one "equity reform" that might help your institution. How could it be instituted?

5. Is there a policy in your school that needs to be reconsidered as a "learning issue"? How might you reconceptualize it as Leslie Thomas did the issue of caps?

Chapter 2

Transformative Leadership as a Response to a VUCA World

David Dean has recently accepted a position as principal of a large, suburban high school—a predominantly White school (73%) with a low-income population of almost 30%. Moreover, in the past few years, the Hispanic population has doubled to its current 14% of the total, and because that sub-group is not meeting expectations in either Math or reading, they are being blamed by the wider community for the school's position on the "academic watch" list. David, however, is experiencing strong support from both the board and the parent community, who perceive his open and collaborative style to be a considerable improvement over the more secretive and control-orientated approach of his predecessor.

Catherine Lake is principal of an elementary school with a declining White population and a large number of classes for students with special needs. She is clear that one of her "non-negotiables" is ensuring that all teachers take responsibility for the learning of all students—and that they do so without reducing student opportunities for either elective subjects or free time. Hence, she and her teachers reject additional noon-hour, after-school, or Saturday test prep in favor of creative and innovative in-school approaches.

John Law is principal of one of America's small public "private" schools—a school located in an exclusive residential community with seemingly unlimited resources and a relatively homogeneous population. His student body of 400+ students is visibly homogeneous, only three non-White students and four students who qualify for free and reduced lunch (two are temporary foster children and two others are technically "homeless" as their mother has had to move in with her parents). John's challenges are very different: how to foster a sense of the globally diverse world in a high performing, wealthy, middle-class community.

All three principals are experiencing the challenges arising from their community-environments as they attempt to exercise "good" leadership. David is working in new ways with his changing school community to promote equitable learning for all students. Catherine has chosen a dialogic approach to leadership in which her whole staff is resisting the current press for test preparation in favor of a more focused approach to student learning—and, not surprisingly, her test scores have also increased dramatically and her school has still met the requirements of Adequate Yearly Progress (AYP). John, on the other hand, is struggling to find a way to help students become aware of their advantage and privilege without adopting a hegemonic "missionary" stance to those perceived to be less advantaged.

Each principal, although very different in personality, style, and non-negotiables, is a "good" leader. Good, as used here and in the rest of this book, refers to leadership that is "effective" in terms of having his or her school run smoothly and effectively according to the criteria and goals he or she has set for the school. Cuban (2003) raises the issue of what constitutes a good school (and by implication, a good leader), and suggests that there are many different ways of conceptualizing this. He writes:

> Different kinds of "good" schools and external social reforms are needed more than ever to embrace the full range of social, economic, political, and private purposes schools are expected to serve. Diverse "good" schools are essential to correct the imbalance in purposes from the present dominance of training for the workplace and increasing an individual's social mobility to one where civic engagement is primary.
>
> (p. 55)

In other words, as Cuban suggests, and as the multiplicity of leadership theories suggest, there are many different ways to be "good." Moreover, Cuban goes on to argue that we need to ask questions such as "good for what?" or "good for whom?" as we consider what each of us means by good.

Although I touch later (in Chapter 5) on the goals and purposes of education (the what), my argument here is concerned with the "for whom" aspect. Some social and political purposes seem grounded in the status quo, in protecting the organization from change, and in keeping things the way they have always been. Although for a particular clientele, the status quo may be seen as "good," in my opinion, this ideology is inadequate for today's complex and changing world. Until and unless we serve all students regardless of social, economic, or cultural background, I believe educators are failing the community, the nation, and indeed, the whole global community. It is for that reason I do not believe it is adequate to be a "good" leader based on calm and efficient performance. Indeed David, Catherine, and John all go considerably farther, grounded in a sense of moral purpose, and working to transform their organizations to create environments in which all students are welcome, included, respected, and are experiencing intellectual growth. In fact, as we shall see throughout this book, I think of the combination of moral purpose, intellectual and social development, and a focus on social justice as going beyond "good" in the traditional sense of effective leaders, but also as "transformative."

To maintain a clear sense of moral purpose, to advocate for those least advantaged in our current systems, and to be willing to both navigate within and sometimes, when called for, to take a stand against, some of the forces of our VUCA context, requires more than an ability to manage effectively. In the above schools, although the specifics are quite different, the principals are forced to acknowledge the *volatility* of the climate and to make an effort to understand the nature, speed, and dynamics of the changes their schools and communities are undergoing (or resisting). Similarly, as they move forward, they recognize the *uncertainty* of doing so in an era of fiscal restraint, increased accountability, and teacher mobility when the bottom line and publically reported test scores seem to take precedence over high quality student learning. In fact, they and other school leaders acknowledge the challenges related to working in a climate of unpredictability. Moreover, the multitude of forces that impinge on each organization's ability to make meaningful change increases the *complexity* of the job. Addressing the micro-political realities of schooling, including an amplified burden of reporting and paperwork, as well as the challenges that come from globalization with its burgeoning new technologies and rapidly changing pace of communication brings an immediacy and a heightened visibility that often seem to be in opposition to the need to carefully and critically reflect on new information and the best way forward (Bogotch, 2000). Negotiating each of these elements and maintaining a focus on students requires strong, ethical, courageous, and transformative leadership.

Educators are bombarded by claims of "research-based" curricular programs, textbooks, test preparation materials, and practices—all purporting to be "best practice"—to promote improved student learning. Implicitly, and often explicitly, these initiatives claim to be good for all times and places; however, they rarely "work" as promised, but instead, enhance the potential confusion as well as *ambiguity* related to desirable outcomes and ways of attaining them. Wheatley (2000), for example, suggests that as many as 60% of reform initiatives fail to achieve their desired goals.

Moreover, curricular demands capture only a very small portion of the realities of educational leaders who must address the specific demands and expectations of local, regional, and national legislative bodies, of diverse constituents, and of students with a wide range of needs and abilities—all within a context of fiscal restraint, increased accountability, and global unrest.

I am sure educational leaders often wish they could simply act as the mythical inn-keeper, Procrustes, who promised weary travelers an outstanding experience—good food and the ultimate night's sleep in a bed especially designed to fit them perfectly. Unfortunately, he failed to inform them that to make the bed fit, if they were too short, he would stretch them relentlessly; if they were too tall, he would systematically cut off some limbs. Wouldn't it be nice, we muse, if we could simply act in similar ways, ignore the changes around us, and push and pull people to do our will, shaping them to fit the policies, to respond as our newest packaged programs suggest they will, or simply to comply with our desires?

Fortunately, despite the early dominance of mechanical and technical approaches, educational leadership is and always has been a deeply moral activity, firmly grounded in principles and values. In 1996, Joanne Ciulla critiqued Rost's earlier contention that "the problem with leadership is that we lack a common definition" (p. 183), and argued instead that trying to construct "the ultimate definition of leadership" focuses on the wrong question. Her contention is that when we ask "what is *good* leadership" we need to be thinking in moral and ethical terms, and not simply in terms of efficiency. In fact, Ciulla stresses that the historic neglect of ethics in leadership theories is at the heart of perceptions of leadership frailty or, worse, leadership incapacity. McKerrow (1997), writing at about the same time, asserts in similar fashion that "it is time to rethink educational administration" and to engage in a "serious consideration of ethics in a profession whose mission is fundamentally moral but whose practice is not" (p. 210). Others argue that it is not simply ethics that is missing but theory in general (Lynn, Benigno, Williams, Park, & Mitchell, 2006) and that perhaps "critical theory provides a lens for interpreting what happens in classrooms and provides conceptual and epistemological grounding for changing the direction of research" (p. 17). In the 21st century we must again reassert that claim: it *is* time to seriously consider what it means to be a "good" leader in the sense of good for all students regardless of their background, their language, their culture, or the degree of influence of their parents.

As we examine the myriad notions of leadership that masquerade as distinct theories, each with its own definitions, each purported to be more able than others to solve the challenging problems of accountability, community, achievement, diversity, and so forth that confront today's educational leaders, we are tempted to ask, with Shakespeare, "what's in a name?" and to respond that distinguishing among them is a futile activity. One might argue, with some validity, that it is exactly the kind of abstract theoretical activity that consumes too much time and energy of ivory tower dwellers.

A Multitude of Theories: What's in a Name?

The primary aim of this section is to describe some ways of navigating the multiple approaches to leadership and to offer some arguments in favor of *transformative leadership* as a theory that may offer promise for deep and meaningful change. Certainly, the proliferation of leadership theories is not new and educators have at their disposal an array of approaches such as bureaucratic, hierarchical, distributed, transformational, democratic, servant, authoritarian, collaborative, or transformative leadership—all intended to improve the organizations in which the leader works. Concomitantly, there are other terms that, while not necessarily *theories*, provide some guidance for directions related to leadership. Here the list is even more comprehensive and includes such concepts as trustworthy, grounded, consistent, charismatic, unassuming, ideological, ethical, focused, and so forth. Scholars and practitioners alike must sort through the maze of terms to attempt to determine if there is an approach consistent with their own belief systems and with their specific ontological and epistemological approaches.

Regardless of our perspective, what is clear is that the world is no longer best represented by the mechanistic 17th century Newtonian metaphor of a clock. We need new ways of thinking about organizations—ways that learn, as Margaret Wheatley urges, from new scientific developments such as chaos theory, quantum mechanics, evolutionary biology, or field theory. (Don't panic, I am not going to veer into the esoteric world of the pure sciences!) But I will argue, with Wheatley, that too many of our educational organizations are still firmly grounded in the 17th century, seeking technical solutions to dilemmas instead of creative and adaptive ones. I am arguing, with Wheatley, that we need to attend to what scientists in other disciplines can teach us about leading organizations and that we need to pay considerably more attention to the patterns that emerge from chaos, to the dissemination of information, to the development of relationships, and to the power of shared vision. In fact, it is precisely because scholars and practitioners alike are increasingly discouraged by reform efforts that are more akin to rearranging the deckchairs on the *Titanic* than to meaningful change that the quest for a more effective approach to leadership continues.

Finding our way among these theories can be both complex and confusing as there is, necessarily, much overlap, and both similarities and differences among the theories. Broadly speaking, I believe leadership theories tend to fall into three main categories.

A Focus on Traits and Characteristics

The first, dating back to very early approaches to leadership, but still common in scholarly literature, focus on leadership *traits*. Images of leaders in the tradition of

Gandhi, or Martin Luther King, or even Machiavelli or Sun Tzu continue to suggest that certain traits will produce better results than others. Most of these theories appear to focus primarily on the solitary leader, enabling one to label a leader as heroic, charismatic, ethical, authentic, spiritual, courageous, etc. In this category as well, we might place some of the current approaches drawn from historic figures: Lincoln, Dwight Eisenhower, Ronald Reagan, Nelson Mandela, Colin Powell, the Navy SEALs, Attila the Hun, or even Jesus or Harry Potter (the list is amazing and exhaustive). Researchers tell us that many of the traits often studied in more technical approaches to leadership—age, years of experience, formal educational training, charisma, and so forth are inconclusive, even irrelevant, for it has long been acknowledged that there are many different types of "good" (excellent and ethical) leaders. Included here are approaches to leadership that emphasize the personality, trustworthiness, or authenticity of the leader. Although it is fair to say that it is helpful and desirable for a leader to be able to develop the support and trust of members of the organization and to have the ability to foster and attain a shared vision, there are no normative traits that permit this to occur. What is important, according to some scholars (Evans, 1996; Terry, 1993), is for the leader to be seen as *authentic* and to be seen as ethical and consistent in his or her approach. Having authenticity requires that there is consistency and congruency among one's stated values, expressed goals, and actions. This does not require a leader to express himself or herself in a certain way, to have a particularly outgoing or humorous or charismatic approach, or a particular style. It certainly does not require that he or she be liked by everyone. But at a minimum, leaders must develop a certain level of trust among those with whom they work and demonstrate that their actions are consistent with their words. One major problem is that this category of theories about traits and characteristics ignores the need for reflecting on the goals of education and for the development of criteria against which to assess our progress. It focuses on a single person in a formal role as opposed to more current and collaborative approaches to leadership.

An Emphasis on Process

A second large group of leadership theories focuses on leadership processes or *how* a leader might approach his or her tasks. Here we see a range of approaches from bureaucratic, command, or hierarchical to more distributed or distributive leadership, servant leadership, situational, or perhaps democratic leadership. We also find reference to leading that is principle-centered, full of energy, quiet, or adaptive. Once again, although there is no doubt that a heavy-handed, command style of leadership with little focus on transparency or respect for members of the organization may be less conducive to a positive organizational climate than more collaborative approaches, these theories also neglect to identify a specific direction, leaving the specific goals either to the whim of the local community or to the external mandates of politicians and legislators. For example, the well-known concept of *transformational leadership* (often advanced by Leithwood, 2010) calls for leaders to set directions, develop people, redesign the organization, and manage the instructional program. Note that although each of these is an essential component of leadership, there is no specification of what direction to set, how to develop people, how the organization might be redesigned, or what management of the instructional program might mean. Thus, a principal might conceivably reduce student elective offerings and add noon-hour, after-school, or Saturday instruction as a way of managing the instructional program in order to enhance the school's ability to meet Adequate Yearly Progress (AYP)—all the while ignoring the learning needs of the most and least advanced students.

Identifying Desired Outcomes

A third group of theories identifies the primary focus (or desired outcomes) of the leadership approach, often (but not completely) ignoring the need for authentic leadership or for processes that are appropriate to the desired goals. Here are approaches such as instructional leadership, change-oriented leadership, leadership for learning, vision-centered leadership, leadership for social justice, transformational leadership (aimed at transforming the organization), relational, or dialogic leadership. These theories help leaders to identify their primary focus as relationships, instruction, dialogue, learning, change or transformation, and hence, move us forward toward an emphasis on desired goals. At the same time, there is no guarantee that a singular emphasis will accomplish the radical change needed to ensure that education becomes a facilitator of social mobility and democratic citizenship as well as intellectual development. For example, as previously indicated, adopting a form of instructional leadership that focuses on test preparation would not necessarily ensure that the leader would engage in an examination of structural barriers or challenge pedagogical strategies based on deficit thinking that marginalize some children while, at the same time, promoting a general sense of well-being and school improvement.

And of course, not included in the previous three categories, are the myriad of how-to books—books that tell us what "leadership pill" to take, what to do during our first 90 days on the job, how to go from values to action—and if none of this works, one can always try "leadership for dummies" (Loeb & Kindel, 1999).

My argument here is that there is a need for a robust approach to leadership that encompasses some individual leadership attributes, some processes, and some goals, one that also has a sound theoretical base instead of a prescriptive recipe-based approach. I firmly believe that *transformative* leadership (sometimes also known as critical transformative leadership, see Quantz, Rogers, & Dantley, 1991), is just such a theory.

Transformative Leadership: A Way Forward

To address the many challenges facing school leaders today (and by leader, recall that I include both teacher-leaders and those holding formal positions of responsibility), I want to suggest that because *transformative leadership* is substantively different from most other approaches, it offers a promising way forward. One major difference is its starting point. *Transformative* leadership starts at the end. It argues, with Foster (1986), that leadership that is "critically educative" not only looks "at the conditions in which we live, but it must also decide how to change them" (p. 185). It begins by recognizing that the material realities of the wider community impinge on the ability of any organization to achieve success and on the ability of individuals within the organization to succeed. It acknowledges that an unequal playing field, in which the gap between rich and poor grows steadily, requires extraordinary effort on the part of impoverished children if they wish to be successful in school. It recognizes that the dominant cultural norms of our society create, as Delpit (1990) has for so long and so eloquently argued, a "culture of power" that advantages some children and marginalizes others within our schools, requiring once again a Herculean effort on the part of minoritized students to master both their home culture and that of the school. It acknowledges that for children, for example those whose sexual orientation (or that of their parents) is not heteronormative, whose belief systems draw from Islamic culture, or for whom their home languages are not English, schools are often not safe places. Thus, rather than bring their lived experiences into the sense-making conversations of the classroom, many children have learned they must hide or negate significant parts of themselves.

It is leadership that begins by recognizing that the inequities that prevent our attainment of a deep democracy not only exist in every community but that these material inequities powerfully and detrimentally affect the possibility of equitable educational outcomes for all students. Transformative leaders combine careful attention to authentic, personal leadership characteristics, a focus on more collaborative, dialogic, and democratic processes of leadership; and at the same time, attend simultaneously to goals of individual intellectual development, and goals of collective sustainability, social justice, and mutually beneficial civil society.

In making these claims as starting points, transformative leadership is firmly grounded in critical perspectives—perspectives that take into account the situations of the marginalized and oppressed and seek to offer remedy. As mentioned in the previous chapter, it is firmly grounded in Freire's (1970) notion of *conscientization*—the need for understanding, and for critical reflection, analysis, and action. The goal of transformative leadership is both to critique underlying social, cultural, and economic norms, but also to offer promise—to find ways to equalize opportunities and to ensure high quality education and civil participation for all. This, of course, requires high intellectual expectations, challenging curriculum and appropriate pedagogy, as well as preparation for full participation in civil society, in a life lived in common and in mutual benefit (Green, 1999) with one's fellow citizens. In this way, transformative leaders start with the goal of transformation—not simply of the organization but of society. Thus, both the beginning and end points are the need to work toward high levels of academic achievement and inclusive citizenship and social justice for all.

Historic Roots of Transformative Leadership

Transformative leadership has its roots in James Macgregor Burns' seminal (1978) work, *Leadership*, in which he differentiated between transactional leadership and a form of leadership he referred to as *transforming*. Subsequently, there has been little disagreement over the meaning of transactional leadership with its focus on an exchange of benefits—"You support my discipline policy and I will give you two sections of Advanced Placement (AP) social studies next year." Transforming leadership, however, has given rise to extensive inquiry and theorizing, and in recent years has led to two related, but distinctly different, ways to think about leadership. Burns emphasized the need for "*real change*—that is, a transformation to the marked degree in the attitudes, norms, institutions, and behaviors that structure our daily lives" (p. 414). For Burns, a transforming leader encourages "followers to act for certain goals that represent the values and the motivations—the wants and needs, the aspirations and expectations—*of both leaders and followers*" (p. 19, italics in original).

Nevertheless, Starratt (2011) writes that "The distinction between transformational leadership and transformative leadership is an important one, not only for the field of education, but also for leadership theory and research in other fields, including public administration, business administration, and leadership in the professions" (p. 127). The first transforming theory, *transformational leadership*, has been well articulated (see Leithwood & Jantzi, 1990, 1999). It is a theory that starts and ends with a clear focus on the organization itself—on setting organizational goals and mobilizing resources to ensure the goals are met efficiently and effectively. As Leithwood and Duke stated (1998):

> this form of leadership assumes that the central focus of leadership ought to be the commitments and capacities of organizational members. Higher levels of personal commitment to organizational goals and greater capacities for accomplishing those goals are assumed to result in extra effort and greater productivity.
>
> (¶16)

With its clear focus on the organization, on organizational problem-solving and organizational climate, transformational leaders are primarily concerned with organizational effects and outcomes. This in no way implies a lack of moral or ethical emphasis, simply a different kind of preoccupation than that which motivates those who call themselves transformative. Blackmore (2011) writes of transformational leadership that "issues of power relations, structures, processes of inequality, and unequal economic resources, or how perceptions of leadership are gendered and racialized, are still pushed into the background" (p. 22); but that transformative leadership "emerges out of the politics of difference" (p. 23) and "views leadership as a social practice aligned with democratic practices" (p. 23). Thus, transformational leaders tend to treat the organization as a homogenous whole, and to focus on the shared expectations and needs of the dominant (and often most vocal) leaders and followers, while transformative leaders acknowledge and attend to the differential backgrounds and experiences of those within the organization. In transformational leadership theory, there are no explicit and intrinsic mechanisms to ensure that multiple perspectives, needs, or aspirations are either addressed or understood. Thus, although in many environments, transformational leadership might be sufficient, it is not adequate for a VUCA world in which schools and their communities are increasingly diverse and in which equity reforms need to be made both central and explicit.

The second leadership theory to emerge from Burns' (1978) notion of transforming leadership is *transformative leadership* (see Blackmore, 2011; Foster, 1986; Quantz, Rogers, & Dantley, 1991; Shields, 2009, 2010; Starratt, 2011). Given that transforming and transformative are listed in some dictionaries as synonyms, it is little wonder there is frequent confusion and confounding of the two approaches. Nevertheless, transformative leadership has very different emphases and underpinnings. Burns began his treatise by calling for a consideration of how both power (composed of motive and resources) and power relationships are central to comprehending the "true nature of leadership" (pp. 11–12) and shortly thereafter stated that "transcending leadership is leadership *engaged*" (p. 20, italics mine), thus pointing the way for a form of leadership that looks beyond the organization itself to begin with an acknowledgment that the school is inextricably embedded in the wider society. The leader, therefore, must also be engaged with the wider society in order to understand how best to educate all children.

If we are to take seriously the need for education to be a positive force for change in today's world, our leadership must become transformative. The concept of *transformative leadership* focuses on specific public goals and broad purposes of education in addition to its processes; it focuses on preparing students to be both individually successful as well as thoughtful, successful, caring, and engaged citizens of the global community (see Quantz, Rogers, & Dantley, 1991; Shields, 2009, 2010; Weiner, 2003).

Eight key tenets of transformative leadership theory include:

- the mandate to effect deep and equitable change;
- the need to deconstruct and reconstruct knowledge frameworks that perpetuate inequity and injustice;
- a focus on emancipation, democracy, equity, and justice;
- the need to address the inequitable distribution of power;
- an emphasis on both private and public (individual and collective) good;
- an emphasis on interdependence, interconnectedness, and global awareness;
- the necessity of balancing critique with promise;
- the call to exhibit moral courage.

To help you differentiate among the theories, Table 2.1 summarizes the key distinctions among transactional, transformational, and transformative leadership. The first three of these tenets will be elaborated in Chapter 3; the issue of power in Chapter 4; the concepts of public and private good in Chapter 5; and the interdependence and interconnectedness of the global community in Chapter 6. Then, in Chapter 7, I attempt to put the ideas together, demonstrating how the last two themes—the balance of critique and promise and the need for leaders to exhibit moral courage—permeate all of the chapters and the themes and stories you will read in each of them. Although my assumption is that the transformative leadership vision that embraces critique and promise and that calls for moral courage and activism shines through each of these chapters, they will again be emphasized in the concluding chapter—again enhanced with stories from real schools and school leaders.

Overall, the argument is that transformative leaders are not only concerned with what happens within their schoolhouse walls, but with what happens within the wider local, national, and global communities as well. Some might argue that this is not the concern of schools or educators, that we cannot be all things to all people, and that it is up to the politicians or private industry to rectify the inequities in the wider society. They express concern that any appeal for educators to be concerned with the material realities of students beyond school expands what is already an impossible job. Here I am not arguing that transformative leaders need to make it their cause to change what occurs outside of schools—although they may well be engaged in multiple ways in alleviating injustices and inequities in their communities. What I am arguing is that transformative leaders must pay attention to what happens to students and their families outside of school. They must understand how the totality of students' lived experiences affects their ability to learn, their identity construction, their sense of belonging and being welcomed or valued within the

Table 2.1 Comparison of Three Major Leadership Theories

Charactistic	Transactional leadership	Transformation leadership	Transformative leadership
Starting point	A desired agreement or item	Need for the organization to run smoothly and efficiently	Material realities and disparities outside the organization that impinge on the success of individuals, groups, and organization as a whole
Foundation	An exchange	Meet the needs of complex and diverse systems	Critique and promise
Emphasis	Means	Organization	Deep and equitable change in social conditions
Processes	Immediate cooperation through mutual agreement and benefit	Understanding of organizational culture, setting directions, developing people, redesigning the organization, and managing the instructional program	Deconstruction and reconstruction of social/cultural knowledge frameworks that generate inequity, acknowledgment of power and privilege, dialectic between individual and social
Key values	Honesty, responsibility, fairness, and honoring commitments	Liberty, justice, equality	Liberation, emancipation, democracy, equity, justice
Goal	Agreement, mutual goal advancement	Organizational change, effectiveness	Individual, organizational, and societal transformation
Power	Mostly ignored	Inspirational	Positional, hegemonic, tool for oppression as well as for action
Leader	Ensures smooth and efficient organizational operation through transactions	Looks for motive, develops common purpose, focuses on organizational goals	Lives with tension and challenge, requires moral courage, activism
Related theories	Bureaucratic leadership Scientific management	School effectiveness School reform School improvement Instructional leadership	Critical theories (race, gender) Cultural and social reproduction Leadership for social justice

Source: This table is adapted from the table originally printed in Shields (2010).

learning context. It is for these reasons that attending to the social and cultural contexts of schooling is so important.

To achieve the *goals* of individual development as well as the preparation of students to fully participate in civil society, transformative leadership recognizes the need for leaders to bring to their work certain types of individual *characteristics* as well as to make use of specific *processes*, thus combining elements of other leadership theories. The goal is equitable and excellent education for all and, through it, learning that promotes individual development and global awareness and responsibility. Although transformative leadership acknowledges that there are no inherently necessary traits, no one right way for leaders to proceed, and no single most appropriate style of leadership that each leader must adopt, it is critically important for each educational leader to be *authentic* (Evans, 1996); or as Parker Palmer (1998) advocates, to know oneself first, to have the *integrity* that comes from knowing one's *inner self*; and to, as Palmer describes it, "live divided no more" (p. 163).

When it comes to processes, transformative leadership is equally attentive. However, once again, there is no singular focus on the need to collaborate or distribute leadership, on the need to be democratic or less hierarchical, for sometimes an ethical leader must go against the grain and make unpopular decisions alone. What is essential is that processes be used that are consistent with the values expressed and the goals articulated. Often this will require the use of dialogue (Bakhtin, 1984; Shields, 2009; Sidorkin, 1999), a focus on relationships (Thayer-Bacon, 2003; Wheatley, 1999), the development of transparent ways to share information, and to challenge inequitable policies and practices in order to achieve greater liberty, equity, or civic participation. The processes evoked here are not vacuous labels but ways of promoting deep and equitable change that creates more inclusive and optimistic environments for all students.

Finally, to fulfill their understanding of the moral purposes of schooling, transformative leaders require the courage that permits them to become advocates of equitable change and educational and societal transformation. Indeed, transformative leadership embodies the new VUCA characteristics of vision, understanding, clarity, and agility. It is a robust, critical, theory-based approach that combines personal traits or authenticity, specific processes, and discussion of desired and explicit goals or outcomes. *Transformative* leadership is not a theory for the faint-hearted, but it does hold the potential to change the landscape of educational leadership and of educational institutions in the coming years.

To begin to demonstrate the validity of my claim, let us briefly examine the practice of each of the leaders introduced above and observe one way in which they are exercising transformative leadership in their context.

Embodying Transformative Leadership

David Dean's school is a prime example of chaos and uncertainty. He reports to an assistant superintendent who was formerly in his position. As such, some of his colleagues (perhaps especially some fellow administrators) tend to circumvent him if they suspect he may not accede to a request and go directly above him. Some associate principals, favored by his predecessor, even seem to have negotiated for themselves multi-year contracts—something he has not been able to acquire for himself. The uncertainty is palpable. And to compound the usual pressures faced by a principal of a large, diverse, secondary school, he is overseeing the construction of a new building scheduled to open in the near future. Pending decisions about requests for specific classrooms, equipment, and other privileges add to everyone's uncertainty. Mr. Dean's dedication leads to his presence at the school and school activities for a normal 14-hour day and, as we shall see later, to several controversial decisions such as giving students his cell phone number and conducting home visits when students are identified as in danger of being "lost."

Catherine Lake has a clear focus on equitable educational offerings and opportunities for all students. When she arrived at the school, individual classes celebrated holidays, successes, and special events as they saw fit. With an increasingly high minority population and growing numbers of students living in relative poverty, she decided to put an end to a practice that had become inequitable. Having observed that some classes had lavish celebrations, with parents donating prizes and food, while others could only afford to rent a movie, she implemented school-wide celebrations instead. At that time, and similar to most other schools today, parents volunteered primarily in their own child's classroom. Catherine instituted a different approach, supported by her teachers: she now has a parent volunteer coordinator who helps to both train and assign volunteers so they can be an integral part of the instructional program and help where they are most needed. Although she has successfully deconstructed prior expectations and practice, and reconstructed a new knowledge framework about parental involvement, she still has to courageously face complaints by parents who want to volunteer in their own child's classroom.

Catherine's moral courage and ongoing willingness to make difficult decisions for the good of all is legendary, but the continued grievances on the part of a few disgruntled parents and teachers take a heavy toll. Another example is telling. During team meetings, as staff examined student achievement data and discussed how to meet the needs of students who were still underperforming, Catherine suggested they should bring their lesson plans to the next team meeting as a basis for discussion. Following some awkward silence, she discovered that despite having a 40-minute planning time during each school day, teachers were not "planning." Requiring teachers to show evidence of planning during their assigned free "planning time" brought a union grievance—a time-consuming challenge that, of course, Catherine "won."

John Law's challenges seem, in some ways, minor compared to those of Catherine. He has all the space, resources, and materials he needs in a well-maintained modern building. His test scores are superb and few, if any, disciplinary issues ever reach his jurisdiction. This gives him and his teachers the luxury of being able to include interesting activities without the pressure of covering the curriculum or preparing for the test. For example, this year, one group connected via Skype with students in India; another with students in China; still another read a book about a Muslim student and capitalized on the opportunity to invite a local parent to talk about Islam. Parents are very willing to support any fund-raising endeavor he suggests and were completely supportive of a "who is your neighbor?" day in which classes engaged in activities to learn about students in other countries. Moreover, the "Who is your neighbor?" day occurred the day before statewide testing with slight push-back from only one teacher and none from parents. One parent even made a point of telling him she was happy they had relieved the test-taking pressure instead of heightening it. Nevertheless, John is constantly aware of the parental expectation that few if any controversial topics will be addressed by teachers. When a report of two male penguins in Central Park Zoo tending an egg and raising a chick (Smith, 2004) was discussed as part of a science unit, parents complained about the acceptance of homosexuality and its discussion in their school. This was not an isolated example; John struggles constantly to find ways to help students understand their privilege and concomitant responsibility to those less advantaged in ways that are meaningful and not patronizing. He knows that parents of his students have deep pockets but that donating money (as helpful as that may be in a crisis situation) does little to promote global awareness and citizenship.

Audrey Burns, as do David, Catherine, and John, addresses challenges that are specific to her context, although her school appears, on the surface, to have few challenges. Her small student body, numbering approximately 350 students, achieves well on state-mandated tests and hence enjoys a "fully recognized" status. Approximately 20% of the students (65% of whom are White, 12% Hispanic, 8% Black, 10% Asian, and 5.5% multi-racial) receive free or reduced-price lunch. Nevertheless, as the White population has decreased, the percent of students meeting or exceeding expectations on the tests has declined in the past 10 years from 98% to 83%, raising concerns for both educators and the general public. Of increasing concern to her is the fact that the numbers do not reveal that 5% of her students are classified as "homeless" under the provisions of the McKinney-Vento Act, many of whom are in the group failing to succeed in school.

When Audrey pays attention to students who are homeless, who are not achieving, or whose circumstances are, in some way, more challenging than her historically typical population, a few of her teachers challenge her efforts, telling her the focus is inappropriate and that she is neglecting the students whose parents have influence in the community. Nevertheless, Audrey's eye is firmly on the goal of equity and social justice; and hence, regardless of complaints, she is clear about her responsibility to all children.

Although she recognizes that in a time of increasingly tight budgets and underfunded mandates, having to provide transportation and school supplies to homeless children may constitute a financial burden, the needs of the children must outweigh the fiscal considerations of the district. She is therefore increasingly dismayed by the attitude of some other school and district leaders whose goals seem to be to restrict student enrollment and deny anyone who cannot prove official residence in their district. She is, however, acutely aware that under the McKinney-Vento law, anyone who has previously attended her school and subsequently become homeless has the right to be enrolled in school—without having to wait for a birth certificate, previous school records, and so forth. In fact, there are provisions for leaders to assist families who are having difficulty with documentation. Unlike many of her colleagues, she does not relegate enrollment of new students to a secretary or counselor, but does the task herself, using it as an opportunity to gain and provide information and to begin to build relationships. She is so committed to these goals that she often picks up the phone at the beginning of a new school year, courageously saying to the next principal, "You are receiving one of my precious graduates who happens to be homeless. Would you like me to remind you of the terms of the McKinney-Vento Act?" and, without taking a breath, she summarizes some of its key requirements.

What sets each of these principals apart from their peers is not necessarily their actions (although as we shall see later, in some cases, their actions are dramatically different), or even the programs offered in their schools. It is the degree of clarity about their goals for both individual and civic growth and responsibility, their reflectiveness, and their courage to take a difficult stand. In subsequent chapters, as we examine in depth each of the characteristics of transformative leadership, we will revisit these principals and learn more about how they approach the challenges each confronts. And, as we get to know each better, we will gain a clearer understanding of the tenets of transformative leadership and its ability to effect significant change. Because they are inextricably intertwined, we start, in the next chapter, with an exploration of the first three tenets outlined above: the mandate to effect deep and equitable change; the need to deconstruct and reconstruct knowledge frameworks that perpetuate inequity and injustice; and a focus on emancipation, democracy, equity, and justice.

For Further Reflection and Action

1. How do you define a "good" leader? Does it require moral courage in today's complex and changing context?
2. Discuss what you understand to be the differences between transformational and transformative leadership and consider which most clearly exists currently in your organization and whether modifying the approach might help to meet transformative and equity goals.
3. How can the use of dialogue, a focus on relationships, and the development of transparent ways to share information, help to challenge inequitable policies and practices?
4. Do the situations of David Dean, Catherine Lake, and John Law resonate with you? Can you identify any issues in your workplace that require you to demonstrate clarity of vision and/or moral courage to address them?

Chapter 3

Changing Knowledge Frameworks to Promote Equity

> They just need to let go of the past. Residential schools ended half a century ago; why do they keep bringing it up?
>
> (School principal)

> You always get the parents you don't need to see at these parent–teacher interviews. The ones you really need to see, just don't care.
>
> (Teacher-leader)

> If they would only try to be more like us, and respect our ways, it would be easier to include them.
>
> (Curriculum consultant)

> This school is inclusive. We accept all kinds of kids here but we can't let same-sex couples attend our graduation prom. It just goes against community values.
>
> (School principal)

In previous chapters, I emphasized the volatility, uncertainty, complexity, and ambiguity of today's world and suggested that transformative leadership is a way forward. In Chapter 2, I also clarified the distinctions between transformative leadership and other theories and approaches and identified several key characteristics of transformative leadership. In this chapter, I elaborate on the first three characteristics: the mandate to effect deep and equitable change; the need to deconstruct and reconstruct knowledge frameworks that perpetuate inequity and injustice; and the need for educational leaders to promote emancipation, democracy, equity, and justice. They are obviously inextricably interconnected.

It is common for schools to develop mottos, mission, or vision statements along the lines of "All children can learn," or "We provide every student an opportunity to achieve to his or her highest potential" or "Our goal is to provide a quality education in a caring setting." What is common about these statements is that they express the conviction, indeed even the moral imperative, for schools to be places where all children can achieve their potential, where all have equal opportunities to successfully meet academic and social goals, and where all are (or should be) equally valued and respected.

Unfortunately, as I suggested earlier, this is not the case. Some students are successful, included, even privileged by our existing systems of education, while others are less successful, excluded, marginalized, and even disadvantaged. As I have described in more detail elsewhere (Shields, 2009), it is incumbent on all educators and educational leaders to determine who is in which group, why this may occur, and to make informed and essentially moral decisions about what to do about it.

In this chapter, I will first examine some ways in which schools reproduce inequitable situations by marginalizing and disadvantaging some children while advantaging and privileging others. This obviously provides the mandate for deep and equitable change and begs the need for new knowledge frameworks that focus on equity and social justice; it requires the transformative stance of focusing on emancipation, democracy, equity, and justice. Then I will offer three keys to overcoming this marginalization—all of which involve the deconstruction and reconstruction of existing knowledge frameworks. The three are rejection of deficit thinking, engaging in democratic discourse and difficult conversations, and opening the curricular space. Each of these will be developed using some current educational theories and elaborated by examples from real schools in order to help school leaders think critically about the situation and challenges to their own schools.

Understanding Educational Marginalization and School Failure

Some argue that, historically, education has served three main functions: a custodial function; an intellectual one; and a communal one. The custodial function becomes salient, especially for elementary children, on days when the normal educational routines are interrupted—snow days, teacher job action, even during days of early dismissal or professional development for educators. Parents complain that their routines are disrupted, they do not have child care, they cannot take time off work to care for their children, and so on. The intellectual function is well understood. Schools are the only institutions in society whose primary responsibility is the intellectual development of citizens. To be sure, the function is shared by the home, churches, and social organizations, but for all organizations except schools, it is one function among many. The communal function of schools relates to the development of citizens—teaching all students ways to get along in society, to participate fully in its democratic processes, and to gain an understanding of what it means to be socially responsible. This last function (like the other two) is not intended only for those who think or look like the teacher or administrator but for all who attend a nation's public schools.

All children deserve to be safe, cared for, and completely respected in their schools. We can no longer consider some ways of thinking, being, or relating acceptable while other lifestyles are rejected, marginalized, oppressed. This is not to say we have to agree with any position we find unacceptable; we do not. It is to say that in publically supported institutions we must find ways to accept, respect, and include everyone. We cannot legislate belief, but it is the role of educators to develop knowledge frameworks that are inclusive and respectful of everyone. And it is the role of transformative educational leaders to ensure that practices and policies demonstrate respect and caring (regardless of individual beliefs).

It is clear that our increasingly diverse and complex schools are populated by many people who do not come from what might be called "mainstream families"; some students are very successful in school, university, and future career; many others are not. Often, we point to the successful members of a given group and suggest that because they have been able to achieve, often to "pull themselves up by their bootstraps," others should be able to work equally hard and also succeed. (Sometimes, people point to President Obama's success and attribute this possibility to all other African Americans, for example, without regard to context or individual circumstances.) Unfortunately, this individualistic interpretation is misguided for several reasons. First it assumes that it is normal, natural, and acceptable for any system to require that African American (or other minoritized) students have to work harder than their White peers, and hence it ignores the deeply entrenched and systemic structural and institutional factors that make it more difficult for many members of minoritized[1] groups to succeed. In accepting this argument, we are, in fact, agreeing that it is tolerable to create conditions under which it is easier for one group to succeed than for others, in fact, perpetuating the privilege of the dominant group. Under this argument, if children from minoritized groups need to try harder, work harder, struggle more, take more responsibility for figuring out the meaning of the curriculum than others, we agree that is not only acceptable but "normal." Further, if a child, despite hard work, fails to succeed, using this argument lets us off the hook. We can safely retreat behind our (incorrect) assumption that the failure was the child's instead of having to examine the deep structures and beliefs of our organizations. At least in North America, where almost everyone has the opportunity to attend school, we too often accept the argument that it is up to each person to find the motivation to achieve.

And yet, fortunately, when the stark reality is described in terms of making it harder for one group than for another to succeed, most educators strenuously object saying, "That's not right! I don't accept this as normal!"

Often without thinking, we accept that if people fail to achieve, they just did not try hard enough—and worse, we blame them, thinking that there was something inherently wrong with them or their approach in the first place. In Detroit (where I now live), I often hear people explaining the continued failure of students in Detroit public schools with the statement that because, in recent years, many middle-class citizens (Black and White) have moved to the suburbs, only those who do not understand or care about education are left in downtown Detroit. This kind of thinking is often known as "deficit thinking" and is one of the major causes for the lack of success of many minoritized students—an issue we will return to below.

Many scholars have discussed school failure as stemming from a mismatch between the social, economic, or cultural capital students bring to school and that which is promoted and valued by the educational institution itself. Bourdieu and Passeron (1977) explain that the *field* of education, like other fields, perpetuates and is perpetuated by what they call *habitus*—a collection of norms and traditions that over time have come to establish the boundaries of what is acceptable and "normal" and what is not acceptable within the educational context. Thus, they and others (see Delpit, 1990) would argue that when what students bring from home differs significantly from what is "acceptable" to the school (i.e., taught within the curriculum, openly discussed, valued, even assumed to be present), they will have more difficulty negotiating the curriculum than will students for whom there is a greater match. To better understand this concept, and to reflect on its validity as an educational explanation, in the next few paragraphs we examine how this might play out for various marginalized groups of students.

Marginalized by Race

Some time ago now, educators and textbook publishers became aware that most of the faces in textbooks were White, that most of the stories students read focused on White middle-class family experiences. This meant that many of the increasingly diverse members of the student body were not visually or conceptually represented in textbooks or, for that matter, in the formal curriculum. However, the attendant change was mostly symbolic and superficial. Members of visible ethnic minority groups began to be represented pictorially, although core concepts were rarely adjusted. When textbook writers and publishers acknowledged the necessity of expanding the curriculum, they tended to add sections at the end of chapters: contributions of women, contributions of African Americans and so forth, failing to recognize that these "contributions" were always seen as add-ons to the core mainstream curriculum.

For example, discussions of Columbus Day and Columbus' discovery of America were rarely expanded to include mention of the atrocities conducted against Native Americans by Columbus and his followers. Instead, the myth of benign discovery was allowed to continue, but with the additional mention of the foods or musical instruments or dances "contributed" by Native Americans. Rarely were the hegemonic assumptions underlying the banning of these same dances and ceremonies discussed; yet, it is widely acknowledged that the urging of missionaries and government agents who considered it would prevent civilizing and Christianizing the Indians was at the root of outlawing these indigenous ceremonies. Of course, consideration of whether the Native Americans might have been better off without having been "discovered" or "evangelized" was similarly never present.

Somehow, the sordid history of governmental attempts in many countries, including the United States and Canada, to literally destroy the culture and language of indigenous populations through the assimilationist policies and practices of residential schools has never made it to mainstream history books. The fact that members of several generations of citizens were often snatched from their families and brutally transported to residential schools where they were forbidden to wear their clothes, maintain their traditional long hair, speak their language, or engage in cultural ceremonies is ignored. Worse still, perhaps, was the damage done to traditional relationships and family structure. Parents had no contact with their children. Children grew up wanting to take their place in society as responsible and caring adults without ever having had role models, without ever having the experience of learning at their parents' knee, without ever having experienced discipline at the hands of loving parents. Is it any wonder that the next generations experienced difficulty adapting to family life, to social responsibility, to school? The school principal quoted at the beginning of this chapter is not alone. I have often heard people expressing the wish that *they* (referring to multiply ill-treated groups) could simply put the past behind them. But until the loss is acknowledged, and missing emotional, social, and spiritual values and information are restored, how can this be done? This is the message of a 1996 Royal Commission on Aboriginal Peoples conducted in Canada (Minister of Supply and Services Canada, 1996). It is also the powerful message contained in a number of films such as *Rabbit-proof fence*, *Walkabout*, and *Whale rider*—all of which demonstrate the competence and resilience of indigenous peoples and the need to understand and confront a country's history of repression and prejudice before it can be overcome.

Similar issues exist, for example for those African Americans whose parents or grandparents experienced the horrors of slavery, the prejudices of reconstruction, or the continued exclusion on the basis of race from what have become known as sundown towns. Hispanic Americans have their own history of inconsistent messages, of suffering the norms of manifest destiny, and of ongoing barriers to the use of their language in the United States. All of these experiences have caused (as Ogbu, 1992, might argue) large groups of people to be treated as second- or third-class citizens. Moreover, as the marginalization and prejudice continued, fear and mistrust grew to the point where unreasonable fear, mistrust, and suspicion affected, and still today continue to affect, racial interactions. Societal conditions are reproduced in schools that are microcosms of the wider community. The impact is subtle, and often not well understood either by members of majority or minority groups. Sometimes, as I have discussed elsewhere (Shields, 2009), we take the stance that we should be "color-blind"—ignoring the very real differences in the daily experience of people whose skin pigment is not white. In fact, this is a form of what has come to be known as "color-blind racism."

A manifestation of this form of racism is described by one of my students, himself now a successful employee of an institute of higher education, who recently wrote (in discussing an article about minority parent involvement):

> The article struck a chord with me because I lived through the shame and anger of not having actively involved parents (on school terms). The shame came because I often believed that I was a bad student for not being able to bring my parents to teacher/parent nights, to award ceremonies, to field trips, among other things. I experienced anger for not being able to share stories about how my parents helped me with a school project, took me on museum trips, or took me along on vacations to other countries or states. It was not until senior year of high school that I let go of that shame and anger. The reason I took that long was that during the summer of my junior year of high school I finally saw why my mother was often absent in my educational experience. Growing up in a Mexican household, I never understood much of the outside world, until I realized that the reason my mother insisted on me getting good grades despite her absenteeism was because she wanted me to get away from the vicious cycle of underemployment that affects many Latinos.
>
> (Carlos)

This student's experience is not unique. Many students whose families come from non-White, non-middle class, non-English speaking backgrounds, tell of similar experiences and feelings. Although their parents were not able to be present at many school functions, they cared deeply about the success of their children and believed in the potential of education to be their path to social mobility. We do them a huge disservice, therefore, when we dismiss them as uncaring and unsupportive of schooling.

It becomes important for school leaders to understand how this kind of marginalization of many students continues and to take steps to ensure the creation of inclusive, respectful, and more democratic learning environments. Thus, the fusing of concepts from critical race theories (CRT) into theories of educational leadership becomes essential (Parker & Villalpando, 2007). CRT began as a way of acknowledging that the legal system is not color-blind, but that members of visible minority groups were too often over-represented in legal action, arrested and incarcerated in dispro-portionate numbers relevant to the size of the population in the wider society (Bell, 1995; Ladson-Billings, 1996), and so forth. Similarly, it demonstrates that in education, lack of academic achievement, excessive dropout rates (or perhaps better described as push-out rates), disproportionate suspensions and disciplinary incidents for visible minority students all seem to point to something structural and systemic rather than simply to student inability, lack of motivation, or effort.

Overcoming these structural and systemic barriers cannot and must not simply be the responsibility of those who have suffered. Those who have benefited (unwittingly and historically) from these situations must play a role. This is not to say we must beat ourselves up with guilt, or renounce our wealth or positions (although some may choose to do so). We must, however, acknowledge our privilege, our benefit, and, with compassion, stand in solidarity with those who have been marginalized or oppressed. It is up to us to acknowledge the injustices and work to create the conditions under which those who have suffered may be empowered and liberated from our misplaced beliefs, assumptions, and prejudices.

Marginalized by Social Class

Marginalization with respect to social class (including economic disadvantage, low levels of formal parental education, unskilled labor, and so on) is more subtle than marginalization due to skin color because class is, in many ways, invisible. Nevertheless, it exerts a strong and persistent pressure on the ability of students to succeed in school. In fact, in 1995, scholars Knapp and Woolverton found that "there is an enduring relation between social class and educational outcomes" (p. 551) in that students from high status families tend to have "high levels of educational attainment and achievement [while] low social class correlates with low levels of educational attainment and achievement" (p. 551). Note that they write about correlation and *not* causation. Lower social status and deprivation do not cause poor educational outcomes (although poor levels of nutrition and the increased stress of living in poverty may certainly contribute to a child's inability to concentrate). Worse still is their finding that "these correlations hold over time and cultures" (p. 551).

When we think about it, the findings of Knapp and Woolverton make sense. We know that students from families who have the ability to travel, provide private music lessons, attend cultural performances, and have the luxury of time to talk about what is happening at school, in their community, or in the world do better in school than children from families without these opportunities. Yet, too often we fail to understand that even though these are family activities valued by schools, all children come to school with a wealth of cultural capital. Other children, who may come from families struggling with poverty, disease, homelessness, for example, may have learned to cook meals, clean the house, negotiate the local bus system, care for younger siblings, and so forth—all skills that have enabled them to survive, but not necessarily those that help them interpret and make sense of the typical "middle-class" school curriculum. This means that, as educators, we must learn to value, and make connections to, a wide range of experiences and cultural capital. It is not sufficient to focus on what students do not know; instead, it is critical to emphasize and build on what it is that they do know and can do.

Too often we hear educators make comments like the teacher-leader comment cited at the beginning of this chapter, indicating their perception that parents who do not attend school events and parent–teacher conferences care less about their child's future and success at school than those who attend. Unfortunately, the experience of shame recounted by Carlos (above) is repeated over and over again in homes of American school children. Consider this reflection by another student, also now an accomplished professional:

> My parents were manual laborers and they never had the time to teach me the alphabet, numbers, or how to write my name. They always felt that school was a place where I would learn all of that. For a 5-year-old my last name was difficult to spell. I remember being placed in timeout because I was not able to fully write it out on my papers. It was a name that no other person had outside of my family; it was unlike other students who may have seen their names written on street signs, campaign posters, in television or radio broadcasts, or heard their parents being addressed as Mr. and Mrs. So-and-So. My last name was unfamiliar to me, but the teacher saw it as a lack of my parents' involvement in my education. Instead of timeout being a space to reflect on how to spell my last name correctly, I understood it as punishment for having such a different last name.

Despite his parents' love and care, teachers communicated their inaccurate perceptions that they were actually remiss—and somehow this impression was so strong it became dominant in his young mind. This is the kind of perception that must be challenged by every caring administrator wherever and whenever it is voiced. Some parents (like teachers themselves) have salaried positions that permit them to take time off during work without losing pay. Others work hourly-wage shift work that does not provide the luxury of time off without pay, and that requires they work at times when many school events are scheduled. If a parent is also the sole wage-earner, has several children in different grades, with activities scheduled at different times, he or she may not be able to repeatedly take time off to come to the school. If they work an evening shift, they may not be able to help their children with homework. And if they are struggling financially to put food on the table and keep a roof over their heads, they will almost certainly be unable to buy craft materials and/or food to support the many school projects often requiring parental assistance.

Sometimes, when impoverished or less advantaged parents do come to the school, their concerns are not taken seriously and they are dismissed for not understanding the system or for making unrealistic requests. Sophie, as we shall see further in Chapter 8, was a child who grew up in poverty, often not knowing where her next meal would come from, sometimes absent from school when her parents had to pick up or cash their welfare check. During one particularly difficult year, in which the family had moved a lot and Sophie was miserably failing math, her father believed that circumstances dictated she should drop out of school and wait until the next year to get a fresh start. At the beginning of the next year, when Sophie was assigned to the same teacher's class, her father went to the school to request a change. The response was less than sympathetic. "It does not matter what teacher we put her with," the principal explained, "we are really just baby-sitting that girl anyway." Fortunately, but far into her future, Sophie met a much more empathic and respectful educator whose support and encouragement led to her actually becoming an educator herself.

Educators make many thoughtless (and unnecessary) comments or requests that result in children from economically disadvantaged families being further disadvantaged in their quest for academic success. Consider the child who, on the first day of school, has to wear second-hand clothes, carry school materials (perhaps an incomplete supply) in a plastic grocery bag, and sees around him or her the excitement of class-mates reveling in their new possessions. The shame and embarrassment are repeated when children are asked about what they did during summer holidays, how they spent the weekend, to bring something for show and tell, and so forth. School pictures are not free, but costly for some families; pizza days, additional field trips, and so forth—all present a challenge to students, some of whom simply pretend they have forgotten to return permission slips. All of these experiences communicate a subtle message that school is not really designed for these students. Despite the fact that some persist, swallowing their pride, and asking for assistance, this should not be a requisite for succeeding in school.

There is no excuse in a "democratic" nation in which education is supposed to be "free and universal" for marginalizing students based on the economic status of their parents. Especially in the VUCA social milieu of the 21st century, with record gas prices, the constantly rising cost of commodities, housing foreclosures, homelessness, high unemployment rates, and so forth, countless families are struggling to survive. Educators must be particularly careful not to exacerbate the educational challenges children face when their parents are struggling financially.

Marginalized by Sexual Orientation

Another hidden factor marginalizing students is sexual orientation—an issue that has received increasing attention in recent years, due to high-profile press stories about graduation proms, discrimination cases, and an excess of bullying and victimization for students whose sexual orientation is not heteronormative. Often school leaders who accede to requests from students or teachers to publically acknowledge safe spaces, to support gay pride activities with "silent" support such as the wearing of T-shirts, or to permit the sponsorship of gay–straight support groups and alliances find themselves in trouble with superiors or with their surrounding community. Here again, it is important for the school leader to know and understand the statistics as well as the individual stories of members of the school community. Tooms (2007) writes that we need to understand how "heteronormative power effects [*sic*] school leadership (and therefore schools) on a day-to-day level in terms of student and faculty safety (Capper, 1999; Sears, 1996), pedagogy (Britzman, 1995; Kumanshiro, 2001), and politics (Lugg, 1998, 2003, 2006)" (p. 1). Those whose sexuality is not heteronormative, whether students or teachers, too often experience a lack of safety, respect, or acceptance in our schools; and neither the current pedagogical nor political practices adequately address the issue.

Being sensitive and age-appropriate, however, are sometimes used as codes for skirting the central issue. I recently asked a group of teachers how they would handle it if, after asking a group of kindergarten children to draw a picture of their families, one child showed himself or herself with two mommies or two daddies. A teacher quickly responded, "I would talk about how there are different families; some children live with grandparents, some with aunts and uncles, etc." This is an excellent starting point, but in order for the discussion to address the central issue, it is also important to include in the conversation that some children have two mommies or two daddies. The important question is whether the chosen approach allows us to get to the heart of the issue and to validate the child in question or to skirt the issue, leaving her vaguely humiliated and embarrassed that her family configuration was not really included in the subsequent discussion of multiple family clusters.

A transformative leader will warrant that the topic be addressed, in a non-judgmental and matter-of-fact way, to ensure the respectful inclusion of all children in the learning environment. In the particular discussion, the staff had just finished a brief exploration of an incident that one teacher had encountered on the playground. She had come across a group of fifth-grade boys apparently rough-housing, grabbing one child, slapping him around a bit, and then dragging him across the yard. When she asked the boys what they were doing, she was taken aback by their forthright reply: "Playing 'Catch the Illegal Alien'." She was astounded and wondered what might be an appropriate response. As we explored the issue, one staff member suggested he would ask the boys why they were being so rough, whether they liked it, and whether one of them might actually get hurt. As we explored the possible outcomes of that approach, it became evident that it avoided the core issue of illegal aliens—something we often do when we are uncomfortable with a somewhat volatile subject. Someone else suggested. "I'd ask them, 'What is an illegal alien?'" The first teacher then indicated that, in fact, that is what she had asked, and had received the simple response, "A Mexican." Now, the staff realized, they would need to confront the difficult central issue. More questions could ensue: what is a Mexican? Where is Mexico? Who lives there? Are all Mexicans aliens? What might make someone go into a country without proper documentation? Is it justified? How might it be handled? Are all Mexicans illegal? What about all Mexicans living in America? If a parent comes into this country illegally, is it a child's fault? and so on—in appropriate depth for the age group engaged in the conversation.

Because of this exploration of illegal aliens, when the issue of Sally having two mommies was raised, one of the teachers, after a few minutes' thought, asked, "If we simply talk about different family configurations, isn't that really like just asking the kids about playing rough? Doesn't it simply avoid the central issue?"

Sometimes one hears educators ask about the norms of local control, raising the following question: if the community is against homosexuality, perhaps for religious reasons, is it ethical, permissible, or desirable for the school to address the issue, in essence, going against the will of the community? My argument is that it is the only moral and ethical way to proceed, given that there *are* children within the school who are either gay or questioning or whose parents may be in a homosexual relationship. Beliefs that exclude or marginalize others cannot be acted upon in a public forum, no matter how strongly they may be held.

Marginalized by Home Language, Religion, or Country of Origin

The above discussion of race and ethnicity, social class, and sexual orientation is applicable to all students whether they were born in their country of residence and schooling or not. Nevertheless, students whose home language is other than the language of instruction, whose religion is not Christian (despite the claims of separation of church and state), or whose country of origin is not seen as friendly to the United States, often experience additional pressures and challenges in our schools.

Too often inability to speak fluent, unaccented English is associated with dullness of intellect, lack of understanding, or lack of commitment to American values. The situation is compounded if the language spoken by the student is not considered a "high status" language, for educators need to acknowledge there is a hierarchy of additional languages. Because, in the United States, Spanish speakers are often associated with undocumented citizens, with border breaches, or with some of the drug-related violence frequently reported in Mexico, there is a strong political movement in some states to prevent or restrict the occurrence of Spanish–English bilingual programs—programs well known to promote the academic success of students (Cummins, 1989). At the same time, schools that teach advanced classes in Russian, Mandarin, or even French rarely experience similar political pressures to curb their activities, because, for the most part, the latter are examples of high-status languages.

In recent years, since what has come simply to be known as "9/11," an increase of Islamophobia has been noted by many. Protests in states such as California, Michigan, Wisconsin, or Tennessee when a group of residents want to build a mosque have become almost commonplace. The widely publicized congressional hearings, sponsored by Peter King, to discuss the radicalization of Islam in America, reduced Keith Ellison, the first Muslim elected to the US Congress, to tears as he described the death of a Muslim paramedic working as part of the rescue effort at Ground Zero and the subsequent false rumors that he was one of the attackers. Similarly, too often in schools, Muslim students experience lack of understanding and even frequent taunts of being terrorists or "suicide bombers," as well as additional challenges related to completing requirements for physical education, or engaging in extra-curricular events if their cultural practices come into conflict with those of their school.

What is important for school leaders to know is that we *construct* our impressions, images, and conceptions of those whom we consider to be Other. Many of my friends from Middle Eastern Arabic countries, for example, tell me that until they arrived in North America, they had always considered themselves to be White. Only when they learned that we do not typically see them that way, that North Americans tend to think of them as Brown, did they begin to consider themselves Brown. They have been "Othered" and have begun to construct their personal images of themselves, based on our views that they are different from us. Thus, those who might easily align themselves with "us" become Othered, as, once again, they find themselves excluded, marginalized, rejected. Ultimately, this leads to discouragement, frustration, withdrawal, a concomitant lack of school success, and sometimes even "radicalization" (Apple, 2001).

A powerful example of how marginalization can lead to negative and even confrontational behavior may be found in a stunning prize-winning dissertation (Sayani, 2010). The author examined the condition of students known as the "Brown boys" in a Canadian high school. These students were, in general, second-generation Indian or Pakistani youth who felt disaffected and disengaged in school. He found that instead of creating spaces where these students were accepted, teachers actually feared them and wanted to prevent them from gathering together in the halls or cafeteria. So excluded did these students feel, they often admitted exacerbating their own situations by fulfilling the image others had projected on them. Sayani (2010) cited a "Brown" teacher who said:

> The Brown guys are the ones who do most of the stuff. Look at the example of the guy who put a firecracker in the toilet and it blew up; that was a Brown guy. No one else did that. All the stuff that has happened, like fights and stuff—that you see on U-tube—they were done by Brown guys but I don't think it's fair that when any bad thing happens, they [teachers] go there to the Brown guys first and blame them. I can see why they think that but I don't think it is fair. You can also see why the Brown guys are so pissed and continue with stuff like fighting.
>
> (p. 338)

The boys repeatedly confirmed her impressions, acknowledging that if "something bad happened," people immediately assumed the Brown boys were at fault. They acknowledged, however, "That's true sometime but not all the time that people think. It's usually easier to be this way than to change history" (p. 343). Another also agreed:

> we've had many examples of how . . . our parents who were younger . . . were bullied and excluded and suffered racism because of being Brown or having an accent or dressing in a certain way . . . We won't let history repeat itself. We are taking control; it's like we may not be the majority but we can take the power. Who's going to stop us? If we have the power then they can't do stuff to us. We will bully you [people who once had power] and not let them bully us like before or the way they probably want to even right now.
>
> (p. 165)

Comments like these are important reminders to educators that if they do not address incidents of racism or bullying that lead to students feeling marginalized and excluded, then the cycle of exclusion, negativity, and even of increased violence is perpetuated. Students begin to act as they are "expected to," whether in positive or negative ways, and take control where they can. Unless we are careful to provide opportunities for students to exercise agency over their learning, citizenship, and community relations, they will often use their power in anti-social, negative, and even self-destructive ways, increasing the volatility and complexity of the school community.

Overcoming Marginalization: Making Schools Inclusive

The point of the previous discussion is that if educational leaders are to be successful in making schools places of liberation, equity, and social justice for all students as well as sites for academic and intellectual growth, they must deconstruct the images of students as problems, as Others, as unmotivated and uncaring and replace these negative images with an understanding of all students as individuals worthy of respect and support (Apple, 1996). In short, they must create the conditions for the development of caring and supportive personal relationships that will overcome fear and suspicion.

Eliminating Deficit Thinking

The starting point for holding all students to the same high standards is the deconstruction and rejection of what is known as *deficit thinking* and the reconstruction of positive images of able and engaged students. Deficit thinking is another way of saying that we blame the students or their families for their lack of school success because we see them as being in some way deficient. In other words, we equate difference with deficiency and place the onus on them to change. Although they might not use this transformative leadership language of deconstructing and reconstructing knowledge frameworks, many scholars argue for the necessity of rejecting deficit thinking and holding high expectations for all students. Almost 20 years ago, Wagstaff and Fusarelli (1995) conducted a study in which they found that the *single* most important factor in the academic achievement of minoritized students is the principal's explicit rejection of deficit thinking.

Other scholars have also found that when educators reject deficit thinking and start, instead, with the assumption that all students are capable of learning to high standards and able to play an active and agentic role in their own learning (Bishop & Berryman, 2006; Shields, Bishop, & Mazawi, 2005), the outcomes change positively and surprisingly rapidly. Bishop and Berryman, for example, in their New Zealand program called *Te Kotahitanga* (see http://tekotahitanga.tki.org.nz/) found that when teachers stopped blaming Maori children and their families, and took responsibility for the learning of all children in their classes, the Maori children performed as well as the mainstream White, "pakeja" students.

Nevertheless, deficit thinking is still pervasive, as demonstrated by Shields, Bishop, and Mazawi (2005), and as described by Valencia (2010) in his award-winning book that explains how to dismantle contemporary deficit thinking. Often when I speak to school leaders about helping all students learn, I ask them to mentally select a student who is unsuccessful in their current context and to brainstorm with their neighbors the reasons for the lack of success. As I gather some of their responses, I often hear "They just don't try"; "Their parents don't care"; "Their home is too chaotic and they don't have a quiet place to do homework"; "Their parents really don't value education." I then point out that all of these responses fall into the category of *blaming the victim*—placing the blame for the child's lack of success either on his family or on the child himself.

Too often, even after I have discussed the concept and used the term *deficit thinking* multiple times, educators come up to me asking questions about "that kind of thinking you described." Similarly, a colleague (herself a school principal) reports that, at a conference of educators, she "heard a group of white educators from a predominantly African American community argue that 'these kids aren't able to think critically . . . they just do not come to school with the necessary background'" (Bieneman, 2011, p. 228). She went on to write:

> At present, few educators are even aware of this construct and its unintended, yet destructive, effects. Recently, I served as adjunct faculty at a private university. I taught in two separate master's programs—one for reading specialists and one for administrators. During the course of that year, I introduced students to the research on deficit thinking. None of the nearly 80 educators were even familiar

with the notion of deficit thinking, and none had examined pathologizing practices in their own classrooms and schools. Becoming aware is a critical first step for transformative leaders.

(p. 299)

Very recently, at an international academic conference, I was part of a panel of scholars, researchers, and practitioners who had been working with concepts of transformative leadership in high poverty schools for over a decade. Despite our data showing that children from impoverished homes can learn, and the insistence of many urban school principals that this was indeed so, one member from the audience insisted that it is impossible to successfully teach children from disadvantaged situations in today's schools. His response is all too common.

It is undeniable that some social and structural factors contribute to the lack of success of some students. Children who are well rested, well nourished, and assisted at home are undoubtedly well positioned to succeed at school. Nevertheless, educators must take responsibility for what occurs during the school day and there is much that schools can do. Is the child placed with a teacher who is just putting in time to retirement or with one who is innovative, patient, and knowledgeable? Does the school or classroom have the appropriate resources to teach each child (appropriate reading material for example)? Does the school have the ability to provide food for children who come to school hungry? Do school policies permit children whose home language is not English to converse quietly among themselves in their first language until they are sure they have understood both the instructions and the content, and then, are they encouraged to respond with a solid response in English? The issue is that transformative educators cannot wait until society's ills and disparities are resolved before we take responsibility for educating all children.

Unfortunately we know, from numerous studies over the years, that we can still predict school success and achievement in kindergarten only by knowing about the family's socio-economic status and living conditions. If this is to change, if schools are truly to play a role in helping all children to learn, in promoting social mobility, and in helping to equalize future opportunities, then educators must understand it is one of their duties to help children overcome the limitations of their home situations—limitations that the children have not created and for which they are not responsible.

Transformative educators must, therefore, understand that when they place the blame for lack of achievement on the child, they are abrogating their own responsibility; they are engaging in deficit thinking, and longing wistfully for someone to first "fix" the child so that they may teach her. Once educators have begun to reflect on how to overcome blaming the children and their families and have indicated willingness to learn to teach differently, taking responsibility for the learning of all children, they can begin to examine their own roles and responsibility and develop new strategies for teaching all children.

Wagstaff and Fusarelli's (1995) finding (cited above) bears repeating: the single most important factor in the academic achievement of minoritized children is the explicit rejection of deficit thinking—not just on the part of one teacher, or in one classroom, but school-wide—initiated and encouraged by the school leader. The point is so important I dwell on it here for it is one strategy, one way of deconstructing and reconstructing knowledge frameworks that is within everyone's grasp, and capacity. Deficit thinking lets us off the hook. If the deficiency is in the child, we cannot be expected to "fix" or teach him.

If, however, the child is not deficient, but we have just not figured out how to adequately reach and teach her, then we are not only complicit in the failure, but responsible for it. To deconstruct deficit thinking, no special equipment is needed, no new program, almost no training necessary—simply a dedicated, consistent, and concerted effort on the part of every educator to resist blaming the child or family for lack of success. What is necessary is that every educational leader make his or her staff aware of the need to address and overcome deficit thinking.

It can be done. I have been in schools and listened to conversations in staffrooms that are full of complaints about students and their families. But I have also visited schools in which the conversation is about how teachers have adapted the lesson, what strategies they have tried, how they have found a new and creative way to teach a concept. In these schools, if a teacher slips, and begins to place the onus on a child, I have heard teachers hold each other accountable, literally saying to one another, "Careful, you seem to be in deficit thinking now." In one elementary school I know in an impoverished area, teachers, recognizing that children do not learn well when hungry, went against conventional wisdom, and set out food and a microwave oven in the back of the room. There was no particular time set aside, children did not have to seek permission to eat, but children were allowed to eat when they were hungry. Several times a day, teachers who participated noticed a few children quietly getting up and helping themselves to needed nourishment. Teachers reported that children did not abuse the privilege; moreover, they were not seen as deficient—only, in this case, hungry.

Catherine Lake (one of the transformative leaders we met in the last chapter) believes this is so important in her school that she often asks her teachers to engage in free writing. She throws out a question like, "Why is there an achievement gap in math between the African American students and others in our school?" "Why are students for whom English is a second language doing better in math than our African American students?" Her contention is that if children who are operating in a second (or third) language can succeed in her school, then children who are learning using their home language should be at least as successful—unless they are targets of inappropriate assumptions and deficit thinking. Once, when she heard teachers blaming the children, she suggested she planned to have banners made proclaiming the inevitable "truth" that "in our school 98% of White students will succeed; 79% of Hispanic students will succeed; and 52% of African American students will succeed." Naturally her teachers were horrified, and once again, took to heart the need to take responsibility for figuring out how to reach all children.

Again, this is not to suggest that home factors don't matter. Of course they do. In fact, as long as the curriculum and assessments of our schools primarily emphasize the traditional Eurocentric, middle-class knowledge perspectives, then some children will come to school having already learned at home many of the necessary basics for making connections and interpreting the material. Other children, from various other cultural backgrounds, will have learned other valuable lessons at home, but the teacher may need to teach these children information they have not yet had the opportunity to learn. For example, although many children who live in economically impoverished homes may not have had the opportunity to travel widely or far from home, they have often learned to navigate public transit on their own. Thus, to be more inclusive, discussions of travel should include the local as well as national and international. This is also an important point. Educators need to understand what it is that children have learned and what competencies they bring to school that may not necessarily be valued in our current curricula in order to help students connect new learning to what they know.

Address Challenging Issues through Difficult Conversations

In the discussion referenced earlier in which teachers explored, in a brief 45-minute meeting, the issue of the "illegal alien" and of "two mommies," we saw that even having a brief opportunity to begin to explore how to respond to complex issues helps teachers to reflect and to formulate strategies for addressing issues head-on. There the key was that the school principal had created the space to deal with issues instead of being afraid of a backlash from the parent community. Yet, backlash there might well be. The principal and the staff recounted that when a Muslim parent from the community had addressed a fifth-grade class a few months previously, to explain some of his Islamic beliefs and practices, several parents complained directly to the superintendent and others had gone directly to him—one particularly upset that his son had been told that Islam was a religion of peace. Holding difficult conversations takes courage and knowledge, but it is the central task of an educator wanting to construct new knowledge frameworks, reject deficit thinking, and open the curricular space. Engaging in difficult conversations is key.

Gutmann (2001) has a useful way of responding to such questions. Her argument is that public schools should help students learn to live with conflict and tension. She asserts that the fundamental test in a democracy is whether knowledge and information may be freely disseminated and discussed. Hence the test of what can and should be discussed in public schools is the test of whether or not a topic is repressive or discriminatory. She uses the controversial question of "evolution or creationism" as illustrative of her point. First she states that "the content of public schooling cannot be neutral among competing conceptions of the good life, and if it could, we would not and should not care to support it" (p. 226). For that reason, everyone has the right to believe whatever they want at home, but in a public discussion, anything that is not repressive or discriminatory must be permitted. She explains, "Repression entails restriction of rational inquiry, not conflict with personal beliefs, however deeply held these beliefs" (p. 227). Using this guideline, even if a parent community wants to repress discussion of homosexuality, schools should not accede. To do so would repress legitimate inquiry and foster discriminatory attitudes and behaviors related to same-sex families. Hence, as in the situation to which I alluded previously (the penguins in Central Park Zoo), no group should have the power to insist that the discussion be repressed (although it must of course be conducted with sensitivity and in an age-appropriate way).

Oakes and Rogers (2006) and others argue that, in today's complex and uncertain context, current conceptions of reform are inadequate to effect equitable education in that they do not focus on equity. They argue that there are components missing in ways of thinking about school improvement or strategic planning that are necessary to consider if deeper, more equitable reform is to be initiated. Freire (1970), for example, argued that "The oppressed must be active participants in their own liberation," because if they are not, then they will only be "objects which must be saved from a burning building" (p. 65). Foster (1986) argued the need for more critical foundations of educational administration, in other words, concepts from critical theory that suggest leadership needs to focus on being educative, critical, and developing understanding. He believed that leaders cannot be satisfied to simply look at the conditions in which people live, but that we must be willing to become engaged in the fight to change them.

Other scholars who identify with the concept of leadership for social justice emphasize the need to address marginalizing structures (Theoharis, 2007), to focus on curricular and pedagogical practices (Reyes-Guerra & Bogotch, 2011), to work toward deep democracy (Green, 1999), to take respectful account of indigenous knowledge frameworks and theories of place (Smith, 1999), to engage critical feminism (Blackmore, 2010), or critical race theory (Bell, 1995; Parker & Villalpando, 2007), and so forth. McKenzie et al. (2008) proffer a framework for social justice in schools in which educational leaders develop critical consciousness, engage with teaching and learning, provide proactive systems of support, and create inclusive structures. Each of these comprises a useful and important approach to furthering equity and justice in schools.

Sometimes, in order to be a transformative leader in this VUCA world, we need to convince people of the importance of being inclusive, and of reconstructing the ways in which we think about children, families, cultures, the curriculum, or the wider society. To do so, it is important to engage in meaningful and often difficult conversations. Sometimes, this takes real courage on the part of an administrator; often it takes prior reflection and consideration of how to facilitate what Singleton and Curtis (2005) have called "courageous conversations." Sometimes it is a matter of discussing the meaning of democratic schooling, and of suggesting that it is not simply a means of governance in which everyone has a vote (although that is also necessary), but a way of thinking about and preparing children to live in common in society in mutually beneficial ways.

Riehl (2000) identified three broad categories of tasks that create an inclusive environment. Those tasks include "fostering new meanings about diversity, promoting inclusive practices within schools, and building connections between schools and communities" (p. 59). She argued that one of the key strategies that principals can employ to accomplish these tasks is "democratic discourse within the school community" (p. 61). Others (see for example, Burbules, 1993; Shields, 2009; Shields & Edwards, 2005; Sidorkin, 1999) have posited the need for dialogue to accomplish a similar end. Regardless of the term used, educators must be prepared and willing to enjoin difficult and often sensitive topics in order to create inclusive, safe, and respectful learning environments for all students. Engaging in dialogue, holding difficult conversations, like rejecting deficit thinking, is simply a foundation for the ongoing task of opening respectful learning spaces in which all children (and the totality of their lived experiences) are valued.

Opening the Curricular Space

Once educators have understood the importance of rejecting deficit thinking and of holding high expectations for all children, the next step is, of course, to work to create more inclusive and deeply democratic (note the small "d") communities of learners. An important step, I have suggested, is for the leader to engage staff in difficult conversations, modeling, teaching, and giving explicit permission for them to do likewise in their classrooms.

If this is to occur naturally, educators will have to carefully consider the appropriateness of their pedagogy. Educational leaders will have to ask themselves if they do all or most of the talking during staff and/or team meetings? Are these meetings opportunities for deconstructing existing knowledge frameworks and for co-constructing new ones? Are they opportunities for real learning and dialogue or are they simply occasions for transmission of information to teachers? What, in fact, are they modeling? Transformative teacher-leaders will have to ask themselves if, in their classrooms, they are still too frequently engaged in a transmissive approach, in which they "tell" students what they think they ought to know and students passively listen to a lecture, at most taking notes at what they perceive to be important junctures? Are they focused on test-taking rather than student learning? (For despite our current emphases, they are not the same.) Have they reduced their own teaching to covering the curriculum in terms of what they believe is required by the state standardized test? Or have teachers taken seriously the need to engage students in thoughtful and critical examination and reflection on the topic under consideration?

There are several aspects of this latter approach worthy of discussion. Parker Palmer (1998) argues that it is inappropriate for classrooms to be teacher-centered, an approach sometimes known as being the sage on the stage, for this pedagogy rarely engages students and certainly does not create space for students to bring their own understanding to the table. He also argues that it is inappropriate for teaching to be totally student-centered—that is to let students determine what they want to learn, when, and how as is sometimes done in classrooms purporting to be "progressive." Instead, Palmer claims that teaching ought to focus on the "Great Thing" in the center of the room—the issue, topic, question under consideration. Here, teacher and students together comment, question, challenge one another, as they explore the topic from multiple angles, each bringing his or her insights to the communal learning, and in the process being enriched and enriching the understanding of others. This permits every student to contribute something of interest and personal relevance whether he has heard his parents complaining about "illegal immigration" or whether she is "undocumented." Starting with the open-ended topic of "immigration" in the center is a way of being inclusive and respectful of each child's lived experience.

In many ways this approach is similar to recent definitions of curriculum. Pinar (2004) has called curriculum simply "complicated conversation." Grumet (1995) states that curriculum is not a "certain set of texts, or principles or algorithms, but the conversation that makes sense of these things" (p. 19). "Curriculum," she says, "is that conversation. It is the process of making sense with a group of people of the systems that shape and organize the world that we can think about together" (p. 19). What is exciting about this concept is that it creates space for individual students to bring the rich diversity of their lived experience to the conversation. It opens spaces in which each student may be included, rather than shut out. It frees the teacher from the impossible pressure of trying to know each student's background and cultural history and to teach it, or incorporate it into the lecture or conversation. Under this approach, each student is the expert on his or her cultural, religious, historical, or family perspective. Each student uses what he or she knows to help make sense of the material under consideration.

Accepting the notion of curriculum as conversation permits the instructor of a social studies class learning about elections, for example, to not only ensure students understand how the electoral college and US federal elections work, but to explore how elections may operate differently in other countries. Why, for example, is there not a fixed term in Canada, and why is a federal campaign limited to 30 days? What of the experience of a student recently arrived from Pakistan or Afghanistan where the hands of voters are stamped and ballots are sometimes pictorial as well as textual? What does the concept of free and fair elections mean in each setting and is it a sufficient explanation of what constitutes democracy? Rather than having a dry class in which students memorize various roles and functions, the conversation is lively, and every student's experience and perspective is valued. Here, of course, there is potential for the conversation to veer into topics with which the teacher is less familiar, topics that may become heated and even controversial. Is democracy the best form of government? A student recently arrived from China may want to extol the virtues of communism, arguing for more central control and authority than most American students are comfortable with. There is no one right way to proceed, but student engagement with the topic and understanding of one another, are sure to lead to increased understanding of central concepts for the test as well. In fact, repeated studies have shown that when we stop focusing on covering the curriculum and preparing students for the test, emphasizing instead, engagement, understanding, critical reflection, and meaningful connections, test scores improve as well.

This latter point is important. Many people think that having open-ended conversations is something one can only do if and when one has already covered the curriculum, if time permits, or in schools where students are already "meeting expectations." Grumet (1995) is clear; the "conversation that makes sense of things" IS the curriculum and studies affirm the effectiveness of this approach.

Scholars like Salinas and Garr (2009) have found that learner-centered instruction is more effective, especially for minority students, than traditional teacher-centered instruction. They report other studies that demonstrate, for example, that "learner-centered schools are more effective than traditional educational settings in promoting traditional indicators of school performance such as achievement (Fasko & Grubb, 1997; Ovando & Alford, 1997; Perry, 1999; Matthews & McLaughlin, 1994; Alfassi, 2004)" (p. 227). They go on to cite studies that also report better graduation rates, more motivation, improved self-regulation, self-efficacy and self-esteem, increased creativity, and more tolerance toward diversity (p. 227). In their own study, Salinas and Garr compared the achievement of 236 majority and minority elementary-school students taught by traditional, teacher-centered and more "progressive" learner-centered approaches. They found that there was:

> a large performance gap between minority (M = −.27; SD = .85) and non-minority (M = .20; SD = .94) students in the traditional educational model (t = 2.83, p < .005), but no significant difference whatsoever between the minority (M = .11; SD = .70) and non-minority (M = .08; SD − .103) students in the learner-centered model (t = .161, p > .87).

(pp. 233–234)

This finding is consistent with Cummins' (1989) "empowerment model" and with that of Bishop and Berryman (2006) in New Zealand who report that when teachers learn to use a more interactive pedagogy, the academic achievement gap between Maori and non-Maori students narrows considerably.

If the goal of educational leaders is to transform the learning experiences and outcomes, with particular emphasis on those who are currently the least successful students in our schools, it is essential to open up the learning spaces by changing the dominant classroom pedagogy. Thus, if we want to narrow the achievement gap, we must engage students in their own learning in authentic ways.

Summary

In this chapter, I have emphasized various ways in which the current ways of thinking about and "doing" schooling often marginalize and exclude some students, making it difficult for them to compete on what is, still, a very uneven playing field. I have suggested that it is unfair, inequitable, and undemocratic to require some groups of students—because of their particular group affiliation—to work harder, longer hours, and under greater duress to accomplish the same goals as those whose home lives more easily facilitate their learning.

Thus, to be transformative leaders, it is essential to acknowledge the uneven playing field, and to work to overcome it. To do that requires change that is deep instead of superficial, change in which current assumptions and knowledge frameworks are challenged and deconstructed and new ones put in their place. To accomplish deep and equitable change, we cannot simply rearrange the administrative structures of a school; we cannot simply introduce a new program, or offer another packaged professional development session that addresses a peripheral issue but does not get at the core of inequity and injustice in the system. To bring about real change, Oakes and Rogers (2006) emphasize the importance of producing knowledge and using new frameworks to effect change (p. 3). It is the relationship of deconstructing existing knowledge and reconstructing knowledge to effect deep and equitable change that we have explored in this chapter. Indeed, these are the only proven ways to create learning environments that are more democratic, equitable, and socially just.

We have seen that this requires turning some of our current assumptions on end. We must stop all forms of blaming the victim and deficit thinking. We must find the courage to engage in difficult and sometimes uncomfortable conversations; and we must open up our understanding of curriculum to ensure that all students are able to bring, without shame or fear, the totality of their lived experience into the sense-making conversations of the classroom and school. In one way these changes are not easy, for they often challenge the core of what we do and what we believe. The good news is that they can be introduced anywhere—in schools that are rich or poor, small or large, relatively homogenous or extremely diverse—by school leaders who are willing to take on the challenge. And they do not require expensive programs, materials, or facilities—they do require a large dose of political will and courageous action.

Oakes and Rogers (2006) add, however, that to engage in equity reform, we must be aware that "educational equity is entangled with cultural and political dynamics that extend beyond the school" and that "therefore, equity reforms must engage issues of power by extending beyond the school" (p. 31). They go on to argue that because "distribution of power is never explicitly addressed, technical change strategies tend toward consensus rather than conflict. They aim at engendering a sense of ownership among all members, rather than a fundamental realignment of advantage" (p. 32).

These are some of the transformative leadership issues that will be addressed in the next chapters. It is critically important to challenge the inequitable distribution of power as well as to understand how issues of power and privilege play out in schools, if we are to successfully create more just, excellent, and inclusive schools.

For Further Reflection and Action

1. Can you identify any ways in which your school or workplace reproduces inequitable situations?
2. How do you define cultural capital, deficit thinking, color-blind racism, and minoritized? Do these concepts resonate with you and, if so, how might you help others to understand and address them?
3. Do you think it is necessary for marginalized groups to "put the past behind them"? How can this be accomplished with compassion and equity? What is the role of members of dominant or privileged groups?
4. Identify ways in which educators punish children for their family circumstances and discuss strategies to overcome them. Which children are "Othered"? How? How might we overcome this?
5. What do you think are the main purposes of education? Which do we do well and which need further attention?
6. What are some free writing prompts you might use in your context? What other difficult conversations do you need to hold?
7. What do you understand by "curriculum as conversation"? Is it useful and, if so, how could it be implemented?

Chapter 4

Making Power a Positive Force

My friends say I am just like them. But when I look in the mirror, I see difference. My skin color is different; my eyes look different. And my daily reality is different. Don't they realize that when they ignore who I am it is just another example of racism in the guise of color-blindness?

(Mike, second-generation Canadian)

We're fighting for our lives here. Isn't it remarkable that a small group of wealthy parents can hold a whole school district hostage—especially when their real reasons have nothing to do with education?

(Superintendent, Hillside School District)

The two quotes that begin this chapter are indicative of some of the many ways in which people in organizations use their power to perpetuate the uneven playing field of the status quo and to ensure their privilege at the expense of others. These are hard words with which to open a chapter—inappropriate use of power, perpetuation of privilege—but unless transformative educators understand the systemic and institutional realities of the organizations within which they work, transformation will be impossible.

As schools become more diverse, sometimes already being what is strangely known as "majority-minority" schools—the VUCA (volatile, uncertain, complex, ambiguous) nature of the school context becomes even more obvious. Majority-minority is a term that (without even acknowledging it) pertains to the dominance of power elites in our schools. If people are in a numerical majority, one would logically think they would have some degree of legitimate power to make rules, determine policies, and so forth. Too often, however, it is more appropriate to think of these numerical majorities as minoritized populations because, unless they also have access to power structures, their populations are still treated as if in the minority.

An excellent example of this comes from schools on the Navajo reservation in southeast Utah, where most of the schools' populations are between 98% and 100% Navajo. At one point, as visitors from the state capital wrapped up their visit to the high school, they said to the school principal: "This school looks exactly like a school you would find anywhere else in the state" (unfortunately, it was meant as a compliment). Fortunately, the principal was savvy enough to know that the school should not look like any other school, but should likely reflect its own demographics and cultures. And she set out to make changes—the construction of a Navajo hogan in which meetings might be held, an ethno-biology project to grow native plants and vegetables, the raising of churro sheep and a rug-making project, the decorating of the school's pillars and façade to reflect Navajo themes and culture.

Shortly thereafter, I happened to visit the elementary school a few miles down the road, to find it deeply immersed in activities for "Native American week." When I asked what this would look like in a school that was totally Native American, I was greeted with strange stares and told it was a week to celebrate Native American culture. I asked why, in a Navajo school, Native American history, culture, concepts, and perspectives would not necessarily be part of everything they do, permeating the curriculum, the activities, and the pedagogy. Instead, native culture was still seen as an add-on. The regular curriculum was the traditional curriculum of the dominant White majority and looked and sounded as it would almost anywhere else in this country. Further, there had been no realization or discussion of the incongruity or mismatch or of how the lack of space for the daily lives of the children clearly marginalized and excluded them. It is obvious that, despite being in the large numerical majority, the Navajo students' knowledge and culture were still not highly valued in school. This minoritized them—treated them as minorities despite their numbers. It was clear that their culture was not the "culture of power," even in their local schools.

Hence, I believed there was a clear need for transformative leadership to address issues of power so these children could be fully included, respected, and accepted within the culture of the school. Too often, as I talked with teachers on the Navajo reservation, I heard evidence of the deficit thinking discussed in the last chapter. Too often, they attributed the high percentages of students not attaining state standards to families who "don't care" or who "don't value schooling" or to the children's lack of motivation and enthusiasm for school. In fact, I never heard anyone (including school leaders) identify the fact that the Navajo were still minoritized within the schools as a factor contributing to their low levels of success.

Let me explain further. When children in these schools were taught American history, their texts still discussed the "discovery" of America by Columbus. Failing to explicitly acknowledge that that Native Americans had been here first and had not needed to be "discovered," there was no recognition of the well-established cultures that had been virtually destroyed by the newcomers, no discussion of how things might have been different had Columbus arrived two centuries later (or earlier), for example, no discussion of imperialism, colonization, and so forth.

Now put yourself in this classroom of children learning about American history. They begin to read with some excitement that Columbus encountered people who looked like them six centuries ago. They wait, knowing that, finally, they can talk about their place in American history—only to find that, in a curious mixing of Columbus' arrival with that of the pilgrims, their culture is reduced to teepees (not at all related to traditional Navajo ways) and to contributions to a Thanksgiving dinner.

Once again, these students receive the message that although they are compelled to attend school, school is not really designed to include them and, once again, they receive the subtle and implicit message that they really do not belong. Without knowing it, they are victims of what Lisa Delpit calls the "culture of power" (1990).

In this chapter, I want to look at power in a number of ways because, as Delpit so clearly delineated it, a "culture of power" exists in all organizations whether we are aware of it or not. I have written about this elsewhere, but because it is so important,

I return to the topic here, in part because the concept seems difficult for many to grasp. As suggested above, power inappropriately understood and used is the underlying force that continues to marginalize students in our schools and to perpetuate structures, practices, curriculum frameworks, and even beliefs that comprise barriers to equitable reform. The above example of the Navajo schools clearly illustrates the presence of power, its pervasiveness, and its perpetuation as a systemic quality of educational institutions. At the same time, power and its negative consequences are frequently hidden, even unintended, and its impact frequently unknown to those who actually benefit from it and perpetuate it.

In this chapter, as I examine ways in which the culture of power plays out, I will show how power traps us in current sets of assumptions and mindsets in ways that are often unintentional and of which we are unaware. Then I will examine how this culture of power sustains an unnatural sense of entitlement and privilege that school leaders must find the courage to address if we are to be able to initiate meaningful and equitable change.

The Culture of Power

In a well-known and often cited article, now almost a quarter of a century old, Lisa Delpit (1990) wrote about how there is a culture of power in every organization. Moreover, she identified what she called the rules of power of which we must be aware. On occasion, when we discuss her article in my graduate classes, my students ask an obvious and important question: if we have known this for so long (almost a quarter of a century), why has so little been done about it? And I believe the answer is both simple and disturbing. Those of us who have power are not particularly interested in sharing it, weakening it, or giving it up. In fact, although we would like to think that we are reasonable, thoughtful, caring human beings, who, once we become aware of inequity and injustice, would be glad to take steps to redress it, research tells us this is not the case. In fact, sometimes (perhaps too often), the urge to react, to protect, and to dig in takes precedence over altruistic values and results in an entrenchment of disparity rather than redress.

Delpit posits that some of the injustice and inequitable uses of power are so ingrained in organizational life, so inherent in the *habitus* mentioned earlier (Bourdieu with Passeron, 1977), that most of us are not even aware of them. Delpit's first rule of power is that "issues of power are enacted in classrooms" (1990, p. 86). And, although she focuses on classrooms, I would extend the statement to argue that issues of power are enacted throughout educational organizations. When a primary school teacher says to her class, "I like the way Johnnie is sitting," or insists that "Sally is sitting nicely," she is exercising an implicit rule of power. The comment is not intended to simply praise the student singled out but to inform the rest of the class, implicitly, that this is the way to behave. When she asks, "Would you like to take your reading books out now?" she is not simply asking students about their preference, or giving them a legitimate choice. Instead, she is issuing a directive—one that many students understand implicitly but that others find confusing, "Why is she asking if I want to do this?" they may be thinking. I don't want to, but if I say that, I will likely get in trouble.

Similarly, when a school principal asks if she can see teachers' lesson plans, the request does not permit a negative response, because in fact, it is not a request at all but a command. Teachers are conditioned and soci[ali]ze[d t]o understand this from the outset (although some may attempt to resist); stude[nts and] parents—especially if their home culture is not congruent with that of the scho[ol ma]y have a much more difficult time. And this is Delpit's second "rule": There ar[e codes] or rules for participating in power; that is, there is a "culture of power" (p. 8[7). A]gain, the rules are implicit; they are unwritten, but exist as ways of dressir[g, way]s of interacting, and ways of communicating with one another.

In one high school, for example, a group of students had been learning about developing résumés, and discussing how to interview for a job. In an attempt to make the learning real, mock interviews were scheduled for the next day and the teacher informed the students to come "dressed up—in their best clothes" for their interviews. Imagine his surprise when a group of Hispanic girls dressed in colorful skirts, shawls, and peasant blouses—their typical "best" festive dress. Only as we discussed the concept of a culture of power in his graduate class, did the teacher find the vocabulary to understand what had happened. His assumption about "dressing up" for an interview came from his membership in the dominant culture, ignoring that other cultures might interpret the directive quite differently. To ensure that all students "hear" and receive the same message, it behooves us to clarify the meaning of phrases like "dress up" rather than to assume everyone knows the proper attire for a formal job interview.

The third "rule" of power identified by Delpit is that "The rules of the culture of power are a reflection of the rules of the culture of those who have power" (p. 87). This is almost self-evident. If I am part of the dominant group, I can make the rules and others will have to comply, and, over time, we forget how the rule came into being and assume it is just the way things have always been and should always be. Although few educators would state it this bluntly, this is generally the way schools and other organizations operate. Moreover, this seems to be the way in which the wider political process works. If I am a member of the majority and of the dominant elite, I can make the rules; for example, introducing house bills to prevent gay marriage, to reject bilingual education in favor of an "English only approach," or to reduce the power of a union of which I am not a member—at the same time leaving my way of life unassailed. Likewise, I can make rules about swearing, clothing, and homework that do not take into consideration their impact on students from home situations different from what I perceive to be the norm.

The next two rules are particularly important: Delpit (1990) affirms that "If you are not already a participant in the culture of power, being told explicitly the rules of that culture makes acquiring power easier" (p. 87). In other words, making the request for all students to sit up with their feet on the floor and their hands folded on their desks instead of saying she likes the way Johnnie is sitting makes the expectation clear for all students. Similarly, talking about what kind of clothes are appropriate for a job interview instead of using the more ambiguous phrase "dressing up" clarifies the expectations. It avoids misunderstanding on the part of those who expect communication to be unambiguous; it helps those whose first language or culture are different from the language or culture of instruction, not to miss a subtle nuance. It overcomes the confusion of parents who are told their child does not follow the rules at school, but who are convinced that, at home, he willingly does as he is told.

Anyone who has lived in a different country for any length of time has experienced this situation. We do as we do at home, unconscious that it may cause offense to someone else. It may be as simple as sitting on a chair with our legs crossed at the knee, unaware that showing the soles of our shoes is considered rude in Arab cultures. In Singapore, where it is customary to reject a proffered gift three times before accepting it, a too hasty acceptance of a refusal may become a significant faux pas. And of course, sitting on any surface where one might put food (such as the edge of a table) is offensive to the Maori in New Zealand. Often we need to be told the rules because we are so used to our way of thinking or acting that it is easy to overlook the fact that we are the only one behaving in a certain way.

Finally, Delpit reminds us that "Those with power are frequently least aware of—or least willing to acknowledge its existence. Those with less power are often most aware of its existence" (1990, p. 87). When I ask my graduate students—all practicing educational leaders (principals, curriculum specialists, assistant superintendents) to role-play this rule as it applies to their organizations, they are at a loss. What kind of activities do we have at our school that perpetuate the culture of power? Is it a matter of sharing the school rules, about discipline perhaps, with newcomers? If I ask them to role-play greeting a new Muslim family wanting to enroll a child in their school (as I have on occasion), the immediate inclination is to stand, walk towards the door, arm outstretched ready to shake hands with both parents—little realizing how awkward this gesture might be when, in most cases, married Muslim men and women are not permitted to touch someone of the opposite sex who is not their spouse.

Overall, what Delpit has suggested is that unless we take care to understand different perspectives, to identify and understand the implicit rules, and to overturn inequities, organizational cultures will continue to reflect the uneven playing field in the wider society. In turn, this perpetuates the privilege of some at the expense of others.

Perpetuating the Culture of Power

Moreover, because we so rarely recognize the culture of power when we are part of it, we tend to think that everyone's experience is similar to our own. This misunderstanding of the culture of power in organizations has led to many "politically correct" but hegemonic notions in our schools. Some of these are programmatic; others relate to subtle, perhaps even more important, attitudes and perceptions.

The notion of color-blind racism, mentioned in Chapter 3, is one such concept. Too often in recent years, we hear people in relatively diverse organizations proclaiming proudly that they "do not see color." In their minds, this sends a message that they are open-minded, that they are not prejudiced, and that in fact, they see everyone alike. The focus, they say, is on their common humanity and not on their visible differences. The problem, of course, is that some differences *do* make a difference. Well-known experiments in which people of different races and ethnicities attempt to rent a house or apply for a job demonstrate that there is still tremendous prejudice with respect to race in our society. This *racism*—it is important to call it by its name—is reflected in the daily experience of people of color who report that taxi drivers lock their doors, security guards follow them in stores, and police pull them over with considerably greater frequency than their White counterparts.

I recently spoke to a man who was an educator, a musician, a tutor, and a father who had some time ago moved into a community where his was the only Black family. He recounted that one day as he was mowing his lawn a neighbor approached and asked what he charged for lawn care. His quick response was that if he considered the cost of his mortgage, taxes, and upkeep on his house, he could likely calculate an hourly rate. The embarrassed neighbor quickly withdrew; nevertheless, the message had been delivered once again: "You don't really belong here. We don't see you as one of us."

Color-blind racism that fails to recognize the ongoing discrimination and prejudice faced by non-White members of our society is a form of power. It conveys the message that in "our" society (whatever that might be) workers have dark skin while the professionals, who hold the power, are White. It explains why Mike, at the beginning of this chapter, seemed so confused when his friends did not see that he was, in meaningful ways, both similar to and different from them.

Moreover, when we remain silent about differences that make a difference, we are perpetuating the uneven and hegemonic "culture of power" in our organizations and society. It holds true when we argue that each child has equal access to education and that all they have to do is work hard and they will succeed. It explains, in part, why Satish (in Chapter 1) had such a difficult time in school after his family's expulsion from Uganda. It was not simply that he could not afford skates or that his family ate curry, but that he did not know how to negotiate the rules of power in the school. He did not know that the typical school lunch comprised a simple white bread sandwich and, hence, brought ridicule on himself as he ate his Indian food with his hands. The culture of power explains why Danny (also Chapter 1) is likely to drop out of school because of his homeless situation. The dominant culture tells him it is not all right to be homeless; that his father must not be a caring, positive role model, and that he must hide his fear at not knowing, when he leaves school each day, where he will spend that night. The culture of power makes him ashamed of his inability to provide a lavish spread of Florida produce and typical southern food during the class "state" project. Worse, the culture of power often leads teachers to dismiss as "just childish teasing" the racist bullying that resulted in Amy's wish (in Chapter 1) that she could renounce her cultural heritage. It results in too many children who come from impoverished homes feeling the prejudice of teachers and the rejection of their classmates because they have come to believe, as in Sophie's case, that they are incapable of success. And it has resulted in countless homosexual youth being embarrassed, teased, and bullied about their sexual orientation.

Transformative leaders must put an end to these implicit but powerful and damaging messages. They must start by identifying the implicit rules of power in their organization. They must, as we saw in the previous chapter, reject deficit thinking, engage in difficult and courageous conversations, and create curricular spaces that are inclusive of the lived experiences of all students. We will find further examples of transformative practices in the next few chapters as well as in the stories that appear on the website. One particularly useful illustration is that of Mrs. Carla Cox's response to a student who was being called "terrorist"—a story to which you will be introduced in Chapter 7.

Understanding the Systemic Nature of the Culture of Power

So far, the discussion has focused on individualistic examples of how the culture of power can marginalize, reject, or oppress people. In each case, the message is that any challenges faced by those in the minority are, therefore, unique to each individual and not the result of systemic barriers or injustices. And yet we know this is not the case. Loewen (2005), for example, in his study of the American sociological phenomenon of sundown towns, demonstrates how pervasive they were right up until late in the last century (and even extending, in some cases, into this one). His research demonstrates that between 1863 and 1890, "blacks moved everywhere in America" (p. 9), but that "between 1890 and the 1930s, however, all this changed . . . Most astonishing, from California to Minnesota to Long Island to Florida, whites mounted little race riots against African Americans, expelling entire black communities or intimidating and keeping out would-be newcomers" (pp. 9–10).

After I introduced this concept of sundown towns in class one night, a student wrote at length in his weekly journal about his own experience, growing up in a town he had only that evening realized fit the definition of a "sundown town." Zak wrote, "I am embarrassed to admit the first naive thought to cross my mind when I recently encountered the term 'sundown town' was 'they must have amazing sunsets.'" Then he continued:

> I know about the racist practices designed to keep blacks from moving into certain neighborhoods . . . I was mortified into a state of shock when I saw my hometown listed as "probably still a sundown town." How could this be? It is true that I was born and raised in a small rural, culturally homogenous community . . . I telephoned my 84-year-old mother and asked her if she had ever heard of such a policy in our town. A resident of the area for the first 60 years of her life, she confirmed that indeed my hometown had an unwritten "no blacks after dark" policy. She was, however, quick to point out that it was a long time ago and she had only heard mention of its existence. "Put my sister on the phone," I said uneasily. My sister, a life-long resident of the town and local nurse, knows just about everyone in the area. "How many people of color currently call our town home?" I asked with great trepidation. Her answer confirmed my worst fears . . . My hometown is *not* famous for its fantastic sunsets.
>
> (Zak)

For those who grew up in such communities, their homogeneity appeared, and often still appears, normal—even to the extent of denying its existence and wanting to perpetuate this abnormal reality at all costs.

This is reflected in the second quotation at the beginning of this chapter. A small group of wealthy families, who live in a neighborhood of very expensive homes on large, manicured lots, decided it would be to their advantage to petition their local school board to be permitted to change its school boundaries to permit their children (most of whom currently attend private schools) to no longer be considered within the boundary of their local district, but to be able to attend school a few miles down the road, in a neighboring district. Their ostensible reason was that their children would be able to receive a better education if the "detachment" from Hillside District were to be permitted. (It would also raise the value of their homes and permit their children to attend a more homogeneous school.) There was no doubt that their designated high school (with its 63% White and 31% low-income population) was more diverse than the school to which they wished to belong (with a minority population of 20%—11%

of them Asian, and a low-income rate of 4%). Additionally, it was a matter of public record that the standardized test scores of the requested new district were higher than those of Hillside. Granting permission to this group of parents to "detach" would result in a relatively small decline of district income in the vicinity of 500,000 dollars a year—and yet, the superintendent perceived they were "fighting for their life."

Despite the fact that both schools had graduation rates of approximately 96%, dropout rates of 0.2% or less, a similar number of Advanced Placement (AP) and honors courses, and equally well-trained teachers, the perception was that the quality of education would be higher in the second district—even though no petitioning parent had been willing to guarantee that should the petition be granted, their child would move to the new school instead of remaining at the private school they currently attended.

What was actually behind the move? One can only speculate, but the lack of interest in sending their children to a public school and some of the questions asked at the detachment hearing were revelatory. One person asked to testify about the programs and quality of education at each school was asked whether the test scores of the desired school indicated that the quality of education was high. (Indisputably.) The plaintiff's lawyer then asked if having a homogeneous school was therefore a positive, and conversely if diversity in a student body was a negative. To this question, the witness, testifying for the defending district, explained:

> You can certainly get a good education in a homogeneous school if you are talking about test scores, but because education has a civil, citizenship function as well, it is important for students, in an increasingly diverse country and globe, to encounter and learn to understand perspectives other than their own. In fact, democratic education requires helping students understand alternative views, including ideas about the curriculum, social issues, politics and so forth. It may even be essential for students to encounter different perspectives while they are still living at home to run ideas by their parents.

Not surprisingly, the response did not appear to please the plaintiffs who ultimately won a split decision from the regional hearing board.

Perpetuating Privilege

The foregoing is an example of how people who have always held the power and who have experienced the world as they want it to remain believe they can exercise their power to perpetuate their privilege. Unfortunately, as in the Hillside detachment decision, those with power were rewarded and permitted to continue to act in ways that perpetuated their privilege and continued to disadvantage others. When a community defines itself intellectually based on sameness, there is an unspoken implication of excluding others. This insidious fear of otherness in the context of a community based on sameness maintains an elite sense of entitlement and privilege.

In the case of Hillside school district described above, the challenge is that if this petitioning group of parents is permitted to leave the increasingly diverse district, then others (also wealthy and White) who do not want their children to attend school with "those" _____ kids (you fill in the blank) will also have the ability to petition for detachment, ultimately leaving their schools impoverished in terms of reduced diversity, fewer knowledge perspectives, and obviously, considerably less money for programs and materials. This is the downside of local control. When a jurisdiction is divided into small units, all governed by local control, then those who have the power continue to make the rules and establish the boundaries, regardless of the detrimental impact on others. The more rapidly the demographics of districts appear to change, the more likely the resistance to the changes, and the more likely those in power are to want to separate again, to preserve their privilege.

Another startling systemic example of how the culture of power serves to marginalize and exclude groups of students came to my attention recently. One of my students—an experienced teacher—began, during her doctoral seminar, to refer to something she called "the brown line" in her local high school cafeteria. Her classmates and I quickly reacted. "That isn't something people say is it? There really isn't a brown line, is there?" To our surprise, she responded, "Yes." And then she explained that although she had explicitly asked about it, she had been told that students who received a free or reduced price lunch in her school had to go through a different line because they received different hot food. Moreover, because the large majority of students in that school who received free and reduced lunch were Hispanic, the line had become known, by students and teachers alike, as "the brown line." The practice was so entrenched that no one thought anything of it—and even when this particular teacher asked about it, the practice continued without apparent concern about the ways in which students from impoverished families were being singled out. Please note, however, that as she persisted to ask questions over a couple of years, awareness was heightened and, ultimately, the brown line was dissolved. Transformative leaders persist with moral courage, raising awareness, developing clarity, and gaining support for what may at first seem to be hopeless causes.

I hope it has become evident that power is closely aligned with privilege—and that holding social, economic, cultural, and legislative power in our country provides clear opportunities for the exercise of privilege. Privilege confers a sense of entitlement in which those who have power are often unwilling to support changes that increase equity but that they perceive to increase their competition. This plays out in numerous ways, including a resistance to ending academic programs that enhance the opportunities of the privileged or to providing additional resources for those who need it. Consider, for example, the outcry when resources for gifted programs are being decreased, or when additional resources are provided for students whose home language is not English.

Ever since Thomas Jefferson composed the Declaration of Independence, the American dream has represented a clear tension between activities that advance collective public good and those that promote and perpetuate the private good of individual attainment for those who already have power. Moreover, those who are in positions of power and privilege have found it expedient and perhaps relatively simple to argue that AP courses, and gifted programs are a public good—preparing the "brightest and best" for future positions of leadership in our democratic society. Too often, the definition of "brightest and best" requires that students so identified look, behave, and sound like the school's dominant power elite. Too often, the argument goes unchallenged, because society has come to expect, indeed to accept as normal, our typical hierarchical organization in which some people are more naturally assumed, for example, to be candidates for gifted programs than others.

And too often, the voices of a powerful group of parents are allowed to dominate the debate, ultimately resulting in what is sometimes touted as a "win-win" situation. We need to be clear, however, that when we attempt a win-win solution to a situation that is inherently unequal, the resulting solution invariably perpetuates the inequity that existed in the first place. Oakes and Rogers (2006, ch. 2) provide a disturbing and true account of a California high school they called "Woodrow Wilson High School." There was strong pressure to address the "two schools problem"—inequitable resources and funding—with fewer resources provided to the school's (predominantly African American and Latino) "regular" programs and additional resources provided to the "honors track" that attracted predominantly White and Asian students. However, after a series of acrimonious meetings, the agreed-upon settlement offered only a slight redistribution of resources intended to pacify some complainants but not to fundamentally change the "two schools" situation.

Similar examples are presented in Larson and Ovando's (2001) extended case study of Jefferson High School or Fennimore's (1997) study of parent-initiated concerns over the inequitable programs in a largely re-segregated high school. In the latter school, a group of parents became concerned that the largely White, magnet program had considerably more resources, newer books, and smaller classes, than the "general program" that housed most of the African American and Latino students. After an acrimonious committee meeting, it was decided that the two parent groups would meet and present their perspectives separately. It is not surprising that, as reported by Fennimore, "the actual resolution focused more on achieving 'peace' through altered retention of the original inequitable structure" (p. 61) than on finding an equitable solution to the problem. There was no true attempt at dialogue, no desire to understand, only a desire on the part of those in power to protect their advantage and on the part of the school district leaders to maintain the peace and a semblance of equity. Fennimore goes on to make an extremely important point. She argues that in situations that at the outset involve fundamental inequities, attempting to find a win-win solution is too often, in our already unequal and hegemonic society, another way of perpetuating the status quo. She concludes: "Those with the power to influence the resolution of these conflicts must question whether both sides can or should 'win' in a situation where injustice brings the central commitments of democracy into question" (p. 63). In other words, compromise may be most appropriate when the playing field is level at the outset; otherwise the inequity remains once the compromise is in place.

I understand this notion of privilege and the desire to perpetuate it very clearly, having grown up in what I must now name as a situation of "privilege" with grandparents who were university educated, parents who worked in professional capacities, being able to live in a comfortable home, to travel to other countries, and to spend leisurely summers at our summer place on an island. As a teenager, I was vaguely uncomfortable when my grandfather stood on the shore, shouting to my uncle (his son) across the small bay, whenever a stranger with a fishing rod ventured close to "his" shore. Only years later, as I learned to name our privilege, could I name my discomfort. We were privileged; the water and shoreline did not "belong" to us and it was a blatant and false expression of exclusionary rights, to suggest that no one else should fish near our cottage. My grandfather was known to be a kind and generous man; however, the power of privilege can be blinding, as his exclusive attitude clearly demonstrated.

I am grateful to those who helped me understand this point, so that, once I finally understood and acknowledged my own privilege, I ultimately also came to recognize my responsibility to name power and privilege where it occurs, to acknowledge the often ignored ways in which it perpetuates inequity including the ways in which I may be complicit, to speak out where that inequity is found, and to align myself in solidarity with those who, through an accident of birth only, may have less access to decision-makers and power-brokers in our wider society. This is one of the many tasks of transformative leaders; they must help those in power to understand their privilege, so that we may stop acting with a sense of entitlement and, hence, stand in solidarity with those who have less power and privilege. Elucidating issues of power and privilege are simply first steps in a complex process. Once those in power recognize their erroneous assumptions (the shoreline is for everyone; the waterways are not for the exclusive use of those who have been there the longest), their next step must be to engage in more equitable and inclusive practices and discourses.

The Panopticon of Power and Performativity

Another form of power resides with those who are placed in supervisory roles over others or whose role it is to enforce accountability mechanisms, and of course, this includes educational leaders. Perryman (2009), in an exemplary piece of research, investigated the ways in which "inspection" and increased surveillance and accountability in British schools led to fabrication of results and to increased cynicism and alienation among educators. She draws, theoretically and metaphorically, on Foucault's use of Bentham's Panopticon—a circular prison designed architecturally so that inmates can never know whether or not they are being observed from a central observation tower. Ultimately, Perryman noted that instead of improving results, the very threat of surveillance served to increase rehearsal, pretense, and "performance" on the part of educators:

> Teachers in schools in danger of "failing" inspection need to behave as if they are being inspected all the time so the performance becomes second nature, and thus the disciplinary mechanism is internalized. There is also the experience of inspection as not just constant but all-seeing. To use the panoptic metaphor, even if a school is not being officially inspected, "the dark central tower" of [the inspection agency] is always invisibly watching. The result is increasing conformity to perceived expectations, the acceptance of the discourse as demonstrated through performativity. Inspection seems a constant threat and teachers can feel that they need to modify their behaviour in a permanent way "because the constant pressure acts even before the offences, mistakes or crimes have been committed."
> (p. 617)

Unfortunately, Perryman's finding is repeated all too often, as many people (educators and others) can easily identify with the preparation of extensive binders of well-formatted, illustrated, and graphed reports, documenting whatever items are under scrutiny, with little if any attention subsequently being paid to the actual content or quality of the program being inspected. Regrettably, accreditation, standards, and assessment too often fall prey to the notion of scrutiny and the power of the Panopticon, as participants attend more to avoiding scrutiny than to significant and meaningful quality. Once again, power is being misused to perpetuate the status quo rather than to introduce substantive and equitable reform.

Combating the Oppression of Culture of Power

We reflected, in the last chapter, on the need to eliminate deficit thinking, to deconstruct inappropriate assumptions, and to engage in difficult conversations. Above I have outlined some of the ways in which those who finally acknowledge their participation in the culture of power can take steps to redress the wrongs. Those with power are complicit, often unknowingly, in the perpetuation of structures, policies, and attitudes that marginalize and oppress those with less (or different kinds of) power. Hence, we must act.

A familiar mantra of some political parties in the second decade of the 21st century is that we must "reclaim America." I am not sure what they have in mind—reclaim what part of American history or culture and for whom? I do agree that reclaiming the democratic values on which America was founded may be a good idea—if by that we mean reintroducing a form of democracy that is *thick* rather than *thin* (Strike, 1999); and that is *deep* rather than *superficial* (Green, 1999). If, by reclaiming America, we are calling for a return to restrictive and exclusionary practices (such as English only, restricting the building of mosques, or withdrawing advertising from programs about immigrants), then it is a call transformative leaders will have to challenge and resist. These and other examples suggest that, too often, "reclaiming America" is code for perpetuating the power and privilege of those already in power as opposed to enhancing this kind of understanding of community life. Here we must resist and speak out.

Green argues that purely formal democracy is limited and "essentially unsustaining and culturally unsustainable" (p. vi). Moreover, it "contrasts with *a deeper conception of democracy* that expresses the experience-based possibility of more equal, respectful, and mutually beneficial ways of community life" (p. vi, italics in original). Transformative leaders ensure that the democracy they promote in schools and colleges is a deep form of democracy that is inclusive of everyone.

Delpit (1990), after thoroughly explaining the rules of power, emphasized that helping people understand and access the rules of power so they, too, can access fully the benefits of a particular organization is not enough. She argued persuasively that although those steps are necessary, it is equally necessary to work to overturn the norms of society that continue to marginalize so many people. This is not an afterthought or an add-on. It is the important second step of a two-part process. It is not enough to simply help people access power; we must make the very pillars of power and privilege in our society more equitable and available to all. And, of course we start by acknowledging our own power and privilege and working to mitigate its negative impact on others.

Does this mean, for example, that we must eliminate all gifted or advanced programs? Absolutely not (in my opinion). But we must eliminate the sense of entitlement and exclusion they often perpetuate. Labaree (1997) emphasizes the competitive nature of schooling, noting that the desire for social mobility and attainment shifts our concept of schooling into the role of a commodity; a social system that provides "individual students with a competitive advantage in the struggle for desirable social conditions" (p. 42). If we are to ensure that the competitive advantage is based on ability and not on a sense of entitlement and birthright, we must acknowledge that there are as many bright children living in poverty, coming from families whose second (or third) language is English, or coming from visible minority groups—as from the dominant group. No single group has a corner on intelligence. Hence, one appropriate response is to broaden the identification procedures for "gifted" programs, ensuring they reflect intelligence and not prior opportunities to learn.

In order to reduce the impact of privilege, do we have to introduce affirmative admission procedures that reduce the quality of applicants for college or for a job, or that lower our standards? Again, not necessarily. But we must acknowledge that if we say we want to diversify our workforce, it will mean broadening our sense of "fit" and acknowledging a wider range of appropriate knowledge, skills, and attributes. Diversity must not be a code word for finding someone whose background, speech, mannerisms are just like ours—but whose skin color may be slightly different. As we widen our criteria for admission, we may need to consider prior experience as much as Grade Point Average (GPA). We may need to implement policies such as those attempted in a few areas, that eliminate the need for competitive GPA scores, but accept students who graduate in the top 10% of their local high school class (Tienda, Alon, & Niu, 2008). The rationale, again, is that students from minority groups, despite common beliefs, may not have truly had full and equal access to a high quality high school education, with high quality teachers who held high expectations for them. Here, it is not a matter of watering down the standards but of recognizing the social reality of disparity and inequity and the ongoing disadvantage incurred by members of some minority groups.

Earlier we met Leslie Thomas, principal of a diverse secondary school that has recently won a national College Board Award, in recognition that it has increased its percentage of minority students taking AP courses, while, at the same time, maintaining or increasing their actual scores. In other words, becoming more inclusive has not lowered standards, but has opened doors and increased the achievement of many of the school's minoritized students. She recounts that it "had been a huge effort for the school's social justice committee to get more minority students into AP." She explained, "But we dropped those low level, low expectation courses. Think about it. We dropped our remedial courses. So we pulled people up, but we gave support. We also had all kinds of support." This is the kind of approach needed to ensure equity of access and outcomes to all students.

In Chapter 3 I discussed three key elements of transformative leadership—eliminating deficit thinking, deconstructing inappropriate assumptions, and engaging in difficult conversations. These three leadership roles take on even more importance in light of the many abuses of power found within organizations and within society. It is not simply that some people misuse their power to attempt to control people, to threaten inappropriate action, or to reward people arbitrarily. The essential understanding leaders must take from this chapter is that power is not only individual but collective, that it is expressed in individual words and actions, but also in societal norms, beliefs, values, and collective acts. To address this misuse of power requires, once again, tremendous moral courage, for it often means going against the norms of the group within which one was raised. This is the role of the transformative leader—to find the courage to challenge inequities wherever they may be found and to work to ensure fully inclusive learning communities for all students as will be further discussed in Chapter 6.

This is what the teacher who recounted the "brown line" story recognized as she explored her experience with me and her classmates. She had stopped her inquiry after raising the issue with the cafeteria staff and the school administrators, believing that she was powerless to institute change. Nevertheless, as she engaged in dialogue with her classmates, she realized that she could not stop short of working to overturn such a marginalizing and inequitable system, and the following year, she persisted until the practice was changed. In many other schools, a practice that required students receiving free or reduced price lunch to have a different color lunch ticket has been stopped, and replaced by pre-paid tickets that all look the same, to ensure no shame or embarrassment is associated with eating lunch.

The "brown line" is not simply an isolated example. I recently heard of a similar practice in rural east Texas where children who participate in the free lunch program are separated into different educational tracks based on the assumption that all low socio-economic status (SES) children "need extra help." When educators and school systems assume lower educational performance from a group of children based on their SES, ethnicity, appearance, or any other characteristic deemed as different, they foster a sense of incapacity within the children that, despite being well intentioned, may shackle them for life. This is another hegemonic use of power that must be eschewed. Rejecting such practices is not only a requisite for transformative leadership, it is an essential step toward offering fellow human beings what Starratt (1991) would call "absolute regard" that supports their ability to be successful.

Summary: Using Power Positively

There is no doubt that in a world that is increasingly diverse, in which volatility, uncertainty, complexity, and ambiguity reign, failing to address the "culture of power" in schools is a sure way to continue to marginalize and exclude increasingly large groups of students. Schools can no longer afford to do things the way we always have, to teach the same concepts in the same ways we always have—without recognizing that we need to open up our spaces and our cultures to be more inclusive of the diverse perspectives of the students in our communities. In fact, failing to address the "culture of power" within our schools, and perpetuating the exclusionary nature of many educational institutions, may well increase the levels of volatility and uncertainty of organizational life rather than help us live productively within them.

In this chapter, I have argued (with Delpit, 1990) that a culture of power exists in every organization. I have further argued that this culture of power is a reflection of ways in which a sense of entitlement and privilege often play out in individual relationships and of how it is deeply entrenched in the structures of our society. Most importantly I have argued that this culture of power must be addressed in order for every child who attends school in this country to receive an equitable and high quality education.

Since the 2008 election of Barack Obama, Americans have often heard criticism of him, for not acknowledging and promoting a sense of "American Exceptionalism." For that, I argue, he should be praised, because we often misuse the phrase, assuming it has positive and desirable connotations. Further, no country, state, or group of people should be able to claim, because of their history, their birth, their financial or military power, that they have an inherent right to govern, to make decisions, or to promote their beliefs or lifestyle throughout the world. Exceptionalism should be retained for those whose contributions are truly exceptional—those who have taken extraordinary measures to promote the welfare, peace, or security of humanity—not a form of government, specific cultural values, or a dominant philosophy. "Only in America"—a phrase parroted by members of the media and general public when a woman runs for president (Hillary Clinton), when a member of a visible minority is elected (Obama), when someone who grew up in poverty becomes rich and famous (Oprah)—is not only misguided, it is patently wrong. Other countries have had women leaders (Britain, Canada, Pakistan). Other countries have had leaders from marginalized and oppressed groups (South Africa comes to mind). And people from abject poverty throughout the world have risen to positions of power where they have made significant contributions. The perpetuation of a sense of entitlement that comes with that version of American Exceptionalism is indicative of the need for dramatic change. It is a call for a renewed understanding of the tenets of our democracy—a way of life in which the people—*all* the people—have a voice, have equal opportunities for success, and have the right and responsibility to participate fully in decisions affecting our way of life. This does not mean that we should minimize the truly exceptional achievements of which there have been many in the history of America and Americans. Nevertheless, we must also recognize that our history is both uneven and, in places, somewhat sordid, and that it behooves us to examine it with realistic as well as patriotic zeal.

Transformative leadership advances an understanding of democracy in which power is used for mutual benefit (Green, 1999), and hence, in which more people are more willing to redistribute the economic, social, political, cultural, and educational benefits of our way of life to all members of society. This understanding of deep democracy is also a way of life in which, because a greater cross-section of the population is involved in decision-making and in creating the rules and policies which guide our daily activities, the fear of the gaze of the Panopticon should be reduced, the need for performativity instead of meaningful performance should be eliminated, and people can work together for their mutual good.

To accomplish this once again, we need transformative leaders. We need leaders who are willing to look beyond the walls of their organizations to the needs, wishes, desires of their community at large, and to see how the current "culture of power" continues to marginalize and exclude some to the detriment of all. Transformative educational leaders will have to acknowledge their own power and privilege. They will have to carefully and critically examine their own use of power to ensure it is a positive force for equitable change. They will have to courageously challenge inequity and stand up to privilege where it is detrimental to our democratic values, and ensure that the goals of education encompass both private and public good.

Transformative educators are not simply concerned with leveling the playing field within their organizations; they are certainly not simply concerned with test scores, or activities that ensure that a school meets AYP (although there is a responsibility to attend to these issues). Transformative educational leaders must be more concerned with learning than with testing, with the holistic development of their students than with school statistics, and with the good of their community—school, local, and even global—than with the celebration of individual exploits. These are the tasks that will be elaborated in the next chapters.

For Further Reflection and Action

1. Discuss Delpit's "rules of power" as they apply to your organization. What kind of activities do you have at your school that unwittingly perpetuate the culture of power? What might need to be made explicit to enhance accessibility?

2. Identify some differences that make a difference in your community? How can they be addressed in your school?

3. Do you have to acknowledge a position of power and privilege? If so, what implicit rules that you have supported might need to be overturned? If not, how has the privilege of others affected you?

4. Can you identify with the notions of Panopticon and inspection and how do they affect your educational practice?

5. Can you identify two ways in which you need to use your power to challenge an unjust practice in your school or workplace?

Chapter 5

Promoting Both Private and Public Good
Creating Inclusive School Communities

If we reduce the number of courses offered, then more students who are not qualified will sit in AP classes with *our* university-bound children, and the quality will be reduced.

(Professional parent)

That year we talked about how we could make it so kids saw themselves as equal, so the experience wasn't dependent on your teacher or your family. And that was one of the first years we started doing festivals, whole school festivals, and during the day, so that it also didn't matter if your family couldn't come at night. Every kid got to be a part of it and get something out of it [instead of having individual class parties].

(Catherine Lake, elementary school principal)

In Chapter 1, I stated that the goal of *transformative leadership* is to prepare students both to be individually successful and to be thoughtful, successful, caring, and engaged citizens. In the previous chapter, we reflected on what Delpit (1990) has called the "culture of power," examining the ways in which power and privilege create systemic barriers to the equitable development and inclusion of all students, and how we can begin to break these barriers down. Here, we extend and delve deeper into this topic to reflect on the need for transformative educational leaders to incorporate goals related to advancing what is often called "the public good" in addition to goals related to the private good of individuals and their specific groups.

Private good, as I use the term here, is reflected in outcomes that enhance the self-confidence and competence of the individual, opening doors of opportunity to increase the possibility that the student can attain whatever individual success he or she desires. It is often associated with statistics about the earning power, longevity, and physical and mental health of those who complete undergraduate or graduate degrees compared to those who do not. It is associated with the essential goal of ensuring that all students have equal opportunities to learn and develop to similar high standards of excellence and, hence, to pursue whatever dreams they may have for their future.

Public good, on the other hand, refers to outcomes that positively affect society as a whole. This includes preparing students to contribute (individually) to the social, political, and economic welfare of society as well as to creating collectively a more equitable and more democratic society to the benefit of all. It also refers to the promotion of attributes that help to create and sustain an educated middle class and civil society in which "the people" can, together, create the kind of healthy, prosperous, inclusive, and caring society which is mutually beneficial. Labaree (1997), in discussing some of the multiple goals of education, suggested that the tension between public and private good is primarily *political*. He wrote:

> I argue that the central problems with American education are not pedagogical or organizational or social or cultural in nature but are fundamentally political. That is, the problem is not that we do not know how to make schools better but that we are fighting among ourselves about what goals schools should pursue. Goal setting is a political, and not a technical, problem. It is resolved through a process of making choices and not through a process of scientific investigation. The answer lies in values (what kind of schools we want) and interests (who supports which educational values) rather than apolitical logic.
>
> (p. 40)

In other words, the selection of which goals education should pursue is not a rational or empirical question, but rather, one grounded in different (and usually competing) ideological stances and questions of what we, as a society, either value or should value. Thus, one of the first tasks of a transformative leader must be to help his or her community clarify the kind of school it wants and the values on which it should be built.

The first quotation that introduced this chapter expresses a conception of privilege and power that relates to what is often known as "private good"—the welfare and advancement of individuals or of the specific groups with which they affiliate, to the exclusion of the general welfare of a society. This comment and similar ideas are often heard in parents' meetings when a school is attempting to address its achievement gap or the under-representation of minoritized students in advanced or gifted classes; it suggests the ways in which education, instead of opening doors of opportunity to all students, sometimes perpetuates the privilege of children from historically dominant groups. In contrast, increasing access to higher level classes, in turn, is sometimes seen to increase competition for positions in prestigious universities and expand the pool of potentially well-educated employees in a given field. For some, this increased access is welcome; for others, reducing the hierarchical and stratified nature of schooling is thought to be a threat that reduces opportunities for their own families and friends to prosper. Labaree (1997) explained:

> Parents are well aware that the placement of their children in the right ability group or program or track can give them an advantage in the competition for admission to the right school and the right job and as insurance against early elimination in education's process of "tournament mobility" . . . As a result, they actively lobby to gain the right placement for their children, and they vigorously resist when educators (pursuing a more egalitarian vision) propose elimination of some form of within-school distinction or another, such as by promoting multi-ability reading groups, ending curriculum tracking, or dropping the gifted and talented program.
>
> (p. 53)

Catherine Lake, the elementary school principal whose quotation also appears at the beginning of this chapter, took a very different approach. She stated, in a recent interview, that one of her goals is to "create an excellent educational environment for kids where all kids are successful" and that her other goal is to "create a strong sense of community." To do so requires leveling the playing field and ensuring an environment in which all students, their parents, and extended families are equally welcome and included. Talking about her approach to gifted programs, she explained:

> when parents who make the most noise get into it [the gifted class], even though their kids don't score at that level; then I'm pushing some other kids out. And it usually is the kids whose parents don't come and make a lot of noise who typically tend to be poor and of darker complexion, who are pushed out.

The need to make sure all children are treated equally and that all have access to similar challenging content, similar high levels of expectations and achievement is fundamental to ensuring that schools address the goal of advancing every member of the school community. As discussed in the previous chapter, fulfilling these dual goals of ensuring both private and public goods is made more challenging by the stance of those whose sense of privilege and entitlement make opening the structures and processes of schooling challenging for educational leaders.

In this chapter, I explore these tensions in greater depth, drawing on both historic and current conceptions of the goals and purposes of education. As before, I will draw on examples from schools and insights offered by transformative school leaders to show how these tensions may be balanced and some challenges addressed. As I address the concept of complex goals, I want to examine the role of commercially packaged programs in today's climate of high stakes testing and reform and to show how they may inhibit the promotion of both private and public good. Then I want to examine the importance of relationships (Bakhtin, 1984; Buber, 1970; Thayer-Bacon, 2003) as basic to a more inclusive and equitable form of education and as a significant alternative to an excessive programmatic emphasis. Finally, I will examine how notions of post-modern community (Beane & Apple, 1995; Furman, 1998; Shields, 2003a and 2003b)—community that takes into account changing demographics and multiple and conflicting values—can enhance the promotion of public good.

The Issue of Goals

Issues of goals and values are fraught with tensions, complexities, ambiguities, and even paradoxes. As Labaree (1997) pointed out 15 years ago, education in America has historically "been a tale of ambivalent goals and muddled outcomes"—"an arena that simultaneously promotes equality and adapts to inequality" (p. 41). Transformative educational leaders constantly live with this tension, while at the same time, striving to reduce the inequities and inequalities and to promote goals related to both private and public good. This is a difficult task, because often, the notion of public good has been lost, despite the recognition in such widely disseminated reports as *Nation at risk* (1983) that "a high level of shared education is essential to a free, democratic society and to the fostering of a common culture" (p. 7).

In Chapter 3, we noted, in passing, three historic goals of education: a custodial function; an intellectual one; and a communal one. Labaree (1997) frames them a little differently, identifying tensions between social mobility (a private good) and democratic equality and social efficiency (public goods) (p. 39).

The custodial function, a function one could associate with both private and public goods, is rarely made explicit, although it is still bolstered by arguments for summer programs, intersession activities, and in some cases full-day kindergarten or extended year programs. Similarly, complaints about school closures for snow days or the concern that early or late school schedules for teachers' meetings disrupt child care arrangements are indicative of this continued implicit role of schooling. We do expect most schools to look after and care for our children during the day. In recent years, the second goal of promoting social mobility through intellectual development seems to have become subservient to an almost anti-intellectual goal in which learning takes a back-seat to testing, and in which the purpose of education is formulated in terms of all students (and sub-groups of students) passing the mandated standardized tests and all schools attaining the specified standard to meet "Adequate Yearly Progress." However formulated, this is the goal that tends to dominate policy and practice early in the 21st century. Similarly, the communal goal (also expressed by Labaree's democratic equality and social efficiency) seems to have largely fallen victim to the fierce individualism and highly polarized political nature of American society (as De Tocqueville, 1835/2000, warned over 180 years ago).

Recently, at the beginning of a university fall academic term, as I introduced a course for aspiring school principals, I asked, "What is the purpose of education?" I was met by blank stares. I waited. I rephrased my question, "What are the goals of education?" Again, silence. Finally one young teacher tentatively suggested, "to ensure that all children pass the tests." Students looked to me for affirmation, and gradually, began to affirm their colleague's response. I observed that it was early in the school year, and asked whether any of them had had this conversation during a school-opening workshop, only to be told that not only had it not happened that year, but they had never been asked that question or had a similar discussion about the goals of education— either in their teacher preparation courses, or in their schools.

It was my turn to be astounded. And yet, the silence over the goals of education was informative. Their silence helped to explain the trends I had been noticing—the reduction and simplification of much academic content, the narrowing of the curriculum, the replacement of learning by testing, the reduction of teaching to data analysis related to preparing students to successfully take tests. The truism that what is tested is what is seen as important, and becomes what is taught, came to mind. Further, if testing is associated with high stakes, then it follows that without critical reflection or challenge, testing becomes the be-all and end-all of education. No wonder so many people speak and write about an educational crisis in America, I thought! And no wonder it is so important for the transformative leader to encourage conversation about educational goals.

Catherine Lake, whom I perceive to be a truly transformative principal, reiterated this theme, saying:

> It's like this gaping hole. And it's not just this district. I've been in a number of districts as an administrator. There's just no discussion of what are the underpinnings of what we do, what's the theory behind what we do, what does the research say about what we do. It's usually, well I heard about this other district that is doing this. Well, five districts are doing it. Maybe we should look

at it. Well, a friend of mine gave me this. We should do this. It's never asking, "Is this instructionally good?"

If teachers and future educational leaders have not spent time reflecting on the goals of education, and if there is rarely discussion about the theoretical or ideological underpinnings of what we are doing, then, in a time of increased accountability and performativity (discussed in Chapter 4), it is unlikely that unstated goals will receive much attention. Too many leaders are busy "putting out fires," reacting on a daily basis to localized events, addressing the demands of the current accountability systems, or even implementing the reform du jour—and hence, they seem oblivious to the limitations of the perspectives they have expressed. Identifying the community's desired goals does not ensure their implementation but is certainly a starting point.

Packaged Programs, Educational Reform, and the Public Good

Earlier, I made reference to the high stakes that have come to be associated with much of the culture of testing that dominates education today. Depending on how long the situation has persisted, schools that fail to meet the goals of Adequate Yearly Progress are forced to either offer the choice to students of attending a nearby more successful school, of participating in a supplemental education program such as tutoring paid for by the school, or, if they require "corrective action," are forced into mandated school improvement or "restructuring plans," and required to meet a list of additional reform criteria.

In recent years, in part as a response to the need to restructure schools, and in response to the need for clarity, a proliferation of expensive programs has dominated the reform agenda. As Catherine's concern about implementing new ideas implied, this programmatic emphasis suggests to many educators and members of the general public that if only we could find the right program, we could increase test scores and solve all of the problems associated with failing schools and education in general. Despite the fact that, in the 2002 iteration of the Elementary and Secondary Education Act (commonly known as *No Child Left Behind*), there are many options for meeting the terms of corrective action, school improvement, or restructuring, policy implementation has often taken a programmatic approach, seeking prescriptive and packaged programs that purport to fulfill the guidelines of being proven effective, data-based, and emerging from replicable empirical research. Educators may implement parent-involvement programs, family literacy programs, programs for migratory children, those deemed to be neglected, delinquent, or at-risk, dropout prevention programs, charter school programs, foreign language, technology, or book distribution programs, and so forth— all aimed at fulfilling the purpose of the act, namely to "improve the academic achievement of the disadvantaged." The goal is to be met, states NCLB, through the implementation of 12 major strategies, including the use of "effective, scientifically based instructional strategies and challenging academic content" (*No Child Left Behind*, 2002, sec. 1001:9).

In addition, educational leaders are required to institute programs to improve reading or language arts, mathematics, and science and to offer qualified professional development to staff. Given all of the options available, and the extensive demands for record keeping, data entry, and data analysis, it is hardly surprising that the minimum requirements have become *the* requirements and that academic content areas other than the three specifically mentioned are often neglected. Furthermore, rather than examining or conducting research into what works with a specific group of students, and taking the time to create locally-developed programs, most educators choose to opt for commercially available "best practices." Unfortunately, there are several problems with this approach.

Testing not Learning

The first problem is an over-emphasis on testing rather than learning that is related to the need to prepare students to pass mandated tests in three subjects. This often means that large blocks of time are spent teaching to the test, drilling students in low-level activities, and unfortunately in killing any eagerness students might have for in-depth inquiry. I have visited numerous schools in which, for example, the whole morning is dedicated to language arts, with little or no discussion of how non-fiction or world affairs may be incorporated into reading and writing strategies. Sometimes I have been told that teaching science and social studies has been completely eliminated, or at best, relegated with art and music to a few minutes at the end of the day or week (if they are taught at all), and only if there is time after the test preparation activities have occurred. I worry frequently about the impact of this restriction of curriculum on our ability to promote education's social or democratic citizenship goals.

A rare example from a study of urban, low-income children being taught science through their literacy block shows the efficacy of an alternative approach.[1] One child, whom we'll call Dionte, had previously been involved in repeated disciplinary incidents and visits to the principal's office. However, during his experimental, third-grade, inquiry-based science project, when the principal visited his classroom, she noted he was fully engaged in a challenging learning activity. When questioned, he explained that he was being a scientist. He enthused:

> I'm drawing my science lab and my assistants are helping me do my experiments. Today, we are finding out where the water is going and this assistant here is telling me that the molecules are moving faster and faster because of heat and that makes them turn into vapor and so they can escape. See these dots here? These are the molecules escaping because of heat. I'm a real good scientist because I'm creative and I like to discover stuff, but the best part is that I get to be in charge of the lab and my assistants help me to discover things and have ideas.

Dionte's classmates subsequently described a time when they learned by "running around the classroom" and Dionte exclaimed,

> Oh, yeah. That was the molecule activity. We were up on the rug with Ms. Richter and we were molecules and Ms. Richter kept turning up the heat and we kept moving faster and finally we popped off the top of the water and went moving real fast round the classroom. Larenzo had to shut the door so we wouldn't escape because molecules move really fast in all kind of directions when they get hot.

He went on to explain how when the heat was turned down, they had to slow down; that it then got really cold and they froze close together and solid.

In this example, it is obvious that Dionte and his classmates had learned about the various states of H_2O and how it changed from liquid to vapor to solid. The learning was not based on a packaged program or on having had to memorize a list of dry facts and formulas, but on a changed approach to instruction—one that engaged children in inquiry-based learning rather than requiring them to sit quietly and repeat endless disconnected facts. This example demonstrates, again, the need for educators to work with vision and agility to create learning opportunities that engage all children. Here they were not simply following a script, but had been given the opportunity to be creative as they learned. Moreover, they felt competent—believed they knew what it meant to become scientists, and had built some capacity in that area. Watching and listening to children who had had the rare opportunity to engage in similar kinds of learning, one has no doubt about their ability to answer questions on standardized tests about the multiple states of H_2O. In other words, as numerous studies have found (for references, see again Tienda, Alon, & Niu, 2008), engaged learning does not reduce test scores. Quite the contrary.

Here, however, our emphasis is not successful attainment of standards, but advancing both private and public good. When students are made to feel inferior, deficient, and inadequate, they quickly become demoralized, and the subsequent "dropout" (perhaps better termed "push-out" rates) increase concomitantly. One, among many, examples of this may be found in the Detroit Public Schools, where (although the number is contested), the high-school completion rate is an abysmal 25% and where teachers are reported to be so demoralized with the revolving professional development activities and myriad of programs that teacher absenteeism not only costs the district thousands of dollars a year, but certainly adversely affects student success.

Misplaced Notions of Evidence and "Best Practice"

A second problem with a heavy reliance on packaged programs is that they rely on several misconceptions. One is the misplaced notion that evidence is necessarily generalizeable and that what works in one context is effective and appropriate in another. Hence, although a program may actually be based on data from one context, there is often no evidence that with different teachers and students in a very different location, the same approach will be effective. The misconception has led to the concept of "best practice" that mistakenly suggests that to succeed all educators need to do is replicate the initiative and implement it faithfully.

Although such a standardized approach may work with manufactured widgets where a consistent product is desirable, this is not the case with children. As we institute packaged programs, we ignore the significant differences in learning strategies and capacities related to students' cultural or socio-economic backgrounds. In turn, this often continues to marginalize those described by Catherine as "poor and of darker complexion" and to advantage those from traditionally dominant families and cultures. Ignoring the context and prior learning perpetuates the erroneous deficit assumptions that some groups of children are less able than others.

Moreover, despite the widespread acceptance of the "gold standard" for research-based programs based on empirical, quasi-experimental, and replicable studies, it is important to understand the limitations of such an approach. Eisenhart (2006), a member of the commission that wrote the document *Scientific research in education*, explains elsewhere that:

> experimental research on causal effects isolates variables . . . and investigates their relationship to other variables . . . This procedure will work if the variables being measured do not change over time, are not variably influenced by circumstances and are not affected by human intention or desire . . . The problem is that in education and other social practices all else is not equal, and little if anything remains constant.
>
> (pp. 699–700)

In fact, in education, almost nothing is equal. One cannot control for personality, background, individual style and preference let alone the attitudes and beliefs of educational leaders and classroom teachers that have been shown to be so critical to enhancing student learning (Shields, Bishop, & Mazawi, 2005). Contexts are not equal as we saw in the discussion of schools on the Navajo reservation in Chapter 4. Teachers, as well as students, are affected by outside events and interpersonal relationships. And when we are dealing with schools, it is difficult, if not impossible, to hold variables constant. Contexts not only differ, but are complex and constantly changing in today's VUCA world. A new family moves into the community; the parent comes into the school to volunteer; and many human interactions change. Schools in urban centers like New Orleans or Detroit may all be located in centers which have experienced severe trauma in recent years, but the differences between devastation by a hurricane and decline through economic downturn and corruption may require vastly different transformative strategies. Similarly, a small rural, impoverished, ethnically homogeneous school population in Idaho will require a different strategy from a school in a small, urban, relatively wealthy and diverse university town in the same state. In education, to promote both private and public good, it is important to acknowledge that "one size does not fit all." This argues again for the new skills of *understanding* one's community, of developing *clarity* around goals, and finding ways to respond with *vision* and *agility* in order to promote learning for all students.

To introduce and foster the concept of private good for all students, we must be intentional about the equity of access, standards, and outcomes we are trying to promote. To follow common wisdom and argue that every school needs to adopt the concept of a Professional Learning Community, sometimes referred to as a PLC, implies something almost magical about the concept but it fails to explicitly address shared goals. And, although the associated strategies of working in teams, discussing challenges and possible solutions, and building educator capacity may be inherently positive, they will need to be implemented in context-specific and sensitive ways. If we choose to adopt a professional learning community approach, it behooves us to ask, learning about what? What does it mean to be "professional"? Who is included and who excluded in this concept? How are the goals of the community established? Professional learning communities, by definition, focus on process and discussions of data, without necessarily having previously discussed or established goals; too often they assume the goal is test-passing, rather than equity, inclusion, social justice, challenging content and the like. Thus, the goal may be achieved in a fashion that promotes short-term, but ultimately limited, solutions.

Process-oriented reforms may often appear to be implemented successfully and with fidelity, only to reveal, on closer investigation, that their implementation has been in conflict with the goals of promoting social mobility or democratic equity. One doctoral student, who is a practicing school principal, focused her dissertation research on exploring the relationships between collective efficacy (Bandura, 1997), highly diverse schools, and student learning (reflected by, but not confined to, satisfactory test scores, i.e., meeting AYP). Her starting assumption was that if a school demonstrated high collective efficacy on well-validated instruments, then when she conducted observations and interviews, she would find a strong focus on student learning. Instead, to her dismay, she found that often educators had developed a strong sense of collective efficacy by narrowing the curriculum and implementing a number of remedial programs (e.g., noon-hour test prep, extra reading blocks, after-school and Saturday schools for students on the bubble). Although in her own school, collective efficacy was intentionally developed through dialogue about equity and the capacity-building of students and teachers, the emphasis on "proven" strategies and packaged programs elsewhere led to her conclusion that a school could demonstrate strong collective efficacy without any discussion of the goals of high quality learning by all students. In discussing her findings, she explained:

> I thought that if you had an average level of collective efficacy or a higher level of collective efficacy, you would have had to tackle the deficit thinking and the beliefs systems undergirding it, right? What I found, though, is that, wow, there's a very healthy dose of deficit thinking co-existing with collective efficacy . . . I think the concern is that we're limiting our own belief systems. And so we are saying, "You know what, our group is cohesive and we do a good job and we're able to reach certain goals cause look at what we have to deal with."
>
> (Bieneman, 2012)

Similarly, educators who adopt the popular *Response to Intervention* (RtI) approach that was originally intended to reduce the number of student referrals to special education programs, and hence, to promote the good of all students, often accept its premises without any prior discussion of goals related either to private or public good. Indeed, many states have mandated the implementation of this program without a clear sense of what it is intended to accomplish. According to a document published by the state of Illinois, for example, in which a form of RtI is mandated for every school, RtI "provides a schoolwide model of integrated instruction, assessment, and data-based decision making to improve student outcomes" (ISBE, 2008, p. 5). RtI, the document states, drawing on the work of Batsche et al. (2006), is defined as "the practice of providing 1) high-quality instruction/intervention matched to student needs and 2) using learning rate over time and level of performance to 3) make important educational decisions" (p. 1). But, unfortunately, when the document discusses learning, it uses language of deficiency, of problem, and of remediation rather than language of excitement, inquiry, and possibility. Tier 1 (of the three-tier RtI program) is to be considered "the foundation" and consists of scientific, research-based core instructional and behavioral methodologies, practices and supports designed for all students in the general curriculum. "Across the tiers, the problem solving method is . . . to define the problem by determining the discrepancy between what is expected and what is occurring" (p. 2), and then to develop an intervention plan.

Although originally intended to promote good basic instruction for all students, the notion that all students' learning needs are equated with "problems" and that teaching to all students is reduced to "an intervention plan" is disturbing, to say the least. Further, teachers too often treat each pedagogical strategy, not as a way of creatively improving their teaching through practicing, developing, refining, or experimenting with a new approach, but as something to purchase and "implement." In one school I visited, teachers were heard to say of certain children and strategies, "They need a particular intervention, but we don't have it yet. We won't be buying it until next year."

Unquestioning adoption of RtI leads, once again, to a prescriptive and technical approach to teaching and learning and fails to ask how it is possible that all children come to school with "problems" instead of simply coming with curiosity about things as yet unlearned, and topics as yet unexplored. What has happened to the notion that, developmentally, when they start school, children are curious, competent learners, ready to explore and tackle the world around them—even though they may have different background experiences? Where are the obvious goals of education: to promote intellectual and social development—instead of to intervene and remediate all children?

I acknowledge here that I may be perceived as being too harsh—that the intent behind such approaches as Professional Learning Communities, or Response to Intervention (and I could add a myriad of others) was not for them to be prescriptive, deskilling, or technical reforms—*but* without prior consideration of the goals and purposes of education, this is exactly what they have become. Hence, as I use these programs as illustrative, it is the implementation and not the programs themselves I am critiquing. The following account of one principal, determined to implement RtI as required by her district, makes the point:

> We tried to do the model that's being advanced, which was essentially, "There's something wrong with these kids, let's pile on interventions." We got this system honed to where these kids were pulled from here, these kids were pulled from here, these kids went to 30 minutes of intervention; these kids went to 30 minutes of [different] intervention. All these are programs. They are unrelated to anything; but we did it with beautiful efficiency. My help team . . . had just spot on technical efficiency, perfectly aligned all these schedules, and made sure things were done with fidelity . . . And guess what? Scores went down for two years.

The principal then paused, and reflected on what had gone wrong with this unquestioning implementation of the new mandated program. She observed:

> RTI [should be] looking at what is your Tier 1, what is your core instructional program, and is it consistent? Is it excellent? But as a district, we never looked at our curriculum, in fact we don't have one. So we never looked at the lack of a Tier 1 as the problem.

Although packaged programs may be useful at times, unquestioning acceptance of any approach, without careful examination of how and where it helps to meet the explicit goals that have been agreed upon, leads to simply another disconnected intervention—and certainly not to instruction that helps promote either the individual success and achievement of students or the good of the community as a whole. In fact, it leads to the third problem associated with the current heavy reliance on packaged programs—the obvious deskilling of educators.

Deskilling of Educators

When teachers have come to the point of saying they do not "have" an intervention, something is seriously wrong. When educators have never discussed the goals of education, we are failing, not only our students, but our society. When we reduce teacher training to a series of strategies and skills related to technical aspects of teaching, lesson planning, unit development, and classroom management, we lose focus on creating the kind of exciting and challenging learning environments for students experienced by Dionte and his classmates—and we imply, if we do not always state it bluntly, that we do not believe either educators or students have the capacity or creativity required to succeed.

Those who teach in colleges and universities, as well as those who develop policy related to educator preparation, will need to reconsider their approach, and to recall that the heart of education lies, not with programs, but with people. When, as discussed in Chapter 3, educators focus on facilitating learning, on the elimination of deficit thinking, and holding all children to high expectations related to rich, challenging, and engaging content, they quickly learn that the key to motivating (and hence to teaching) students is to connect to their interests.

I once had a young student who was, I believe, misplaced in his ninth-grade remedial language arts program. He seemed to struggle academically; his attendance was sporadic, and his home life was unpredictable. It would have been easy to assume Aaron was disinterested, and to write him off as another potential dropout. Instead, one day, something amazing happened. As he entered the classroom, we began to chat, and I discovered he was passionate about martial arts, kung fu in particular—something about which I knew nothing. Nevertheless, my casual inquiry about his weekend activity sparked something in him. The next day, he shyly approached me, on his way out of class, with several pages of misspelled, but fascinating writing. Extolling the virtues of his hero Bruce Lee, through a series of complicated similes, it began:

> Bruce Lee reminds me of Alexander the Great, who opened the famed Gordian knot. Gordius was king of Phyrgia [Sic]. According to the legend, he tied a very large knot with the ends hidden and announced that the person who could untie it would become ruler of all Asia. Hundreds of people tried and were unsuccessful. Then came Alexander the Great who took one good look at the knot and hacked it to pieces with his sword and declared that he had fulfilled the prophecy. "Cutting the Gordian knot" is an expression meaning, solving a difficult problem in a simple unexpected way. Bruce Lee cut the Gordian know [Sic] of the martial arts world. While many styles (of Kung Fu) said, "You must do this and you must do that and you must sit in this stance"; "You must do this to become proficient," Bruce looked at the roots of the problem, the simplicity of art, and the principals of combat, and hacked through the knot of ignorance in the martial arts world.

Aaron continued to write in similar vein about Genghis Khan, Gandhi, Houdini, Caesar, and others and concluded by saying,

> But above all Bruce Lee reminds me of Jonathan Livingston Seagull, who kept striving to be faster and was never satisfied with himself until he could outdo himself by being faster and faster. Bruce, like this seagull, kept reaching levels upon levels which others said were physically impossible to reach. When people asked, "How can you get any better?" he didn't even stop to think he just kept on improving and improving, and improved physically, spiritually, and mentally.

Aaron's list of "greats" was long, impressive, convincing. I had no idea where he got his ideas, how he developed his similes, or what they meant to him. How wrong I was that he was disinterested. How many of his classmates could describe the Gordian knot or identify Genghis Khan? How many had read *Jonathan Livingston Seagull*? It is clear to me that packaged programs would not have engaged Aaron. Neither would they have shown Dionte that he could become a scientist, working with assistants in his lab.

Too often, as educators focus on a mandated form of assessment, a prescribed intervention, or on a scripted sequence of strategies and questions, we emphasize the technical, and in so doing, both deskill teachers and lose the heart of education—the relationships—between and among people and between students and the amazing content they have the opportunity to explore. Thus, to develop the capacity of individual students, transformative leaders must recognize the complexity and the variety of interests and personalities in each school and classroom and focus on developing people, rather than attaining test scores. To that end, relationships, and not programs, become key to successful teaching and learning and to the promotion of private, and ultimately also, public good.

Relationships as Key to Equity and Inclusivity

The point I have been making is that if students are not engaged in their learning processes, they become disaffected, and too often drop out of school, becoming yet another statistic in a system that, through its stratification and hierarchical approaches, has failed them. If we accept Labaree's (1997) statement, that "the social efficiency approach to schooling argues that our economic well-being depends on our ability to prepare the young to carry out useful economic roles with competence" (p. 42), then we must ensure that every student acquires the appropriate skills and attitudes to seek gainful employment and contribute to a prosperous and sustainable society. Unfortunately, our present lack of explicit discussion of goals is not conducive to this outcome and it certainly does not argue for a broader interpretation of educational goals or for democratic participation and engagement. We must find a better approach.

Years ago, as I was studying for a specialist certification, I joined a gym full of teaching colleagues one night a week, to listen to a lecture related to instructional strategies. Paradoxically, because I neither recall the instructor's name, nor did he ever learn mine, the only specific piece of information I recall from that course was the following advice: "learn something about each of your students' interests and activities outside of class." Perhaps the instructor was unaware that he was promoting a kind of "do as I say and not as I do" approach. Nevertheless, his words took root. They made sense. Despite the fact that, at the time, each day I was teaching seven 40-minute blocks of French, each with 25–33 high school students, it was this advice that ultimately led me to discover Aaron's interest in kung fu. It is the advice that leads me, still today, to develop positive relationships with my doctoral students, and to know, for example, that one has a two-year-old child recently identified as having autistic spectrum disorder, that another has an adopted son from Korea, or another is a former champion swimmer, or that still another grew up in an abusive foster home. The point here is that it does not matter if we are dealing with kindergarteners or third graders who enthusiastically share information about their families, or adult graduate students who cautiously reveal something about their private lives; in every case, developing relationships facilitates learning.

Most of us are familiar with studies conducted in crowded orphanages in which it was learned that children who were not picked up or cuddled failed to thrive. Similar experiments conducted with monkeys by American psychologist Harry Harlow from the 1950s onwards with cloth and wire "mothers" also demonstrated the importance of warmth and nurturing. More recently a *New York Times* columnist, Dave Brooks (2011), found simply that we "learn from people we love." He cites a study in which researchers found that, in an urban high school, students who were able to name a favorite teacher had greater academic success and higher graduation rates than students for whom the idea seemed implausible. A response such as, "a favorite teacher—I don't know what you are talking about" was, on the other hand, associated with failure to complete school and to graduate.

Educators have known about the importance of relationships for some time although sometimes it seems difficult to find time to enact positive relationships. Some schools have even attempted to develop special strategies to ensure that every child has a regular encounter with a caring adult who will advocate for him or her. The principal of a school with an owl mascot believes that building relationships is central to everything else that occurs within a school and so sums up a new approach in these words:

> We'd like to have owl families. Every single adult in the building will have an owl family: my secretaries, the custodian, the instructional assistants. And in that owl family is a small group of eight kids or so. And we will meet monthly to just talk about things that are pertinent to the social/emotional/behavioral growth of our kids. Things like empathy or bullying or problem-solving, things like that.

Although this may be a useful supplement to an emphasis on relationships, it seems to me that developing strong, positive relationships is fundamentally the task of every teacher and educator and goes hand in hand with creating an engaging and welcoming learning environment.

Thayer-Bacon writes: "I begin with the assumption that all *people are social beings.* Our lives begin and are lived in relationships with others" (2003, p. 7). In reality, unless we are some of the few individuals conceived in a test tube, we are born of relationships—some more positive than others. We grow up in relationship, being suckled and nurtured by parents or other caregivers, learning to speak, and to negotiate our world as we imitate friends and family members. And if we are lucky, we continue to learn in relationship—with educators and other adults when we enter school. It is not the relationship of a friend, or even of a parent, but the best educative relationship is one of "encounter" with other human beings and with stimulating intellectual content. It is a relationship of complete acceptance, in which we are fully accepted for who we are, even though others will often disagree with some of the things we have been taught or that we have come to believe.

Martin Buber, one of the greatest thinkers of the 20th century, was profoundly influenced by his personal relationships with his grandmother and later, by the sharing and sense of community of the Hasidic Jewish community. He is perhaps most well known for his book, *I and thou* (1970)—in which he asserted the importance of relationships that either humanize or objectify, of treating another person as "Thou" (or you) instead of as "it." In other words, objectifying another person is dehumanizing, while relationships are everything. He sums this up in the pithy and often-repeated statement, "All real living is meeting" (1970, p. 62). Through true encounter with another, by opening oneself up to another, one becomes, Buber argued, truly human: "Through the Thou a person becomes I," he wrote in one place. To live, according to Buber, is not only to be in relationship, but to turn toward the other, ready to meet him or her where he or she is. To live is to care deeply for the other.

Freire (2000) extends the discussion of the purposes of education by emphasizing the role of dialogue as well as relationships, saying:

> Education as the practice of freedom—as opposed to education as the practice of domination—denies that man is abstract, isolated, independent, and unattached to the world; it also denies that the world exists as a reality apart from people. Authentic reflection considers neither abstract man nor the world without people, but people in their relations with the world.
>
> (p. 75)

The relationship required of educators in schools and other institutions of learning is complex. It requires opening ourselves to fellow educators, to our students, their parents, and to members of the wider community. Nevertheless, relationships are basic to teaching and learning, to the creation of a sense of belonging, and to our ability to change and grow as well as to facilitate the learning of others. Jerry Starratt (1991) urges that to develop positive relationships with others, we must treat one another with "absolute regard." This means that whether we agree with someone or not, we respect his or her right to hold a particular opinion or belief. We may not approve a particular act or comment, but we must take care, even while challenging inappropriate or illegal behavior, to respect the other's humanity. Starratt (2005) extends the notion of absolute regard by emphasizing the importance of being present in relationships, and urged three different ways of being present—an affirming presence that communicates and affirms the high regard with which you hold the other, a critical presence in which we critically appraise blockages to authentic relationship, and an enabling presence in which we respond to the possibilities of the other (pp. 74–79).

Audrey, the principal concerned about the growing homeless population of her school, exemplifies the concept of presence in her account of an interaction with a mother whose son was acting out, inattentive and talkative in class. Audrey decided to make contact with the home. She describes the conversation:

> I had called home because I had noticed that Billie had worn the same clothes to school for three days—a shirt with a mustard stain on the front. When I called

home, I introduced myself and made some small talk, and then I asked the mother if there was anything I could do to help. I asked if she needed any laundry detergent or anything for the home. Immediately, she began crying on the phone. I felt awful. I told her I did not mean to upset her. She told me she was not upset, but was overcome with gratitude. She stated in her previous experiences, school personnel would call and make judgments. She said no one had ever called to ask how they could help. That is how I found out about the Brownings' experience with homelessness [and subsequently about the Mother's battle with a brain tumor].

(Shields & Warke, 2010)

In fact, subsequent interviews for her dissertation informed Audrey that the news had spread. Hers was known as a school where homeless families would be helped and respected and not marginalized and stigmatized—a reputation that had contributed to the increased number of homeless choosing her school.

The transformative leader must follow Audrey's example. It is not enough to respect someone in the abstract, but we must, as Buber advocated, develop relationships through the "encounter"—in practice on a day-to-day basis. To be fully human, as we encounter our students as "Thou," we must be both open to them, and willing to learn from them. Otherwise, we cannot expect them to want to learn from us. Buber puts it this way, "I felt I have not the right to want to change another if I am not open to be changed by him as far as it is legitimate" (see http://courses.washington.edu/spcmu/buber/buber17.html) . We must make our relationships concrete as we are fully present to the other (Starratt, 2005) and permit them to change us as Audrey was changed by her growing understanding of the plight of homeless students and their families.

Freire also talks about the mutuality of the pedagogical relationship, acknowledging that both teacher and student learn together, with and from one another. At the same time, he clarifies the complex relationship, emphasizing that it does not overcome power differentials, because there are always inequalities between those in formal positions and those who are not. Freire (2000) states:

> Dialogue between teachers and students does not place them on the same footing professionally, but it does mark the democratic position between them. Teachers and students are not identical, and this for countless reasons. After all, it is a *difference* between them that makes them precisely students or teachers . . . Dialogue is meaningful precisely because the dialogical subjects, the agents in the dialogue, not only retain their identity, but actively defend it, and thus grow together. Precisely on this account, dialogue does not *level* them, does not "even them out," reduce them to each other. Dialogue . . . implies a sincere, fundamental respect on the party of the subjects engaged in it, a respect that is violated, or prevented from materializing, by authoritarianism. Permissiveness does the same thing, in a different, but equally deleterious, way.

(pp. 248–249)

It is the act of creating positive relationships that foster one's ability to engage in the kind of respectful dialogue that permits growth, despite—or perhaps even because of—differences, that I am associating here with transformative leadership.

Although some educators find the need for relationships compelling and inherently reasonable, others struggle with this issue. Earlier I indicated that I make an attempt to get personally acquainted with each of my adult students. One way in which I accomplish this is to invite them to my home, or to share meals and activities with them. Yet, I have a colleague who believes this crosses invisible boundaries, who does not believe it appropriate to "fraternize with adult students." Each person must discover for himself or herself how best to forge the relationships that are conducive to fostering trust and to creating a positive learning environment, but it must be done. Without relationships, individuals do not thrive; with relationships, people achieve success.

Catherine Lake acknowledges the importance of pedagogical relationships, saying:

> At the core of [a successful school] is good instruction. It doesn't matter if you have all the fancy bells and whistles, if you don't have good instruction and you don't question what you're teaching and why you're teaching it. I can equip a classroom with every modern technology feature, and if I have somebody in there that doesn't build relationships with kids, doesn't believe that all kids can learn, doesn't have some good pedagogical or instructional strategies or philosophies, that is not going to change a thing.

Others take a different approach. Some, both elementary and secondary principals, develop relationships with their students by being available and present as each day begins. John Law states, "One of the most important parts of my day is I try to be the first face every kid sees in the school every day. And it mostly works because almost all of our kids ride the bus." In his relatively small school, he is also available at recess and in the lunch room, asking children about something they are reading, or writing about, or about their activities. He also has a shelf of books designated for children who are celebrating a birthday. They come into his office, talk about their birthday, and select a book which he then signs and personalizes. The value of the gift is immaterial in his very wealthy community; it is the relationship established that is important.

Interestingly, David Dean, principal of a large secondary school, uses a similar strategy. Talking about the centrality of relationships, he explains how important they are to the building of trust, and to the acceptance of responsibility. He says, "I do it just primarily by being accessible. I'm always down in the main lobby before school. I moved into the community, which I didn't have to, I was not required to." Then, he recounted an unusual step, one that many will find controversial, and certainly one that seems to go well beyond the expected actions of a high school principal. He reported, "On the first day of school the last two school years, I got on the public address system when they were doing the morning announcements, and gave everybody my personal cell phone number."

(Wow. What trust! The principal of a school of over 1800 students, making his cell phone number public.) When I asked if students abused it, he firmly denied it. He explained that his intent was to ensure that all of his students were safe and that if they needed to talk to an adult, they had the ability to do so. Then, he recounted the following powerful and persuasive story.

> You know, I got a text not even a month ago, on a Sunday afternoon. I was sitting home, writing, and a student texted me and said "I think my friend is going to

and, and what should I do?" And I said, "Well, you really need
is student is because I need to ensure that they're safe." We went
because she didn't want to give up this boy's name, but she finally
ad the unenviable task of calling the parents, because I keep a list
's emergency contact information in my vehicle . . . And so I went
, looked the student's parent's name up and called the parent and
a student had called me and was concerned about their child's
ay "commit suicide.") . . . And she said, "Oh my gosh; thank you
heading back home right now; we've had him in counseling, but
haven't been going well for him." So that was my whole purpose—
s felt a sort of certain sense of empowerment so that they could
o me.

onships that empower students is certainly a first step toward
ood. But, as this incident demonstrates, it goes farther. Developing
xhibit trust establish the basis for strong community relations and
sis for the promotion of public good as well.

Community and the Public Good

It is clear that raising academic standards and ensuring that every child has the
opportunity to succeed in every school is a fundamental goal of educators and policy-
makers alike. Nevertheless, it is also important to restore the concept of education as
a public good—one that benefits society as a whole. You may be surprised to learn, as
I was, that the current emphases on testing and accountability were intended, in part,
according to the 1995 National Education Goals Panel Report, *Building a nation of
learners*, to "ensure that all students learn to use their minds well, so they may be
prepared for responsible citizenship" (p. 11). Nevertheless, using their minds well is
simply one aspect of preparation for citizenship. As Bellah and his colleagues indicated
so clearly, building community also requires "habits of the heart" (1985). Or as Parker
Palmer advocated, education must integrate the intellectual, the emotional, and the
spiritual (1998). This does not imply a kind of modernist approach to community in
which everyone thinks the same way, believes the same things, worships in the same
building, or speaks the same language. It does require, as advocated by Shields (2003a
and 2003b), Furman (1998), and others, that transformative leaders work to create a
"community of difference."

A "Community of Difference"

Sometimes, community is associated with people who voluntarily come together
because they share perspectives, interests, geographical proximity, or ideological
beliefs. These voluntary communities are characterized by similarity, by commonality,
and often by a willingness and ability to exclude those who do not share their position.
However, this cannot be the kind of community established in today's diverse public
schools—schools which are often a microcosm of the wider, increasingly diverse
society. Thus, every taxpayer whose child is enrolled in a school is entitled to be
considered a fully participatory member of the school community, regardless of belief

or background. It does not matter whether the dominant belief of the suburb or town in which the school is located is against homosexual relations, or whether traditionally, the locale has been a sundown town, or whether the community advocates Christian, Jewish, or Muslim values; every child and parent associated with a local school must be treated with respect and encouraged to participate fully in the activities of the school community.

Elsewhere I have written at length about this concept of a community of difference (see for example Shields 2003a, 2003b, 2005, 2009). Fundamentally it differs from that of a traditional community in which beliefs, values, and practices are shared. Instead, in a community of difference, the operative beliefs, values, and practices must develop as people come to know, understand, and respect one another. The beginning shared values of a community of difference are regard for one another, and a willingness to change and grow through engaging in extensive dialogue. In a community of difference, new norms and practices are constantly reinvented to be inclusive of all members of the constantly changing community; old established practices and traditions are constantly re-evaluated to ensure that they do not exclude newcomers whose cultural practices may require modes of participation to be re-examined. Hence, when parents in a school-community object (as discussed in Chapter 3) to a Muslim parent's discussion of his beliefs in his child's classroom, it behooves the principal, as John Law did, to emphasize the need for understanding of the diverse backgrounds of all students.

Teach about Diversity

For a deep sense of community to occur, children must be taught, from a very young age, about the rich diversity of the fabric of American democratic community—diversity that children need to be helped to understand. On another occasion, John Law recounted, with some sense of incredulity, an early morning exchange with a third grader in which the child asked him if he wanted to see a picture of his birthday present—a new pony. Assuming the pony would be a toy, John acknowledged his own incorrect assumption, his surprise, and his recurring discomfort with the wealth and privilege exhibited by most members of his school community, when the child showed him a real pony, and informed him it was being cared for with his sisters' horses at a nearby stable. The child was, of course, insouciant about his privilege and the bounteousness of the gift of a pony.

The exchange emphasized for John Law the need, in his school community, to help students understand that not everyone lives as they do, and to learn to value the contributions of others, despite the dissimilarities between their privileged positions and those of many others in society. We may smile at the enthusiasm of the child sharing a picture of his new pony, but on reflection we also recognize, with John, the seriousness of the need for educational leaders in similar communities to help children address assumptions about the normalcy of such privilege. This needs to begin early in elementary school, given the predisposition of children to develop identities related to the beliefs of their parents.

This predisposition was clearly identified in a study in Northern Ireland, in which the researcher showed very young children images of flags and other national symbols. Connolly (2003) found that "there is evidence for the beginnings of an ethnic habitus at the age of three" (p. 174). By six, they were able to articulate and explain some of their thinking. In all cases, the children chose the symbol associated with their parents' national affiliation as positive and others as oppositional and negative. Connolly therefore called for "conceiving of appropriate ways of engaging young children more critically in the ways they are encouraged to think about and experience identity, difference, and diversity" (p. 180). Too often educators assume that children in elementary school are too young to be engaged in deep conversations about identity, prejudice, and social constructions of reality, but in reality, those who have conducted similar research have been able to clearly demonstrate how eagerly and deeply young children engage in conversations about self and other (Pillsbury & Shields, 1999; Smith et al., 1998).

In a previous book (see Shields, 2009), I wrote about the need to democratize practice, and to teach and prepare students *about*, *in*, and *for* democracy. The thesis was that schools are not democracies nor can they be when participation of minors is mandated by law, but that schools must teach students about our governance structures, and what it means to responsibly participate in them; to demonstrate elements of democratic community in which children can participate in age-appropriate activities that help them to learn to live together in respectful and mutually beneficial ways; and to learn ways to engage some of the differences and inequities that present challenges to our democratic way of life that they will need to confront as future adult citizens.

Similarly, there are a number of practices identified by transformative school leaders that can promote the kind of community that prepares students about, in, and for citizenship and that promotes public good. Among these are finding ways to facilitate the participation of various members of the wider community in school activities, engaging the wider community through home visits (sometimes using interpreters), and opening the school to the community in a variety of ways.

Facilitating the Participation of the Whole Community

Even new educational structures rarely encourage the input of parents and community members beyond that which is superficial and symbolic. Too often our communications are one way, telling parents what is happening at the school, how the schedule is changing, what activities their children need to pay for and when, or when their child has not completed his or her homework or needs additional learning support. In recent years, this is often accomplished by having a computerized program that automatically phones a parent or guardian when a child is absent from a class and has not produced a note. On other occasions, notice of a closure for inclement weather or an unexpected power shortage, for example, is left on the answering machine of every family. There is no question that these impersonal strategies are useful in times of emergency or when time is of the essence. Nevertheless, excessive use of such devices repudiates the relationship rule discussed above.

One parent with whom I spoke recently expressed frustration at the excessively long messages she received when she attempted to call her daughter's school. She did not, she informed me, need to hear about all of the schedules, administrative activities, policies, and activities going on in a given week when she called with a specific question for a teacher—and she certainly did not need to hear the same information every time she called. For her, the impersonal message had lost its impact and its utility and had become a barrier to successful communications with the school.

To involve all members of the community in the life of the school requires intentional action often involving personal invitations and innovative strategies. We cannot make the assumption that because the school is there, people either know how to participate or believe their involvement would be welcome (and often it is not). Transformative leaders will have to work intentionally and consistently to create communities of difference.

Facilitating (and Rethinking) Parental Involvement

Sometimes we develop newsletters—or worse yet, "training" sessions to inform parents of our expectations and how they can help their children at home—without ever asking them about their expectations or about how we (as educators) may help them educate their children. We fail to recall that education is also a partnership—and that parents and caregivers are not only their children's first teachers, but that they and their extended families and communities continue to have an influence beyond that of the school. Too often, we reduce "parental involvement" to activities in which parents participate *at school*—chaperoning trips, volunteering in classrooms, an occasional demonstration of expertise or talk about career. Worse, we dismiss those parents who are unable to appear on demand (on our schedules) at a school event (class play, choir concert, or parent conference evening) as uninvolved and, even worse, uncaring. And we hear comments such as, "It is always the parents we don't need to see who come to the interview," or "It is too bad the other parents don't care about their child's education."

Some immigrant families, for example, have come from cultures in which teachers were the most highly educated members of the community and, hence, quite decidedly revered. In those cultures, one would not think to question the teacher or to offer to "assist," believing instead that the educators knew best how to educate each child. Sometimes we hear, again as a criticism of parents' willingness to be involved in their child's education, that as children grow older, parents become less involved and less inclined to come into the schools. I doubt the responsibility lies fully with the parents or adolescents. I often ask, as a rejoinder, what a high school physics or history teacher would expect of a parent volunteer. It is not that parents have nothing to contribute, but in general, educators relegate their participation to assistance with routine duties (distributing materials, etc.) and rarely ask them to participate fully in classroom discussions, sharing their own experience, or contributing an alternative perspective to the conversation. In general, we open our classrooms reluctantly and invite the participation of others cautiously, if at all.

We mistakenly, and to everyone's disadvantage, make the assumption that some parents do not care and that others (for lack of formal education or lack of visibility in the school) may have little to contribute. And we mistakenly describe, define, and explain parental involvement on traditional middle-class terms—confining it to what parents do *at the school*, instead of believing that most parents try to support their children's successful education in whatever ways they can.

One of my sons is a welder (paid by the hour) who works about an hour north of the community in which the family lives and in which the children attend school. His wife currently runs a day-care center from their home and hence is responsible for seven children under the age of five. At one point, I was surprised to hear that my son had to take a full day off work to attend his eight- and nine-year-old children's school plays. (It was not possible for his wife, regardless of how much she wanted to be there, to take her seven young charges from the day care, so the responsibility fell on him.) Upon further inquiry, I learned that one grade level had the activity scheduled for mid-morning (prohibiting him from working for a few hours before attending) and the other child's play was in the afternoon. Fortunately, he and his wife had made involvement in the children's school a priority—even if he had to lose a day's wages to attend—although in some weeks, when there were a lot of activities, the decision did place a strain on the family budget. At the same time, his experience made me reflect again on the challenges that would be faced by less fiscally secure families or single-parent families who might not have the same luxury. Salaried educators often fail to find ways to accommodate those who cannot so easily take time off work, losing wages budgeted for the family's survival. Moreover, teachers often resist the suggestion to stay a few extra hours, to hold class presentations later in the afternoon or evening when more parents might be able to attend.

If transformative educational leaders are serious about creating a welcoming *community of difference* at their school, they must help all teachers to find ways to include and learn *from*, as well as to communicate *with*, all parents and members of the wider community.

Engaging the Wider Community through Home Visits

As suggested above, it is not enough to issue an invitation to members of diverse communities, expecting the invitation itself will be enough to encourage attendance and participation. Moreover, we sometimes fail to realize that inviting people to attend a meeting about which they have little, if any, prior knowledge, in a school culture with which they may have little comfort or familiarity, is not particularly reassuring. For example, even a notice of a parent–teacher conference evening translated into the multiple languages spoken by the school community, will not necessarily inform the parent about what is expected, how long and with whom they will meet, what preparation (if any) is required, what the dress code is, whether or not the student or younger siblings should or should not attend and so forth. Making the rules explicit, as discussed by Delpit (1990), goes a long way toward making people feel welcome.

Sometimes, however, transformative leaders will find it helpful to encounter parents in the safety of their own home or community in order to reduce some of the power inequities that inevitably exist between home and school. A number of principals with whom I am acquainted have taken measures to reach out in this way. One hires a bus on the first day of school and takes the whole staff through the community, pointing out where families live, points of interest, gathering places and so forth—to the surprise of many teachers who often ask, "Aren't you afraid?" Another elementary principal tries "to personalize the start of school" by putting teachers in teams and giving them lists of students' addresses. Teachers then go door to door, welcoming their students back to the school year, and giving parents a flier for the upcoming curriculum night, saying, "We hope to see you here at school."

Another held small morning coffee meetings in a parent's kitchen, and asked the parent to invite a few neighbors who were also members of the school community. Over coffee (and often a cigarette), the principal said she was able to speak about how welcome and badly needed everyone's involvement was, and encouraged parents to come as often as they could into the school. When I visited this principal's school a few months later, I could never tell, when I walked by a room, whether the person who answered the ringing telephone was a teacher or a member of the wider community— for everyone had been welcomed into all of the spaces of the school.

Ways to develop more inclusive communities are myriad. One middle school principal started by inviting parents into a morning coffee conversation at the school. When, during the conversation, one parent asked if she would be willing to go into their immigrant Muslim community to meet with parents, she agreed. Following her first visit, conducted with a translator, she stated that she had "learned more in a 45-minute timeframe" than she had in her four years at the school. For example, when she asked parents if they felt comfortable in the school, she was dismayed to have them tell her they were comfortable coming to open house because they could understand when teachers did the talking. But when they said they would not call in if their kids were sick, and would not come to parent–teacher conferences because of their limited English proficiency, she was dismayed to learn the school had failed to adequately communicate that there would always be a translator available. Another parent told about working three jobs and having asked for 30 minutes off to tell the principal how much she wanted to help her son with his sixth-grade math but not really knowing how. The mother described having driven around to the local teacher stores, and picking up math workbooks so she could teach herself, and help him. Recounting this tale, the principal stated, "It broke my heart; that is our job"—although she also stated that many of her teachers were not convinced of their responsibility and believed she was coddling and making excuses for the parents. For this principal, building an inclusive community is so important that she also makes time to meet with about 15–20 students a week in several focus groups.

That making home visits must often be an integral part of the work of the transformative leader was also dramatically demonstrated by a poignant story recounted by the same high school principal who shared his cell phone number with his students. He had also asked his counselors to identify six to eight students a week whom they were "losing." He explained,

> virtually 100 percent of those students are low SES; some of them live in housing projects or on ___ street, which is an area of blighted homes. One front door was just a big sheet of plastic, nailed to the top of the wall, kept in place at the bottom by a 2-by-4 piece of lumber. My dean doesn't say, "May we come over"; he says "What time is convenient for us to come over," because we don't want them to think it's an option.

He went on to describe how persistent they sometimes had to be in order to gain entry to homes where the parents were either uncomfortable or fearful of their visit. In one home, where the parents spoke only Spanish, the bilingual counselor translated: "The parents are very honored that you would visit their home, but they can't understand why you would be here because their daughter told them when she turns 17 in two months she's getting kicked out of school." Knowing this was not at all the case, the principal asked to see the girl, whom he knew spoke excellent English. When she appeared, he told her she was "busted." He added, "Obviously, I could tell her mother was mad, the father was very hurt, I mean his daughter lied to him, telling them that we were going to throw her out of school."

This and many other incidents I have had recounted to me indicate how important it is to communicate with, and include, parents and families who do not speak the language of the school. We can make assumptions about their attitudes; we can believe we have communicated adequately; but unless we take time to listen and understand, we cannot know either their concerns or their potential to contribute to the school community.

Opening the School to the Community

Once educational leaders have found ways to hear from their teachers and also from students, families, and community members, it is important to ensure that all of the policies, practices, and processes of the school are open and transparent, and that all learning activities of the school are meaningful and inclusive. If the school is truly to foster goals related to public good as well as to individual achievement, every member of the school community must feel included. Thus, strategies must be implemented to ensure that students from disadvantaged financial situations are able to fully participate in school or class trips; parent involvement requirements must ensure that all parents regardless of financial or employment status may contribute even if it is in a non-traditional way or timeframe; governance structures must be inclusive of the diversity within the school and overcome the traditional norms of privilege and power.

In Chapter 3, we encountered Madeleine Grumet's (1995) understanding of curriculum as the conversation that makes sense of things. To fully implement this notion, it is important to include the whole school community. We cannot, as some parents tried to do in John Law's school, prescribe what ideas can legitimately be discussed within a school or classroom and which should be excluded. For parents to press for the exclusion of sometimes controversial topics such as immigration, homosexuality, Islam, or evolution in the name of their own belief system, of preserving the status quo, or of "reclaiming America" is absolutely inappropriate. As we also saw in Chapter 3, we may want to incorporate Gutmann's (2001) criteria for appropriate dialogue in order to offer guidance to transformative leaders wanting to open the curricular spaces to all topics. Her position, again, is that all topics, regardless of how controversial, are appropriate fodder for debate unless they repress or restrict rational debate or unless they discriminate against legitimate members of the community. Every person and every perspective must be welcomed and included if we are to "reclaim" the democratic notion of civil society and civil debate.

School Community as Public Good

In this chapter, I have suggested that if schools are to promote goals related to public good and to the development of the kind of civic awareness that will help students to become fully participating citizens of our democratic society, they must, in and of themselves, become inclusive communities of difference—communities in which all people, cultures, perspectives, and subjects are addressed in open and respectful ways.

One useful way of thinking about schools as communities of difference is to recognize that schools are microcosms of the wider community, and that student communities reflect the changing demographics of the wider community, with all of its attendant volatilities of competing religious and political belief, complexities of language, uncertainties and ambiguities of social, cultural, and political practices. If students are to learn to negotiate the tensions and contradictions of the wider society, they must learn to understand and confront difference within the relatively safe and protected climate of a school community. They must understand how to debate issues and not attack individuals, how to negotiate and mediate differences without the inappropriate exercise of power and privilege, and how to understand differing perspectives without rejecting them out of hand or, alternatively, adopting a relativistic "anything goes" attitude. In fact, as they engage in high quality learning, students need to learn to work collaboratively with those with whom they respectfully disagree, moving forward to complete their assigned tasks in the interest of the common good.

The foregoing are some of the requisite skills students must acquire if public education is to promote both private and public good, and if it is to contribute to the creation of a civil society which will work for the good of all. For schools to foster these attitudes and dispositions requires transformative leaders with a clear moral purpose related to promoting both private and public good. These dispositions are not only essential for creating communities of difference and schools in which the learning environment is welcoming for all students, but they are also building blocks for the creation of a sense of global curiosity and citizenship that is the topic of Chapter 6.

For Further Reflection and Action

1. What kind of school are you trying to create and what are its dominant values?
2. In what ways does your school advance both the private good of individuals and the public good of society as a whole?
3. What has been your experience with "packaged programs"; how have they helped (or hindered) your progress toward achieving your goals as a school? What changes might you need to make?
4. Share how developing a positive relationship with a student or teacher actually resulted in a changed performance and new commitment. How do you develop strong relationships with various members of your school community? If you have ever gone into the community to meet parents outside of the formal school context, share your experience.
5. What are the boundaries your school-community tries to place on free inquiry in your location? How might you extend their understanding of what topics are appropriate as a basis for dialogue? Do you find Gutmann's (2001) criteria to be helpful or not?

Chapter 6

Fostering Global Citizenship

Understanding Interconnectedness in Our Global Community

A baby boy named Le innocently came into this world. His mother was a poor young Vietnamese girl who had taken a job serving drinks in a local bar. His father was an American soldier on furlough. Villagers advised his mother to throw him into the Mekong River but she loved him too much. His teachers beat him and his peers fought him until he could no longer stand the punishment. Throughout his childhood, he knew only long days of heavy physical labor in the rice paddies, deep hunger, and sleepless nights spent alone outside.

(from Zak)

Amjar:	"What do you do when kids are racist?"
Mrs. Cox:	"Why? What has happened?"
Amjar:	"You know I am an Arab, right? They call me terrorist, suicide bomber."
Mrs. Cox:	(wanting to find and punish the perpetrator) "Who does? When? Where?"
Amjar:	"I can't tell you. It's everyone, all the time, everywhere—not just one time."

Madaha is one of the 60 children who are raped each day in South Africa. Experts aren't sure why this continues, but some believe that the myth of what is called the "virgin cure" is a contributing factor to the over 21,000 child rapes reported last year.[1] The virgin cure is a belief that having sex with a virgin is a cure for diseases like syphilis, gonorrhea, or HIV/Aids. You will likely be surprised to know that this myth has a long history dating back to 16th century Europe and that it was especially prominent in 19th century Victorian England.　　　　　(Taylor, 2002)

The three incidents with which this chapter opens demonstrate the need for transformative educators to understand and address issues of identity and interconnectedness. They remind us of the stories of Amy, Satish, and Danny introduced in Chapter 1—all of whom were devalued, marginalized, and diminished in some way. And they may remind us of the hundreds and thousands of students like them, some of whom move to our country and enter our schools; others who for myriad reasons struggle for success in their home countries. While Le's story may be an extreme example of injustice occurring a generation in the past and half a world away, it demonstrates clearly our interconnectedness with people and events around the world and, hence, highlights the need to help students understand their place as global citizens.

Whether we are talking about Le, or Satish, or Amjar, it is clear that when we marginalize children because of differences, either real or perceived, they fail to perform in school to the same level as other children. Moreover, failure to succeed in school reduces subsequent life chances and opportunities and, hence, represses and diminishes them for life. Transformative leaders must exercise vigilance to identify and eradicate structures in our own communities and around the globe that seek to marginalize and diminish individuals.

Transformative leaders must also show concern and raise awareness about children like Madaha. Her story is not in the past, but recurs throughout the world on a daily basis. She is one of the millions of children who never appear in school, and who have little if any opportunity to improve their life's circumstances. I believe we must ask ourselves and our students to reflect on how stories like hers diminish us all, and to consider our global responsibility. Yet, I rarely think about these or similar stories without being reminded of an exchange in a master's level class with aspiring administrators. One woman, after reading about child labor in several countries, commented "Why should we talk about these issues with our students? If we do, they won't even enjoy shopping anymore!" This reaction is disturbing and certainly does not exemplify leadership but it does represent an attitude of insouciance for others and the desire to perpetuate privilege and separation as we discussed in Chapter 4.

In this chapter, I extend the notion of public good to the global stage and examine the role of transformative educational leaders in fostering an awareness of global interconnectedness and of global as well as national citizenship. In a world of rapid and increasing mobility, of climate change, natural disaster including flood and famine, of economic crisis and interdependence, I believe it is important to foster in our students a sense of global curiosity, global understanding, and global responsibility. To do so, transformative leaders need to raise the awareness of all students about their own identity, their interconnectedness with students around the world, and ways in which what happens in one part of the world affect us all. We are, for instance, in some ways complicit in Le's story; we should be both moved by, and concerned about, Madaha's plight. Hence we need to help our students recognize that they are not only citizens of a particular country, but also citizens of the world.

For students to be able to see themselves as engaged citizens of the world (as Socrates did), transformative educational leaders must help them to develop a sense of self that is empowered and empowering, that permits them to empathize with those less fortunate, and to decide when and how to act for mutual benefit. In other words, we must develop *agentic* human beings—knowledgeable about their ability to act, as well as cognizant of when and how to do so in ways that are helpful and not patronizing or hegemonic.

Here I offer a caveat. As clearly indicated by my master's student's comment cited previously, I am aware that not everyone believes this expanded view of education is important, relevant, or even necessary. There are some who believe that America is so important, so powerful, and so dominant, that if Americans take care of their own country and solve its "problems," the rest will follow naturally. Indeed, some educators respond negatively when such questions are raised. One secondary school principal, when initially asked about her school's emphasis on global issues, responded, "America is a vast and beautiful country. I have absolutely no interest in travelling outside of my own country." By implication, she had no interest in teaching or learning about other countries either. On another occasion, I heard an educator ask,

> What difference does it make if the oceans rise a bit or if the glaciers melt or even if some children don't have the opportunity to go to school? What does that have to do with us? We have enough problems in this country. Let's take care of our own.

This is the crux of the matter. Who is our neighbor? Who are "our own?" My contention here is that the world is so interconnected, that there is so much mobility, so much economic interdependence, so many cultural connections that our own backyard truly is the globe—with all of its inherent beauty, challenges, and possibilities. Our backyard is comprised not only of individuals and social groups, but nation-states, and complex ecosystems.

Because of my strong belief, I am convinced that the above comments and many like them represent short-sighted and inadequate understandings of the myriad interconnections between and among nations as well as an abrogation of our privilege and power that begs us to reach out, learn from, and work with, others. Although not all children in America today have experienced the taunts or rejection experienced by Amjar or Le, many children have known bullying, rejection, humiliation, and exclusion. Moreover, in the second decade of the 21st century, children in North Africa are dying from the world's worst famine in over 60 years; children in Norway were murdered (July 2011) by a "deranged radical" who was unhappy with his country's immigration policies; many children throughout the world are entrapped by prostitution rings; and children in China (and other Asian countries) are still engaged in difficult and dangerous child labor—a situation neither the United States nor Canada has signed on to address.

When natural and political conditions in many countries have forced considerable human mobility and displacement, and when America is engaged in several wars in the Middle East, there is little doubt that our students and children from other developed countries have increasingly frequent opportunities to interact with those from different backgrounds than their own. Where the rich and powerful are present, either through military intervention, aid agencies, or simply tourist travel there will undoubtedly be multi-ethnic or biracial children who suffer a fate similar to Le's. How can we not teach our students to care about such situations?

These are all difficult and often controversial topics, uncomfortable for adults to confront, and even more controversial to bring into the curricular spaces of our schools and classrooms. Nevertheless, if we do not help children and youth to understand the underlying causes of famine, disaster, and global unrest in the relatively safe conversations of schools and home communities, then one must ask when and where— when will we be ready to confront these difficult issues and, if not in schools, then where can such reflections occur?

I am arguing that there is a considerable (but subtle) distinction between providing a *socially just education* for students and offering a *social-justice education*—which is, in fact, one goal of a transformative educational leader. The former implies that the learning environment, organizational structures, and educational opportunities experienced by students offer equity of both access and outcomes to all students and is an essential first step. The latter incorporates these elements, but goes further, implying that students are again taught *in* a socially just institution, taught *about* social (in) justice in the world, and are prepared *for* taking a stance against injustice wherever it may be encountered. If we wish to offer an education that is truly transformative—that focuses on both individual intellectual development and collective social awareness, on both private and public good, then it is incumbent on school leaders to ensure that both are included in the conversations and reflections about the goals and purposes of education. In turn, this will help us to prepare students who better understand the relationships between a well-educated middle class and a free, prosperous, safe, and inclusive global society (whether we use the term "democratic" or not).

To promote these broader goals requires that we minimize (perhaps even reverse) today's almost singular emphasis on testing and test scores and to reclaim a fundamentally educative role—to teach students about the world and their place in it.

In this chapter, I want to first briefly reflect on the nature of identity construction and its role in developing global curiosity and understanding. Next, I invite reflection on the importance of understanding the interconnectedness of the global community. Finally, I contend that expanding our concepts of equity, social justice, and citizenship to be inclusive of everyone is beneficial both at home and abroad and is an intrinsic part of transformative education and transformative leadership. Unfortunately, this is not currently seen as a priority, despite the constant availability through electronic media of dramatic images of events in countries around the globe. We (and our students) are vaguely aware that, in 2010, a cloud of ash emitted by an erupting volcano in Iceland affected air travel throughout the northern hemisphere for days and that, subsequently, a similar event in Chile affected air travel in Australia and New Zealand. We know that recently an earthquake devastated the northern coast of Japan, damaging nuclear reactors, but are less aware that the event precipitated votes in both Germany and Italy banning nuclear power, and served to polarize the debate in North America as well.

We know, on one level, that poverty, disaffection, and religious fundamentalism in some countries contribute to terrorism and to vicious attacks in other countries; but are less aware of how our own responses also fuel misconceptions about members of certain cultures and groups and contribute to increased violence. It has often been noted that in America, there has been an increase of Islamophobia since 9/11. Yet, apart from occasional comments that suggest there are extremists within every religion and political ideology (a claim I certainly accept), I have heard little substantive conversation about what it means to be a Muslim in America. What difference might it make to our image of Muslim youth if we were to spend more time discussing the commitment of members of a football team in a Dearborn, Michigan high school who practice daily and play competitive matches depending on their schedule, even during the period of fasting known as Ramadan. Would our image of these boys, fully engaged in the "macho" American sport of football, practicing in the intense heat of summer, and subsequently competing without having had anything to eat or drink since dawn, change the way we think of these youth? Would we continue to see them as young, potential terrorists, or would we attenuate our opinion when we know they are involved in the same activities as other American teens?

Here, I build on the premise, articulated by Dewey, almost a century ago, that "the purpose [of education] is to set free and to develop the capacities of human individuals without respect to race, sex, class, or economic status" (in Green, 1999, p. 56). Despite the current lack of reflection on these and similar goals, and the fact that educators are already overwhelmed by the pressure of accountability measures and the need for improved test scores, I believe transformative educators must help their school communities to inquire deeply about our global assumptions and beliefs. These are legitimate, indeed, essential topics for curricular discussion.

Constructing Identity as a Global Citizen

Identity is a complex but important concept. Giroux's (1998) insight that "how others see us becomes in part how we see ourselves" (p. 15) is significant. Thus, it is important to consider what images of Muslims we might hold, especially in light of reports that major businesses have withdrawn advertising support from television programs about them. It is necessary to reflect on what images of groups such as the Dearborn football players we might hold because, in part, how we think about them affects how they see themselves; what we communicate to them about their place in society affects the roles they take on for themselves. Moya (2000) wrote about identity, saying:

> The significance of identity depends partly on the fact that goods and services are still distributed according to identity categories. Who we are—that is, who we perceive ourselves or are perceived by others to be—will significantly affect our life chances: where we can live, whom we will marry (or whether we can marry), and what kinds of educational and employment opportunities will be available to us.
>
> (p. 8)

Because of the veracity of this statement—that goods and services in every country are distributed according to how we consider people to be needy, worthy, deserving, meritorious and so forth—helping all students construct positive and healthy identities is an important role of transformative leaders.

Although theories of identity construction are often complicated, complex, and contested, the incontrovertible fact is that how we are perceived by ourselves and by others is important. As Moya asserts, these perceptions continue to affect our life's chances and opportunities. Here I do not intend to enter into the debates about the relative tenets or merits of various concepts or theories of identity. Our need here is to understand the importance of the relationship between constructions of identity and life's opportunities and outcomes—both those we create for ourselves and those created (or constrained) by others. Moya continued her explanation by making the following assertion: "We contend that an ability to take effective steps toward progressive social change is predicated on an acknowledgement of, and a familiarity with, past and present structures of inequality—structures that are often highly correlated with categories of identity" (p. 9). To that end, it is important for transformative educational leaders to understand some of the multiplicities and complexities of both individual and group identity construction—for each plays an important role in the creation of school communities of difference.

There are many ways to think about identity construction. In 1993, Philip Taubman suggested that there are three overlapping ways (or registers) through which we come to think about ourselves—the fictional, communal, and autobiographical. The fictional identity register is created by others' perceptions and understandings, and hence, is one that "imprisons the subject" (1993, p. 291). Thus, when Amjar asks his principal, "What do you do when kids are racist?" he is asking her to help him reject the fictional identity of terrorist imposed by others.

In this case, Mrs. Cox asked, "Why? What has happened?" To which he responded, "You know I am an Arab, right? They call me terrorist, suicide bomber." When she persisted, trying to determine who was responsible so the offenders' statements could be addressed, she was amazed when his response was, "I can't tell you. It's everyone, all the time, everywhere— not just one time." Here we see clearly how focusing on a single aspect of race, ethnicity, culture, religion, or social class as the identifying characteristic of a person can be both alienating and objectifying. It is not a joke; it is not, as some of Mrs. Cox's teaching staff wanted to believe, simply the normal teasing of sixth graders, but as described by Amjar, is evidence of a pernicious and persistent underlying rejection of Islam and of Arabs in that school community. Mrs. Cox cannot simply apply the appropriate disciplinary action to those engaged in name-calling, but must address the underlying beliefs and assumptions that harm and marginalize students like Amjar. She and other transformative leaders must address stereotypes and stereotyping in schools if they are to create inclusive communities of difference. And Mrs. Cox set out to do exactly that by having conversations with each of her teaching teams and with focus groups of students.

A second way in which we construct our sense of self, according to Taubman (1993), comes from the communities with which we are affiliated. Group membership not only helps to foster a sense of belonging and membership but also prescribes appropriate actions and constrains others. Being a Muslim football player helps to create a sense of affiliation with both being Muslim and being American, but it also likely constrains the ability of the players to admit easily to one another their love for poetry, their ability to also play the violin, or possibly even their doubts or questions about the necessity of religious fasting.

A few years ago, I had the wonderful opportunity to teach a graduate course in Abu Dhabi, to a class of about 25 students (23 women, most of whom were fully veiled, and two men). After class one day, as I sat next to a female student, each of us waiting for our ride, she suddenly blurted out, "I don't wear my veil at home you know." As I nodded, she elaborated,

> There is no gender equity in this society. I hate it, I don't wear it at work either, and I am a school principal. But my family would only let me enroll in this master's program if I agreed to cover my face.

In that society, despite her sense of being an independent professional in her daily work-life, the community of which she was a part constructed for her a specific identity—one she was forced to accept to pursue her education. Obviously, Elaje's desire to be accepted by her family conflicted with her desire to be seen as an independent professional—but in this case, because of the presence of two men in her class, the communal register dominated.

It was not my place here to probe or challenge, because, as Taubman (1993) says, "It is only in relation to group membership that such identity may be explored" (p. 291). As an outsider, it was not my place to judge the rightness or wrongness of her family's request. It was not my role to suggest that being forced to wear a veil was a way of controlling women in her society, for an outsider cannot know all of the complexities of a specific cultural tradition. Indeed, I needed to remind myself that, despite how much I might condemn a member of my family for a specific action, I am likely to defend him vociferously to outside criticism. Ultimately, Taubman's message is that change must come from within a specific group; hence, if she wanted to break out of this register, Elaje would have to construct for herself, with the help and support of others in her community, a different, more liberatory identity. My role at that time was simply to accept, affirm, and attempt to understand her position.

Another way in which we come to know ourselves is through what Taubman (1993) calls the *autobiographical register*—one that acknowledges the complexities of identity formation and in which "identity emerges as a personally meaningful and continually developing aspect of one's Self" (p. 288). This is the self that will permit Elaje to explore the relationships between her family's desire for her to wear her shela, and her own desire to move in society unveiled. It is the register that will permit Amjar to reject the perception that he is a terrorist, and to develop a sense of his own personal agency within a society that still condones and perpetuates racism. This is the identity that we construct for ourselves as we integrate all of the conflicting images and messages we receive from outside with what we know to be true about ourselves. It is the identity that permits me to be a Baptist, to enjoy a glass of wine, and to love and support my homosexual friends. In other words, as we become aware of the conflicting pressures from other sources, we can also develop clarity about which we will uphold, which we can reject, and how it is that we can remain true to ourselves.

Zak, whose narrative of his Vietnamese-American friend, Le, was introduced at the outset of this chapter, shared with me some of his own story:

> As a boy, I was painfully aware of the marginalization pressures exerted against people like me. I would shrink inside when I heard my friends teasing the unpopular kids and calling them "fag, queer, and gay." Sadly, I was also guilty of hurling the same insults at others in an attempt to deflect suspicion away from me. Fear of rejection, isolation, and the threat of physical harm kept me from admitting my sexuality even to myself for many years. I no more chose to be a member of that marginalized group than a man chooses to be Black. On the other hand, unlike many marginalized individuals, I could conceal my differences from those who would surely persecute and torment me. Because I chose this option, I paid a terrible emotional price. I lived most of my youth in fear of exposure, unable to speak out and afraid to pursue my dreams.
>
> (Zak)

Fictional pressures led Zak to pretend to be heterosexual; his community's rejection of homosexuality led him to join in the taunting of unpopular kids; but as the autobiographical voice—his own—came to the fore, he was able to acknowledge the huge emotional price he had paid by letting others create for him a normative and desirable identity. Zak's story of growing up with a burgeoning awareness of his homosexuality speaks dramatically to the importance of schools helping students understand how to author their own identities in positive ways, not needing to hide from who they are, not focusing on the fictional constructions of others, but as he expressed so eloquently here, able to speak out and pursue their dreams. In his case, the school did not help him to reconcile conflicting messages, but by silencing discussion about alternative realities and perspectives, forced him to deny significant parts of himself. Unless identity becomes part of the educative conversation of schooling, children may, as Zak did, choose an identity that forces them to be marginalized and fearful, even to act in ways that betray who they are in order to "deflect suspicion."

Transformative leaders will seek to overturn the institutionalized structures that continue to marginalize students. They will focus on emancipation, democracy, equity, and justice; and they will emphasize interdependence, interconnectedness, and global awareness. Once students have begun to understand the forces that help them construct a healthy identity for themselves, in their local contexts, they will be able to look beyond themselves to explore global interconnections and influences as well.

Interconnectedness and Global Citizenship

Above, we have seen examples of how "the whole self is constituted by the mutual interaction and relation of its parts to one another" (Hames-García, 2000, p. 103). Hames-García, a gay, Latino academic, adds that "the subjective experience of any social group membership depends fundamentally on relations to memberships in other social groups" (pp. 103–104). His point is that, for himself, his identity is not just tied to the Latino community, but also, and inextricably, to the gay community, possibly to members of his community clubs or sports teams, and to his academic colleagues as well.

The notion of interconnectedness and the importance of multiple affiliations and relationships help us to begin to understand how inextricably Zak's identity development was also influenced by the stories of his friends, Hung and Le, and by their early identity-shaping experiences as group members (or outsiders) a world away in Vietnam. Similarly, Amjar's sense of group membership is intertwined with the ways in which the Muslim diaspora has been constructed and received in North America and elsewhere.

To help all students understand these connections is another task of the transformative educator. Here, to emphasize this point about our global interconnectedness, I share, with permission, an expanded account of Zak's relationship with Le (introduced at the beginning of this chapter) and a second friend, Hung, both of whom emigrated from Vietnam to America approximately 20 years ago.

Nha Trang, Vietnam—March 1973. A baby boy named Le innocently came into this world. His mother was a poor young Vietnamese girl who had taken a job serving drinks in a local bar. His father was an American soldier on furlough in the quaint seaside village nestled between the central highland mountains and the South China Sea. The Vietnamese had a name for babies like him, My Lai [pronounced me lie]. In essence, it means "American child of no concern." These children were not welcome in Vietnamese communities, nor were they welcome in American society. As the tide of the war turned, Saigon fell. The fate of these children is rarely discussed.

The brutal war had taken its toll on both cultures, mentally and physically, for more than a decade. In America, anti-war sentiment had grown steadily. In Vietnam, Communist propaganda painted everything American with a wide black brush. Communist leaders insisted that educators fill Vietnamese children with anti-American sentiment like the steady drip of intravenous poison. The Communist government effectively used the Vietnamese education system to indoctrinate the youth of their society on a dogma of resentment and blame against America and anything American. Thousands of My Lai children suffered this fate. The Communist education system taught Vietnamese students that My Lai children were the product of a prostitute and the devil, therefore not worthy of even the slightest respect. Growing up My Lai in Vietnam must have been a lonely and socially isolating experience. Adults devalued him and his peers considered him the product of pure evil.

The fifth of six children in his family, Hung, born in South Vietnam in 1972, grew up with an understanding that My Lai children were the product of the devil. Hung and his family escaped Vietnam and came to the United States in 1990. Hung graduated high school in Vietnam but was not able to communicate in English when he came to this country. He entered an ESL (English as Second Language) program and eventually became fluent. He has since gone on to become a successful optometrist.

Le would endure an even worse providence because his father was not only an American soldier, but an African American soldier. With his dark skin and nappy hair, Le could not possibly hide his identity. Even the other My Lai children shunned him. Villagers advised his mother to throw him into the Mekong River but she loved him too much. His teachers beat him and his peers fought him until he could no longer stand the punishment. Le fell out of the formal education system by the age of eight. Throughout his childhood, he knew only long days of heavy physical labor in the rice paddies, deep hunger, and sleepless nights spent alone outside. Le and his mother also escaped Vietnam and came to live in the United States. Unlike Hung, Le never learned to read or write even Vietnamese and his formal knowledge of the world is limited to a parochial understanding gleaned through his limited contact with his village. He has tried unsuccessfully to become literate but the deficits of his early life seem too great to overcome. His early years of excommunication fundamentally determined his later station in life.

Le is one of the most kind-hearted, hard-working souls I have ever met. He is anything but obtuse; yet, because of a system of acute marginalization, he had no chance to become educated and to avail himself of the possibilities that follow. Le has helped me to understand educational marginalization and the diminished life chances that result from the perspective of one on the outside.

(Zak, university employee and graduate student)

This story clearly illustrates the topics of this chapter—first, that healthy identity construction is essential and that the experiences of our youth shape us in incontrovertible ways. Second, it demonstrates the need for global understanding in that attitudes and experiences inculcated in communities in one part of the world affect what happens elsewhere. It also shows how reflection on the condition of others can be helpful in coming to an understanding of one's self, and a fuller appreciation of one's true identity.

As individuals and nations come into contact, as is inevitable in today's volatile, uncertain, complex, and ambiguous world, we have a lasting impact on one another. Moreover, our experiences influence others in unanticipated, pervasive, and permanent ways. Zak's insight into how Le's upbringing limited his ability to develop his potential and to become a prosperous and contributing member of society is sobering. For Le, the fictional and communal pressures were so strong that he was never able to overcome them; for him it was not simply a matter of working hard, of pulling himself up by his bootstraps. Somehow, perhaps because his early experiences were different, Hung was able to create an identity that permitted him to succeed.

Thomas West (2002) explains that cultural differences do not "exist independent of social contexts and power relations; they are, rather, signs of struggle, interpretations of human tendencies, practices, features, and customs defined in relationships and struggles among groups of people in particular contexts for particular reasons" (p. 1). And there is no doubt that it was both a lack of personal power and privilege and its excessive use by others that so restricted Le's life's opportunities. As suggested earlier, what is needed is not simply a matter of understanding cultural differences, but a recognition of their location in differences related to power and privilege as well.

Enlightened Understanding and Egalitarian Solidarity

Global understanding is not simply a matter of learning about individuals' stories, but also of considering how whole populations and systems either prosper or decline as power and privilege are exercised throughout the world. Why, for example, have the education and economic systems of India developed differently from those of Pakistan following the fall of British rule and "Partition" in 1947. What are the similarities and differences in the roles of indigenous populations in Australia, Canada, New Zealand, and the United States (and why might they matter)? What are the relationships between privilege and wealth and the rapid decline and destruction of the natural species of the Galapagos Islands—and again why should it matter? What does garbage disposal have to do with equity and social justice—in either developed or developing countries? These and a myriad of other questions come to mind when we begin to consider how we might teach our students about the complex interconnectedness of the world. In other words, I am arguing that we need to attend not only to individual stories, or even simply to human interconnectedness throughout the world, but also to the ways in which economic and ecological issues are related to social justice and human development.

Human Interconnectedness

A number of scholars emphasize the need to understand human interconnectedness. Dahl (2000) emphasizes the need for all students to have opportunities to learn about themselves and the world around them because he believes this is the basis for being able to fully participate in democratic life. This is the learning, he believes, that creates "enlightened understanding" and although he recognizes that "full understanding" is not possible, he argues for the fullest understanding possible of both our own interests and those of others. His concept is somewhat similar to Philip Green's (2001) concept of *egalitarian solidarity*. Green describes solidarity as the "disposition to ally oneself with others not because they are similar to oneself in social background or agree with one's own tastes and values but precisely because they are different *and* yet have permanently common human interests" (p. 177). Both argue that the ability to ally ourselves with others who may be very different in needs, perspective, or background is fundamental to an ability to understand and to participate fully in the world around us. In fact, Dahl calls for "enlightened sympathy in which we try to grasp the desires, wants, needs, and values of other human beings" (p. 181). For Dahl, enlightened understanding requires an "expansion of the institutional protections for many fundamental rights and interests" (p. 187).

This is exactly the point of this section—to argue that the whole universe is our schoolhouse and that we must introduce this concept to our students for their consideration and reflection. As we reflect further on the meaning of phrases such as egalitarian solidarity or enlightened understanding, we might turn to Thoreau's statement that "We are all schoolmasters, and our schoolhouse is the universe." Thoreau, however, added the following statement: "To attend chiefly to the desk or schoolhouse while we neglect the scenery in which it is placed is absurd" (1859). In other words, he was not simply arguing for consideration of our place in the universe, but for taking care of it in ways that are not necessarily happening. This leads to the need to explore not our human interactions but our relationships with the natural world as well. Are we, in fact, attending more to desks than to scenery? Should we? What might be the consequences of additional attention to the "scenery"? This too is part of fostering an awareness of, and concern for, the interconnectedness of the world.

Earlier (in Chapter 3), I discussed the concept of differences that make a difference and argued against the notion of saying that everyone is the same—all members of the human race—and hence, of making comments such as "I don't see color." Indeed, I suggested that such manifestations of color-blind racism were actually hegemonic expressions of power only available to those in positions of dominance in a given society. The argument here for solidarity on the basis of common humanity may appear to be a contradiction, but is, in fact, quite different. It does not minimize the material differences people experience because of the color of their skin or their place of birth. Instead, it recognizes these differences, acknowledges the role of power and privilege in perpetuating them, and calls for a form of solidarity that stands with those whose situations are quite different from our own as we work to both understand and meet the needs and desires of others.

Connecting to the Environment

Some extend the notion of interconnectedness to include our role as stewards of the natural world and emphasize the need for awareness and proactive engagement with such issues as climate change or sustainable development. Recent studies of the impact of climate change (a complex and contested topic, yet one for which the scientific community has expressed almost unanimous support) found that not only had global warming resulted in more and more violent storms throughout the world, but that since the 1970s, the frequency of wildfires has increased at least fourfold, and the total size of burn areas has increased at least sixfold in the western United States alone (David et al., 2011; see also *ScienceDaily*, 2011). Sometimes discussion of the diminution of Arctic ice flows and their impact on polar bears or of the shrinking of glaciers can seem somewhat remote or esoteric to students who may wonder how these changes in far off locales could possibly affect them. Further, students are likely to ask why the melting of glaciers at the foot of Mount Kilimanjaro in Africa is relevant to them, or why the extinction of a species, even one as beautiful and intriguing as the polar bear, is of immense concern to naturalists. At the same time, they may be more likely to become concerned if they realize that an increase in the number and intensity of forest fires, has, in recent years, resulted in an unusually aggressive encroachment upon large North American cities, destroying homes, and forcing the evacuation of hundreds of people.

A study of climate change might lead to discussion of why fewer Americans believe in climate change now than a decade ago. Or, it may give rise to another topic that students may encounter in their study of science—"sustainable development." The popularity of the term comes from the 1992 Earth Summit held in Rio de Janeiro at which leaders of 105 nations agreed on a number of underlying principles. Originally intended to bring together individuals from nations concerned about the loss of tropical and temperate rainforests, the degradation of waterways, the reduction of swamp lands, and the extinction of numerous plant and animal species, participants in the conference agreed on a number of guiding principles. Nevertheless, the articulation of the first of these, Principle 1, seems to indicate a shift from the original focus to a declaration of the rights of the privileged; it states that "Human beings are at the centre of concerns for sustainable development. They are entitled to a healthy and productive life in harmony with nature" (Rio Declaration, 1992). Critics of the principles note that this implies that humans have both the ability and capacity to manage the future of the earth and to care for one another as well as for future generations (Selby, 2002) but that this capacity is tempered by a sense of entitlement. They argue that the agreement was more closely aligned with neo-liberalism, profits, markets, and the conservation of development than with ecological justice and the conservation of nature.

Understanding the Interconnections

In point of fact, despite the ecological connotations of the term sustainable development, it is clear, simply by examining the first principle from the Rio conference, that one cannot think about the environment without understanding the impact of human development on it. The term sounds positive and unproblematic, but many scholars and ecologists suggest that it is important to know what is being sustained and for whom. Which development is under consideration (natural or human)? Recently an advocate for ecological sustainability succinctly summed up the contradiction by saying that the ecologists won the adjective—"sustainable"; but the economists got the noun—"development." In other words, the topic is complex and ambiguous but calls for deeper understanding and clarity if we are to move forward.

Pimm and Lawton (1998) argued that human activity has influenced species extinction rates at least 100 times their natural rates. Moreover, supporting a kind of entitlement for human beings in terms of a healthy and productive life does little to protect the Brazilian rainforests (disappearing at a rate of 250 square miles a month, in part, to supply the growing global demand for meat consumption) or to alleviate the suffering of 800 million people from hunger and malnutrition (when the majority of corn and soy grown in the world feeds livestock rather than humans) (Bittman, 2008). The relationships among work, hunger, famine, or the loss of housing to ecological development introduces, again, the idea of interconnectedness and demonstrates the importance of transformative leaders helping students develop a strong sense of global enlightened understanding as well as of enlightened solidarity.

More difficult to discuss, but perhaps even more important in terms of developing "enlightened understanding," is a topic that ties in to Moya's opening comment about the distribution of goods and services—in this case, the distribution of natural resources. Smith (2000), for example, cites Jones as saying that "the distribution of resources across the world is entirely fortuitous and that it is morally unacceptable that people's lot in life should be determined by this accidental feature" (p. 1155). Educators who want to help students explore the concepts of power and privilege as they relate to this topic might want to begin with a statement such as this. Why are children in Africa so much more likely to suffer hunger and malnutrition than those in North America? Why are children from Asian coastal communities more likely to lose their homes because of floods and tsunamis than those in Europe or North America? What is the relationship between wealth, economic production, and geography? And is there anything that can or should be done to overcome such inequities? Are they simply part of the natural order or do we contribute to perpetuating these disparities?

Rudy and Konefal (2007), using the term "environmental racism," identified the disproportionate impact of pollution and other detrimental environmental effects on "oppressed minority populations" and the "disproportionate representation of oppressed people of color and the poor within the most heavily polluted, toxic, and illegally dumped in areas of the country" (pp. 495–496). Taking this statement as a starting point, it might be useful to have students map and graph the relationships between population distribution (ethnicity, education, income level, etc.) and proximity to garbage dumps, scrap yards, polluting factory smoke stacks, potable water, and so forth.

Transformative elementary principal John Law was so convinced of the importance of global understanding in order to help his very privileged, predominantly White community understand how to exercise their privilege in positive and not hegemonic ways that he began by encouraging a few school-wide activities that ultimately resulted in a number of partnerships between classes in his school and classes in other countries. His teachers began with a survey in which they presented their students with pictures of children from around the world and asked questions about which children they thought were nice, friendly, mean, angry, or which was likely to become a doctor, a nurse, a farmer, a construction worker, etc. They also asked the children to respond to a series of statements such as "having more stuff makes you happier." John reported that the results were pretty much as anticipated and that it was apparent his students needed more information to break out of their stereotypes. As a school, they then engaged in several book studies—books like *Wake up, world!* (Hollyer, 1999) that describes the lives of children in several different countries by following them through their day and showing what their life is like, and books of photographs by Peter Menzel (Menzel and D'Aluisio, 2010; Menzel, Mann, & Kennedy, 1995) that show families from around the world with all of their possessions piled in front of their homes or that show all the food a family typically consumes in a week—books that permitted lively discussions focused on comparing and contrasting lifestyles. This led to another whole school activity, a "who is your neighbor?" day in which each class took up a different activity that was shared with the whole school—and actually took place the day before the statewide testing. (Here John paused in his narrative to talk about how this sent a signal about the relative importance of both the global understanding and the testing.) One subsequent activity, adopted by a few teachers after reading Friedman's (2005) *The world is flat*, connected their classrooms with schools in India and China. Here Mr. Law explained that they were careful not only to discuss significant differences but to show some more affluent Asian children, because they did not want students to develop a sense of pity but to cultivate a wider, and more complex, understanding of the world.

There is no doubt that activities such as these take considerable time, resources, and initiative on the part of transformative educators. It is also evident that they do not need to take time away from teaching and learning that prepares students for mandated tests. Here students were reading, writing, making short presentations, engaging in compare-and-contrast exercises, and so forth. Similarly, activities related to understanding the relationships between poverty and pollution can also prepare students for reading and writing of persuasive pieces, for graphing, data analysis, mathematical computations, and so forth. In other words, I am not suggesting that we should simply throw out state standards or mandated tests (although I do believe they have taken on too much importance). I am absolutely convinced that students may learn to meet required standards through a rich, interesting, and challenging curriculum that teaches them about the world in which they live. In fact, I would argue strenuously that this is better preparation for tests than boring or repetitive rote learning. By broadening the base of our curricular activities and discussions, we can also connect human relationships with environmental and economic issues to develop some more robust and just concepts of sustainability (Gruenewald, 2003; Rudy & Konefal, 2007) as well as of socially just global awareness.

Concluding Reflections on Global Curiosity

We must not treat as acceptable calling a Muslim student a terrorist. We cannot perpetuate the marginalization of multi-ethnic or biracial students, constructing them as exotic misfits or outcasts, as Le and Hung experienced. If we so marginalize or devastate people that, ultimately, they cannot become productive, contributing, or participating members of society, we are all diminished. If we can create inclusive, respectful conditions that support all people—both at home and abroad—in meeting their needs, in receiving an education, and in fulfilling their dreams, we will all benefit. Bourdieu (in Swartz, 1997) thinks of "school systems as the institutionalized context where the intellectual habitus of a culture develops" (p. 102). This intellectual *habitus*, he explains, comprises durable dispositions that become entrenched to the point where they confine and constrain thoughts and actions that are perceived as possible and acceptable within given institutions and societies. It is important that educational organizations ensure that the enduring dispositions they foster are those of respect and curiosity.

We must not perpetuate a habitus of entitlement and elitism in which students believe they do not need each other (either locally or globally). We must carefully reflect on the ways in which our systems of education are fields in which, over time, durable dispositions develop and become entrenched and how they begin to operate as organizing principles that constrain our thinking. Over time, these principles define what can and cannot be seen as acceptable, and hence, perpetuate societal norms, often at a subconscious level. These norms and dispositions comprise the *habitus* of education, too often, in developed countries, making White-middle-class norms, values, beliefs, and cultural practices the benchmark against which all others are measured (and generally found wanting).

To implement democratic and social-justice education, transformative educational leaders must, therefore, expand our concept of what is valuable, useful, and even normal. Journalist and political analyst Daniel Altman (2011), in his recent book, suggests that what has become normal is a kind of narcissism that is contributing to a national as well as global economic downfall. He argues that it is important to teach our children to look beyond themselves and to see that not everything we have or do is wonderful and praiseworthy. Instead, his call is to educate our children less narcissistically and more realistically. To do so requires that educators help students to develop realistic and healthy identities, to know more about the interconnectedness of the world in which they live, and begin to understand that when education develops the capacities of people, as Dewey said, "without respect to race, sex, class, or economic status" (in Green, 1999, p. 56), we do so to our mutual benefit. In doing so, we fulfill the goals of transformative leadership for improving schools.

But this cannot be done unless educational leaders engage courageously with structures, cultures, pedagogies, and policies that inhibit equity and deny all children equal opportunities for success. Moral courage that enables leaders not only to critique inequity but to move forward, ensuring the promise of a better future for all, is the topic of Chapter 7.

For Further Reflection and Action

1. Do you agree with the premise of this chapter that educators must teach students about global issues and inequities as well as local ones? Why or why not? If you agree, share how you promote increased awareness in a way that does not perpetuate hegemonic attitudes.

2. Reflect on how your identity has been shaped by the three registers identified by Taubman—the fictional, communal, and autobiographical—and share how your concept of yourself has facilitated or constrained your personal development and success.

3. How does global understanding permit fuller democratic participation here at home? To what extent do we need to add ecological awareness to learning about other cultures, systems, and societies?

4. How do you think teachers in your school would respond to John Law's approach? What other ideas do you have for increasing global understanding and awareness?

5. Do you agree with Altman we are teaching a kind of narcissism that has the potential to contribute to a national as well as global economic downfall or are you satisfied that our curriculum comprises what North American students need to know in order to face the future with both clarity and agility?

Chapter 7

Putting it Together
Transforming Schools

I worked hard, pushed myself, and had the highest GPA in my high school, but was told there would be a White co-valedictorian to avoid a "big mess."[1]

(Kymberly Wimberly)

I attend a school for street children in Pakistan. We have a wonderful principal who sets up mats in her back yard, hires a few part time teachers, and encourages many volunteers. Before I went to that school, the principal looked out her window one day and saw me looking in her garbage for kernels of corn that might have been left on the cob. She offered to feed me and teach me, but I ran away because I thought it was a trick. Later, I was so desperate and so hungry I asked her again if she was serious.

(Hussein)

The two vignettes with which this chapter opens remind us that although much has changed in the educational landscape in recent years, too many inequities have not been overturned. Despite the rapidly changing nature of our VUCA world, some kinds of change are difficult. In particular, it seems very difficult to effect lasting educational change because of the deeply entrenched social, cultural, and economic nature of inequity and injustice. In this book, I have posited that it is unlikely that real change will occur unless transformative educational leaders engage courageously with structures, cultures, pedagogies, and policies that inhibit equity and deny all children equal opportunities for success. Moral courage that enables leaders not only to critique inequity but also to move forward, ensuring the promise of a better future for all, undergirds this entire book. As we saw in Chapter 1, the final two tenets of transformative leadership which cannot be separated from the previous discussions include the need for moral courage and an activist approach that does more than simply critique and complain but that offers hope and promise for the future. It is easy to critique the current state of education—even easier to grumble and complain, but effecting deep and significant change that leads to the promise of a better future for all students requires courageous action and engagement. Social justice, democratic community, and global awareness do not and cannot happen from a distance.

Here I began with two stories—one in which we see the impact and outcome of a lack of courageous leadership; the other a story of courage, persistence, and promise. Following further consideration of these two stories, we will then reflect on a number of other ways in which leaders with a strong sense of moral purpose have confronted inequities by addressing aspects of their pedagogy, cultures, structures, and policies that have maintained barriers to inclusive, equitable, and high quality learning environments for all students.

Leadership? Perhaps—but not Transformative

Kymberly's story, introduced at the outset of this chapter, is both disturbing and ironic in that it occurs in the very cradle of integration—a community near Little Rock, Arkansas. The first chapter of the story is well known; in 1957 a group of courageous Black students, now known as the Little Rock Nine, steadfastly and heroically maintained their right to be educated in an integrated situation in their local school, Little Rock Central High School. How sadly ironic that 55 years later (and with a myriad of other changes swirling all around us), we learn how little change has really occurred, how short a distance we have come, how far we still have to travel, and how uneven the playing field still is. Kymberly, a young African American student, who is also a single mother, had worked hard, taking a series of honors and Advanced Placement classes, and had earned the highest GPA in her school, entitling her, as she was informed by a school counselor, to be the valedictorian. Her achievement was short-lived as a White co-valedictorian was announced the following day. Despite Kymberly's appeal, on May 13, 2011, graduation ceremonies in McGehee Secondary School were punctuated by two separate valedictorian addresses—some would say, one legitimate and the second, the result of continued entrenched prejudice and discrimination. Future chapters of Kymberly's story are yet untold—but even if the courts offer her punitive damages, the moment to savor and bask in her accomplishments can never be regained.

Wimberly says the school discouraged Black students from taking honors and Advanced Placement classes, "by telling them, among other things, that the work was too hard" (Abel, 2011). When she tried to protest the principal's decision to have a White co-valedictorian to the school board, Superintendent Thomas Gathen would not hear her appeal. His claim was that she had "filled out the wrong form." Instead of completing a request to make a "public comment" at the upcoming school board meeting, he felt she should have asked for "public participation." He ruled therefore that she had to start again, and thus, that she could not appeal his decision until the June 28 school board meeting—six weeks after the May 13 graduation ceremony. The decision demonstrates clearly the negative impact of power wielded to maintain an inequitable position rather than to overturn it. What is most disturbing is the superintendent's unwillingness to challenge what is obviously a deeply ingrained perception that White students would (and should) automatically and continually outperform their African American peers, compounded perhaps by another perception that students who are single parents have no right to be honored for their academic achievements. Although taking a stand might have been temporarily uncomfortable for the superintendent in the wider community, it would have been unlikely to result in a "big mess"—certainly not one bigger than the national prominence of the story and resultant court case; moreover, it was simply the right thing to do. By not taking a stand, neither the principal nor the superintendent exercised moral or ethical leadership; hence apparently permitting the perpetuation of entrenched prejudice and discrimination.

In contrast, educational leaders who are willing to make change that results in justice for all students, to take a courageous stand, to do the right thing regardless of public opinion, provide evidence of the last two tenets of transformative leadership:

- the necessity of balancing critique with promise; and
- the call to exhibit moral courage.

Depending on how you interpret the situation, those who had power in this situation demonstrated either a singular lack of leadership, or worse, a form of leadership that privileges those already in power to the disadvantage of other constituents. The lack is a moral one—raising the need for moral courage, persistent advocacy, and engaged action—all characteristics found in transformative leaders and all attributes that often create backlash and push-back. Moreover, here those with formal authority failed to exercise their power to offer a critique of the status quo and of attitudes, assumptions, and beliefs that might have offered promise of a new and better future for Kymberly.

At the same time, leaders who take a strong stand know themselves what guides and what grounds them—they know their "true North" and their "non-negotiables." They know that change can occur as they lead with courage and persistent optimism and have transformative and inclusive approaches that make a significant difference for members of their school communities of difference. This is the example of Zehra Fasahat, a leader whose example is quite contrary to that of the principal and superintendent in the foregoing account.

A Courageous Transformative Leader

In December 2007, I had occasion to visit Rah-e-Amal school in Rawalpindi, Pakistan, the school introduced by Hussein at the beginning of this chapter.[2] As I entered the yard, I was immediately welcomed by about 150 children, ranging in age from about five to 18, dressed in dark blue sweaters, and wearing huge smiles. I had arrived, it seemed, on the day when the school was presenting a combination Eid/Christmas celebration to parents, visitors, and friends of the school. Almost before I realized what was happening, the mats on which they had been sitting were rolled up, and the children (and visiting adults) proceeded into a large tent that had been rented for the occasion. As I met with Mrs. Fasahat, her husband, and two daughters, they informed me that this was truly an event that had been planned and was being run by the children themselves. I examined the colorful backdrop—amazed to find a brightly painted Christian nativity scene beside a large sign, surrounded by balloons proclaiming Eid Mubarak. I asked about the school's clientele and was told that the school admitted any child who wanted to learn and who was either homeless (living on the street), or who came from a life of extreme poverty—ubiquitous in this large city of over four million people. Really? Any child? Christian or Muslim, male or female? What an unusual and courageous stand to take in Pakistan where education is still predominantly for males and where Christians, who must carry identification cards, rarely interact with Muslims!

As the program proceeded, I watched older boys open the celebration with a Muslim prayer; others enacted a skit; young children speaking in Urdu presented plays about family interactions; children sang, acted, and recited; and girls holding candles performed traditional dances in brightly colored costumes. Some older children spoke in English; others also in Urdu, but what struck me was the self-confidence and accomplishment of these impoverished and often neglected children. One young man spoke eloquently (in English):

> We have been in the rain. There have been some wild animals moving around our class, but it makes no difference to us . . . We are confident—what is right; what is wrong . . . That's what I have learned from Rah-e-Amal. Thank you.

A young teenage woman spoke, "I have been here for the last ten years. I have seen ups and downs, but here we learn how to cope with the difficulties of life. We are taught with great care." For me—a Westerner—the finale was a touching and amusing mix of tradition and innovation, with children singing a version of the carol, Hark the Herald Angels Sing, complete with arm movements and gestures, an enactment of the biblical birth of Jesus with three young boys wearing "pig" masks added to the complement of people gathered around the manger, and, of course, followed by the arrival of Santa Claus. I was particularly moved by the sight of a very young girl, dressed in a white dress, brightly striped stockings, wearing cardboard angel wings covered with aluminum foil, and wearing a silver crown. Small gifts of candy were given to all the children and the event culminated with a traditional Pakistani meal of rice served from huge metal cauldrons.

It is difficult to describe the powerful impression made by these young people who had so little in terms of material goods, speaking two languages, upholding the traditions of two world religions, confident and caring for one another and welcoming to me, a stranger. As we shared the simple rice meal together, a young girl (I judged her to be about 10), shyly proffered a Christmas card she had made for me; then, several boys approached, wanting to practice their English and be photographed with me.

The story of the school's modest beginning with five students, its growth, and its challenges is well told on its website. What is not as obvious is the extent of the contribution, the sacrifice, and the dedication of its founder and director Mrs. Zehra Fasahat and of other members of her family. The school is supported only by donations and largely through hours of volunteer tutoring (at the time of my visit, she said she hired three untrained, but full-time, teachers to teach the children as well as work with volunteers). When I asked about having both male and female students, Zehra, who had completed a master's degree in international relations in Toronto, Canada, said simply that both needed to be educated. When I followed up with a question about having both Christian and Muslim, her courageous but simple response was, "We don't ask." Nevertheless, taking this open stance means that she cannot accept agency or government funding that would require a different student population or a specific curriculum. Thus she remains dependent on the goodwill of others, and only accepts donations without "strings" attached. It is clear from the student comments about rain and wild animals and knowing right from wrong that the curriculum is not focused narrowly on test-taking or test preparation but on the making of citizens. Zehra beams proudly at "her" children, and explains how difficult it is for many of these children to attend school, when their parents often think they should be out begging on the streets or offering to wash the windows of tourist cars for a couple of pennies a day. Instead, she said that many insist on coming to school but spend hours after class contributing to the family income by begging on the streets. And she told me, as she has written on the school's website:

> We are happy to observe the change in the character qualities of Rah-e-Amal students. Initially when asked about their future plans they would say "I want to be a sweeper in a government office," but now, after their exposure in Rah-e-Amal they want to be doctors, engineers, etc.
>
> (Rah-e-Amal, p. 3)

An educational leader who provides her own home and yard, who uses much of her own resources, and dedicates all her time to a school for such destitute children is certainly a courageous and principled leader. To do what she has done in Pakistan, soliciting donations of materials, books, cloth for school uniforms, and so forth from local merchants and teaching all children who come her way is grounded in a deep conviction of the need for critique and promise—silent but effective critique of her country, its approach to educating girls, its approach to offering and funding education, and its lack of services for the poor and destitute, but transformation through her actions that offer hope and promise to her students. By her actions, she has challenged the structural norms of separate schooling, the religious norms of her culture, the political norms of her state, and the transmissive pedagogies that dominate—in order to provide these children with a life-changing education.

Multiple Fronts, Multiple Strategies

The foregoing story shows that it is definitely possible to be a transformative leader, even in a VUCA climate of volatility, uncertainty, complexity, and ambiguity—although few of us will have to face the odds and tackle as many dimensions of needed change as Zehra. To ensure that no one leaves this book believing that I am arguing for such a Herculean effort on the part of everyone, the rest of this chapter will show how a number of school leaders, at various stages of understanding of transformative leadership, have proceeded to implement change using the new, requisite VUCA strategies of vision, understanding, clarity, and agility. Although each story emphasizes one of these skills, it is clear that the need for a combination of vision, understanding, clarity, and agility has been threaded throughout this book, as well as throughout each leader's story. As with Zehra, their stories are not presented as prescriptive ideals but are included here as a way of raising awareness and prompting reflection on various ways of engaging the task. In each case, however, we see a leader who accepts his or her role as being more than ensuring the school meets accountability measures. Each acts with moral courage, either implicitly or explicitly challenging inequities, and offering hope and promise to the students in his or her care.

First, we see Charles Mason, a leader in early stages of understanding, working with his school. This is followed by further reflection on the work of Mrs. Carla Cox, Leslie Thomas, and Catherine Lake (all introduced earlier). Each of these leaders confronted the need to address elements of the cultures and the pedagogical practices of their schools. The chapter concludes with an examination of how principal Lynn Mann challenged some inequitable policies and practices of her board and, as a response, instituted structural change to both support and act as a catalyst for cultural and pedagogical change. Through these discussions, we also reconsider the meaning of the new VUCA skills as ways of thinking and moving forward.

Introducing Equity: Building Shared Vision

Principal Charles Mason has himself recently been introduced to issues of transformative leadership and through a series of serendipitous events has become convinced of the need to transform his school. In the same year, he had begun a doctoral program at a major university, begun his second principalship at a new elementary school, and taken advantage of an opportunity to join a group providing a week of professional development activities for teachers in Cuba. He is aware that, despite a history of excellence, his school has experienced both a demographic shift and a dramatic decrease in test scores. His superintendent has also explained that other schools with similar populations seem to be doing much better, but that perhaps this has been due to a lack of leadership.

Through his doctoral program and his brief time spent working in Cuba, Charles' horizon has been expanded so that he has become keenly aware of the inequities that are playing out on a daily basis in his school as well as in other less developed and less advantaged countries. He has worried about how to raise the awareness of his teachers and spent considerable time reflecting on how to develop a new vision for his school—one that deconstructs and reconstructs current frameworks to focus more on equity and inclusion. Charles is aware, as all leaders must be, that developing a shared vision is not synonymous with the creation of a mission or vision statement—often an empty, performative activity that results in no more than a document filed away in a drawer in case it should be requested by a superior.

Senge (1990), for example, talks about "shared vision" as one of the requisite disciplines for a learning organization. The key here is "shared." Developing a sense of shared vision requires time and commitment—time to listen to all members of the organization, to hear their concerns, their challenges, hopes and dreams. It requires identifying elements held in common, extending them, building on them, and ultimately articulating the new direction. Senge reminds us that if we adopt a vision that is not truly shared we are, in effect, empowering members of the organization for chaos. In humorist Stephen Leacock's (1911) words we, like Lord Ronald, as though all sitting astride one horse, are attempting to "ride madly off in all directions." Instead, as Senge describes his concept of a shared vision, he likens its development to the aligning of dipoles on a magnet: the more alignment there is, the stronger the magnetic pull. Empowerment without clarity of purpose is a recipe for disaster; a strong vision provides the focus for empowerment of the whole school community.

In the spring, as a way of beginning to construct a shared vision, Charles decided to start engaging his advisory committee in an activity I like to call "snowball writing." He asked them to begin by thinking about a student or students who were failing, and to write in silence for five minutes on the topic of why they thought these students were unsuccessful. After five minutes, he asked them to crumple up their unsigned papers and toss them from person to person. The brief hilarity soon turned into somber reflection as people read and discussed the reasons identified for student failure—most attributing the cause to factors related to the parents and home situation.

As they discussed the implications of these explanations that tended to blame families and to exonerate the school, they began to realize the seriousness and depth of deficit thinking that had been expressed.

The ESL teacher began to cry, sobbing that she had for so long been concerned about the ways in which many of the minoritized students she taught had been constructed and represented, yet had not known how to address it. Several others joined in her tears. All indicated that they were relieved that inequities and blame had finally been named explicitly and stated that this was an activity with which they should start the school year with the whole staff in August.

Although Charles would have liked to move more quickly and to have conducted the activity at the next staff meeting, he acceded to the suggestion of his advisory council, knowing that he could use the intervening time period to plant some additional seeds. A few weeks later, he invited his university instructor, who was visiting in the region, to meet for a brief conversation one day after school with any of his staff who might have questions about equity. The assembled group was typical of most suburban staffs—predominantly White, with one Latina and one African American teacher present. As the instructor asked questions about inclusion and diversity at the school, one teacher was insistent that it was sufficient for teachers to role model respect and tolerance and that it was never necessary for issues of race, class, or sexuality to be explicitly addressed in an elementary school. It was at that point that the vice-principal suddenly recounted an exchange she had had earlier with a student. When the student, who had been in the school for several years, first saw an unknown Latina woman, he asked with some boldness, "Who are you?" Her response that she was the new assistant principal amazed and confused him, and prompted the rejoinder that she could *not* be the assistant principal because she was both a woman and Latina. Her presence in a formal position of authority was beyond the realm of his experience and assumptive world; he had no knowledge that a woman from his own ethnic group could hold such a position.

Although she had not shared the surprising incident with anyone on staff for the first nine months of the year, having the opportunity to explicitly discuss issues of equity prompted the vice-principal to share her story. This opportunity then opened the door to explore, and ultimately challenge, the conviction of the vocal teacher and her peers who believed that modeling respect was all that was necessary. They began to understand that some inequities cannot be addressed simply through modeling respect. Here, the underlying assumptions about Latina women, race, and mobility needed to be surfaced; elsewhere it might be assumptions about poverty or religious belief that need to be challenged by teachers, students, and members of the wider community. Ultimately, the staff understood that addressing situations like this as they arise can provide fortuitous opportunities to help students (and perhaps especially other Spanish-speaking members of the community) recognize the implicit barriers and limitations placed on those whose first language is not English and to discuss the opportunities for everyone to become leaders and/or administrators if they should wish. Probing and exploring this brief exchange gave Charles a way to help his teachers understand how to use chance comments to begin to break down barriers and to institute a culture of critique and promise in the school.

Charles' conviction that something needed to be done to change the knowledge base and habitus of his school was simply the beginning of what will be, no doubt, a long journey. However, it is clear that he has taken steps to begin the development of a shared and expanded vision of transformation for his school. There is much he can still do as he plants the seeds to prepare for an expanded understanding. For example, five months after his trip to Cuba, which he had described to his doctoral cohort as "life changing," he had not shared his insights or experience with members of his staff. Taking this as a starting point, and making use of every other natural opportunity to discuss power, privilege, and global responsibility will keep such issues in the forefront of his staff's awareness and will serve to consolidate their commitment to both private and public good.

Fostering Empathic Understanding

Carla Cox's school is somewhat more advanced than Charles' in terms of understanding the need for equity and inclusion to undergird the curriculum, pedagogy, and school culture if they want all students to succeed. She has spent time, over the past two years, inviting speakers to meet with her staff and engaging in extensive conversations about meeting the needs of all students. Not surprisingly, these conversations have emphasized the need for dialogue that focuses on ethnicity, social class, ability, home language, prejudice, and deficit thinking. Four years before, when she had first been assigned to the middle school, she had found that staff meetings were never held, low expectations and reliance on transmissive pedagogy were never challenged, and that teams of teachers never had the opportunity to meet together to discuss shared goals. She quickly instituted monthly 7 a.m. staff meetings as well as daily team meeting time as a way to increase teachers' understanding of her expectations, the students' needs, and to discuss pedagogical strategies to become more caring and more inclusive of all members of the school community.

At every staff meeting, including those to which she had invited speakers, she strategically placed tripods of poster paper divided into four quadrants labeled kudos, complaints, questions, and concerns. On entry into the room, each teacher was regularly given a small pad of post-it notes on which to write notes that, as they left the meeting, they were expected to place in the appropriate quadrant on the poster paper. Soon, whenever parents were invited into the school, they too were asked to provide feedback using the same headings. Carla persisted, despite the concerns of some teachers that when their feedback was taken seriously, parents were being given too much power. Students, too, were empowered to provide input through the use of weekly focus groups (as mentioned in Chapter 6). Immediately following each meeting, the notes were transcribed and shared with everyone so they could be used as a basis for discussion during the day's team meetings.

On one occasion, following an address to the staff, I spent the day at Mrs. Cox's school. With Carla, I conducted brief classroom visits throughout the school, and then met with each teaching team during the day. We commented on what we had seen and asked numerous clarifying questions. Why were students building boats and filling them with marbles until they sank? Although students had assiduously counted and recorded the number of marbles added until the boats sank, they seemed unaware of the key concepts related to volume and mass that the teacher's written lesson plan had identified as the lesson's goal. In another class we asked students why they were learning about tectonic plates. On inquiry, although they knew they had something to do with earthquakes, not one student could tell us why it might be useful to know their location. In another class, we saw a teacher engaging students by asking them to physically line up on different sides of the room in response to various statements and beliefs about government immigration policy. Yet, when one child indicated her enthusiasm for the lesson by starting to recount an incident about her grandfather's immigration experience, the teacher's response had been, "Not now. We don't have time, we have to get through this exercise." Wasn't the point of the exercise to involve students in the topic we wondered? Why had the teacher brushed off the potential contribution of the girl who wanted to tell of her own grandfather's involvement in the topic? What did they understand by "teachable moment" and could they describe one? Follow-up conversation took place with each of these teachers and their teaching teams during the day's regularly scheduled meetings.

In one meeting, a math teacher proudly described how, because her students liked sports, she had given them a work sheet with word problems all related to sports. What she did not know was that we had slipped into her class when she was absent and had received a very different response from the students who said they hated the work sheets. In fact, when Carla asked a group of students why they thought the teacher would give them such a sheet, the quick response was "because she hates us." On exploration, Carla learned that this really was the firm belief of the students—again something that needed to be addressed during the team meeting. It is clear that Carla uses courageous and persistent dialogue with her staff to help them understand how to change and improve their pedagogical practices.

One final example is illustrative of Carla's persistent focus on enhancing understanding that, in this case, addressed how the school still presented some barriers to the equitable inclusion of all students. The discussion turned to ways in which students were sometimes embarrassed either by comments made in class or by activities that singled them out. Yet, as soon as Carla had emphasized the importance of ensuring this did not happen, one teacher proudly recounted how she had extra books that students could come and ask for, if they did not have money to purchase materials. Somewhat frustrated, Carla revisited the principle that materials should be made generally available so that no one would have to "beg" or ask for books or supplies because they did not have the money to buy them. It took considerable discussion before some teachers understood the difference between freely providing materials and making students ask for them if they could not afford them. The first is an inclusive practice; the second, once again, sends the message that school is not really for them, because they are not rich enough to fully participate.

At one point, after Carla had had the exchange with Amjar that opened the previous chapter, she made a decision to attend each team's meeting during the day to listen to the conversation, to ask some questions, and to share Amjar's story. Here, it was the culture of shame and exclusion that she was trying to address. Each hour, the response was the same. First, a teacher responded, "I'll bet I know who called him names." When Carla indicated that it was not just one person, but the repeated and consistent response of his peers, another teacher would chime in, "Yes, but that is just the harmless teasing of adolescents. They don't mean anything by it." Repeatedly, Carla explained how detrimental this teasing would be to Amjar's sense of identity and how harmful it would be to other Arab students in the school as well.

Because she knew her teachers were unconvinced of the seriousness of the incident, she asked them to follow-up with their classes to determine if other students had ever heard anyone in the building being teased. At first, a number of teachers resisted, arguing that they could not afford to take time out of a lesson "to talk to a group of students whom it probably doesn't affect anyway." As Mrs. Cox persisted, reminding them that if no one had heard such negative comments, it would not take long to return to the planned lesson, the teachers reluctantly agreed to explore the situation. A few days later, one teacher who had vocally resisted Mrs. Cox's original suggestion, asked to see her. The ensuing conversation, as reported by Mrs. Cox, was very different.

Teacher:	Mrs. Cox—you won't believe this.
Mrs. Cox:	What?
Teacher:	I had the conversation with my students this morning. Every single student said that they had heard students in our building called terrorist and suicide bomber.
Mrs. Cox:	Really? So what did you do?
Teacher:	We spent the entire period discussing it. Did you know that many of our Arabic students are being called this? Did you know that our Arabic students don't want to come to school because of these comments?
Mrs. Cox:	I can imagine. It's horrible. So what did your class say about it?
Teacher:	We are going to make time weekly to discuss it, but we all agreed that as a school we need to talk about it. Do you think we could make it part of our Advisory lessons next week since it appears to be impacting the school? So many of my students said they feel awful about it but don't know how to address it. I think we need to help them.
Mrs. Cox:	Sounds great. Why don't you put something together for the staff and we can continue the discussion next week in Advisory?
Teacher:	Great, but I really want the students to help me. Is that ok?
Mrs. Cox:	I think it's a great idea. Thanks for your leadership.

Here we have an example of how a school principal encouraged reflection and critique on the part of her teachers, despite their unwillingness to "be involved." Having heard from one student of his negative experience, she was unwilling to accept—without further investigation—that the response was confined to a thoughtless comment on the part of a few children. Instead, her response is an outstanding example of how critique leads to promise—not just for Amjar but for the students who wanted to find a solution and to help raise the subject on a school-wide basis. There is no doubt that this kind of engagement on the part of a transformative leader makes a difference to the climate of a whole school. Changing the environment from one in which a group feels marginalized and excluded to the point of not wanting to attend school to one in which all students are engaged in creating a welcoming and safe learning environment makes a powerful statement regarding the worth of each and every student. It also helps students learn real-world skills that will support their ongoing democratic participation.

Her firm belief in the importance of listening to everyone led to a significant change of practice in the school. Subsequent conversations after her interaction with Amjar ultimately led to the restructuring of her advisory program. She explained:

> Advisory used to be about kids coming into a room they shared with teachers and occasionally talking about grading, specific procedures, or a memo from the

principal. There was very little time spent on meaningful interactions. It has since become a haven designed to specifically address issues that deal with students' lives. We host a scenario-based conversation every Friday. Advisory is now about dialogue. It's about understanding. It's about getting to the root of why these issues are happening.

Thus, she has turned the advisory period into a meaningful strategy to build an inclusive and supportive school community for all students. Carla acknowledges that listening and dialogue are important to the exercise of transformative leadership. In addition, she believes that to be truly inclusive, everyone must have a chance to regularly voice his or her opinion.

Having visited Carla's school, and engaged in dialogue with her teachers and with parents, it became clear to me that some teachers were not fully on board with Carla's goal of creating a respectful and fully inclusive learning community—one in which teachers, parents, and students were empowered to bring their culture, their prior experiences, and a variety of strengths and perspectives into the learning environments of the school. Some persisted in deficit thinking, rigid assumptions, and low expectations for minoritized children. Nevertheless, as the dialogue with her resistant teacher demonstrates, Carla courageously persisted, to the point where, in her fifth year as principal, she could say that teachers were fully on board and those who had been resistant had chosen to leave.

The moral courage and commitment exhibited by Carla to enhance the understanding of her staff exemplifies the dedication and hard work required of a transformative leader to develop the empathic understanding necessary to transform a school's culture and pedagogical practices. Her persistence and willingness to engage in what are often difficult and uncomfortable conversations go a long way toward creating a culture of both critique and promise in her school.

Developing Clarity

As we have previously seen, Leslie Taylor is in her fourth year as principal of a diverse secondary school. Leslie claims that until she completed her doctoral program she did not have the language of social justice, although she had always been sensitive to the needs of the less fortunate and marginalized. As we have seen earlier, Leslie is determined to empower her staff and to share the decision-making and leadership with a number of committees she has instituted and empowered. In so doing, we have seen that Vital High School has won a number of awards. We also noted, in Chapter 1, that teachers who, a few years earlier, might have blamed students or their families for low test scores or lack of achievement, have now taken responsibility for student learning and experience personal distress if they are unable to find ways to help students succeed.

How, one is likely to wonder, did Leslie achieve such clarity of belief and a strong sense of accountability on the part of her staff? Although working tirelessly toward a sense of shared vision and enhanced empathic understanding are no doubt part of the response, and although there are many other pieces of the puzzle that will remain invisible, one major strategy was Leslie's institution of a "social justice committee" at the school. Unlike other committees, this one was open and began with the identification of two staff members who would chair the committee. An invitation was issued, not only to staff, but also to any interested students, to attend the inaugural meeting of the committee. To their surprise, so many people turned out to the first meeting, that a larger classroom meeting space had to be found. As people filed in, they were invited to help themselves to refreshments prepared by the staff sponsors. During the first meeting, principal Leslie gave a brief 10-minute overview of what she meant by social justice, answered a few questions, and then left. From that time on, the committee belonged to the staff, students, and visitors (from community and university) who chose to attend; it had the principal's support, but was conducted without interference.

During the first few meetings, time was spent brainstorming areas of inequity in the school and identifying priority areas for voluntary groups to address. Although present, teachers often permitted students to take the lead as they learned together. One topic that received the support of the whole group was the need to reduce negative language, scathing and prejudicial comments about race and sexuality that were frequently heard throughout the school. By the end of the first year, a group of brave and dedicated students had agreed to present some skits at upcoming staff meetings for the consideration and discussion of the whole staff.

In the following year, the committee decided to create a video addressing the issue of negative and prejudicial language. Not only did they conduct surveys and interview students in the school, they enlisted the help of technicians in the wider community and also obtained permission to use, as part of the video, a clip from one of Wanda Sykes' comic routines addressing homosexuality. Mention of the video is not only found in a prominent place on the home page of the school's website, but every student is shown the video at the beginning of each school year and is engaged in a discussion of what it means to be part of a school community with an inclusive and respectful culture. It is not surprising that this degree of effort has produced considerable clarity around what the school stands for—and has dramatically reduced the incidence of disrespectful language around the school.

The clarity of vision and goals did not develop overnight, but once again, took time, effort, and a clear sense of moral purpose. Leslie's conviction that students and teachers needed to work together resulted in a committee unlike any other in the school—a committee that has grown and flourished—sponsoring numerous activities, taking leadership roles in other community events, as each member proudly wears his or her committee T-shirt proclaiming an unwavering allegiance to social justice goals. Developing clarity around a shared mission of equity and inclusion is hard work, but is fundamental to the success of a transformative leader.

Ambiguity Promotes Agility

In today's world of rapid change and uncertainty, it is also necessary for a transformative leader to be agile and to accept the inevitability of ambiguity. This reality should not be paralyzing, but indeed, liberating, as it frees the leader to make change as circumstances warrant. Because this concept is not necessarily as intuitive as the others, I will first elaborate the need for agility before describing how principal Catherine Lake exemplifies this quality as she engages in transformative leadership.

The need for agility suggests, for example, that too much time spent on finalizing a long-term or strategic plan may not be time well spent because by the time the plan is in place, conditions may well have changed. Further, it is impossible to plan for all eventualities, although it is necessary to develop and understand some shared preparedness principles. We are all too aware of lengthy hours spent in strategic planning meetings, only to learn, once the plan has been completed, that it is no longer useful, and is relegated to a bottom drawer somewhere. Two theoretical concepts are useful here. The first is Fullan's (1993) notion of the need to change from a "ready, aim, fire" mantra to one of "ready, fire, aim." The change reminds us of the need to prepare (ready), but then to act (fire)—taking time after we explore a potential line of action to stop, reflect on it, reconsider and refine it as necessary (aim). Too often we spend countless hours planning, refining the plan, and having it approved, but failing to execute it—as I found to my surprise when I took up my new position. Having been informed that a budget reduction plan of over a million dollars had been carefully crafted to prevent having to lay off any employees, I was surprised (and somewhat dismayed) to find that it had not been implemented—indeed that the deficit had risen to the point where we had to wrestle with approximately 1.7 million instead. The planning had been extensive, but no action had followed, leaving us with the need to start over instead of simply refining what was there.

The second useful concept comes from Karl Weick's (1996) examination of how firefighters manage to survive when fighting a volatile and dangerous fire. He argues that survival in dangerous times is dependent on one's ability to put into place a system of lookouts, communication, escape routes, and safety zones (LCES) (p. 567). In fact, although educational leaders often use the metaphor of "fighting fires" or "putting out fires," his analysis shows that this metaphor may not be particularly helpful, and further that extensive education and training alone are not enough. What is important, he suggests, is the need to be agile, to recognize the importance of small events before they develop into crises. Additionally, it is critical to know what we know and what we do not know and, hence, to remain alert in order to prevent ourselves from being blind-sided. To accomplish this, we need to know when something might be a trigger for discontent, for concern, fear, and so forth.

Weick's advice is applicable to educators as well. Effective transformative leaders will ensure that there are people at multiple locations in the organization who attend to the big picture, always looking out for the resistors and the unexpected backlash, for example. There will need to be excellent communication, "sending clear messages in a timely manner" (p. 573) to ensure agile responses to threats. Then, it is important for there to be at least two "escape routes"—options, revocable action, and the possibility of pulling the plug (p. 574). Finally, Weick argues for "safety zones"—ways of buffering oneself from the "danger"—perhaps by reading an email a second time before sending it, by taking time before responding to a phone call, by floating trial balloons, implementing experimental or pilot projects, and so forth. Any strategies that permit a sober second thought and time for reflection and focused dialogue will be useful. Whatever theories we use—including that of transformative leadership— must also be practical and must permit leaders to be both focused and agile.

Catherine Lake, in her ninth year as principal of her elementary school, exemplifies these characteristics of agility, communication, and preparedness. She explains that she went to the school knowing it was a long-term commitment. She recognized that she could have "been everybody's best friend and brought in everything they needed and politicked and smiled and shaken hands and built her résumé" and that in so doing, she could have introduced initiatives that "were popular and faddish," been rewarded for doing so, and then moved on. Instead, she acknowledged from the outset that she would have to "really look at a lot of difficult issues, talk about a lot of topics that make people uncomfortable, [and] push people out of their comfort zones."

Over the last nine years, the school population has changed from having an 80% Caucasian and approximately 15% low-income population, to being one-third Caucasian and more than 40% low income. In her first four years, when the non-Caucasian population had increased to 64%, with a strong focus on the success of each student (and not on testing), achievement had risen dramatically to exceed, at every point, the district averages. However, the changes were not consistently maintained. Moreover, given that there were still students and groups of students who were not succeeding as well as Catherine knew they should, she did not simply use the success as a stepping stone to other opportunities, but continued to work toward deep and equitable change. She is, thus, quite a bit further along the road to sustainable transformation than some of the other principals, although she still experiences push-back and fear on the part of newer teachers.

Over the years, her focus has been on empowering teachers to "look at what the data say about who's succeeding and who's not." Further, the task is one that constantly needs to be repeated as "the disparity of one racial group versus others comes again to light." Catherine explains that

> it's a disparity that doesn't make any sense. So in the case of looking at the data, it's looking at who's succeeding in our school . . . and noticing that African American kids are doing worse, the worst of all kids in our school. Given that there are so many kids who are second language speakers, how is it that the group who are not native speakers of English are doing better in reading than African American children?

As mentioned in Chapter 3, if children whose home language is not the language of instruction are exceeding the performance of children who speak English regularly at home, Catherine believes something is wrong. Hence, as usual, she has asked her teachers to think about, write about, and discuss this disparity and then to come up with ways of addressing it. If teachers suggest it is because a group of students is poor, Catherine says,

> I give examples of White children whose parents I know—there are single parent homes; I know they're poor. I know, for example, that in some cases the mother or father is mentally ill and unable to be a part of things. And I'll say well how come those kids are succeeding?

In other words, she will persist to show her staff that other children who have similar qualities are doing very well in the school; however, she says, "They just happen to be White, and these happen to be Black." She admits that confronting these issues head-on, instead of "doing things around the edges," has "made a number of people unhappy" but that the solid focus has been a careful examination of what they are teaching, to whom, and how.

Catherine refuses to accept that it is changing or increasing diversity at her school that periodically opens an achievement gap between Caucasian and African American students. Instead, she acknowledges that it can, to a large extent, be attributed to a change in the make-up of her teaching force, to the expansion of her school programs, and the addition of a number of teachers who had not been part of the original conversations and who have not adequately "bought into" the shared vision and pedagogical approaches that had been instituted previously. In her words,

> I think there's a great sense of urgency . . . We reconfigured, got a number of new staff, some of whom come from rather privileged backgrounds and seemed to be able to position the blame on the type of kids we serve here.

And so she starts the dialogue over again, determined not to blame the children or families and to have her staff collectively take responsibility for all children's learning. This commitment is, of course, one mark of a transformative leader.

She accepts that asking "What do we need to do differently?" has offended people, but is firm in her belief that she must persist. Having developed a shared vision and a clear understanding of the parameters necessary to ensure that all children are successful, Catherine empowers her teachers to make the pedagogical decisions. Nevertheless, once teachers decide on an approach (in a recent case, a literacy strategy called "The Daily Five,"[3]) she carefully monitors its implementation so it becomes the core instruction throughout the school, and not subject to the whim of individual teachers to implement at will.

Hence, we see clearly in Catherine's example of cultural and pedagogical change the transformative and VUCA characteristics of developing a shared *vision* related to high expectations and equity; enhancing *understanding* that involves deconstruction of existing knowledge frameworks and co-constructing new ones; developing *clarity* around the need to address the use of power and privilege and to bring new teachers on board; and around the need for *agility*—changes that continually balance critique with promise of the population of teachers and students within the school at a given time. Earlier (and more fully in Shields, 2009), I have also discussed how Catherine balanced private with public goods, introducing and fostering school-wide activities to ensure equity and promoting "community meetings"—weekly Monday morning assemblies in which all students and members of the wider community participate. Throughout all her endeavors, what shines clearly is her courageous engagement wherever she finds an inequity that must be addressed and her deep sense of moral purpose grounded in identifying "non-negotiables" that sustain her in times of conflict and resistance.

Transformative Structural Change

To conclude this chapter, we examine the activities of Lynn Mann[4] whose transformative leadership started with a critique of district policy that was adversely affecting her school. Lynn had been principal of several Canadian middle-class schools in relatively homogenous and affluent neighborhoods and throughout her career had advocated an approach to schooling sometimes known as "full-service"—a concept in which community, neighborhood, and governmental services were all present within the same building as the school and coordinated for students (see Dryfoos, 1996). She seemed, therefore, well prepared for her new assignment at Kenneth Mann Community School (KMCS). However, KMCS was different. It had attained the designation of "community school" after making an application to the school district based on its relationship with its extended community, and hence, had a small budget for a community-school coordinator. The low socio-economic status of many of its students also resulted in the district's designation of KMCS as an "inner city" school. In fact, it recorded the highest proportion of students with special needs, English as second language learners, transient students, students living in poverty, and indigenous students (Canadian First Nations) in the large district of over 18,000 students and 29 elementary schools. Additionally, its English language learner population of 25% dramatically exceeded that of less than 1% found in the community as a whole.

Lynn quickly recognized that the district policies of school-choice and open boundaries were detrimental to the ability of her school to thrive, perhaps even to survive. Yet, during her first year as principal, all impacts were magnified when the district authorized a neighboring school to become a "magnet school," a designation that resulted in only three of a possible 42 families with possible kindergarteners choosing to register at KMCS, leaving only 56% of the children in her catchment area enrolled there. The impact was further exacerbated by the controversial, well-publicized school ranking system established by a national, conservative "think tank" which consistently listed KMCS as the lowest ranked school in the province, ignoring its many community-based, family support, and engagement efforts, and focusing almost solely on test scores. Hence, families had become accustomed to thinking of the school as undesirable—"a loser school" some said—and, as often as they could, requested what was really a pro forma approval for a transfer to another school. Each time a child transferred, the opportunities of those remaining in the school suffered, because of course, the school was funded on a per pupil basis. Thus, for example, a class of 31 children at the magnet school received approximately $8,000 more than the "decimated" class of 23 at KMCS, leaving the educators with the dilemma of how to provide a similar, high quality educational experience.

Teachers could not plan with accuracy; dwindling resources made it even more difficult to meet the needs of the children and families attending the school; and specialist teachers in subjects like art and music had to be released for lack of numbers—aggravating the disadvantage of these children who most needed an enriched curriculum.

Unwilling to quietly accept the negative impact of these policies that reduced the ability of KMCS to meet the needs of the remaining students, Lynn reached out to local agencies, helping them understand the situation, requesting (and receiving) grant funds and donations, and making many appeals to the school district. Additionally she successfully worked with her staff (in a heavily unionized environment) to propose a change to a year-round calendar—a change intended to provide additional intersession support for her students, to reduce the long summer vacation period, and ultimately to address one of the causes of an achievement gap between advantaged and disadvantaged children—summer learning loss (Alexander, Entwisle, & Olson, 2007; Shields & Oberg, 2000). She describes these efforts as a way of implementing Fraser's (1995) recognitive and redistributive justice.[5]

After a number of discussions with her staff, and presentations to the union and to the elected school board, she was given permission to proceed with a three-year pilot—a move that data collection and university-supported research subsequently proved to offer effective support to the student population.

What is important here, once again, is Lynn's willingness to identify an inequitable situation and to confront it in ways that made a difference. Many others before her had decried the policies and the negative reputation of the school, but in general they had found that the job was so time-consuming and overwhelming they had not time or energy left to implement change. Despite the fact that Lynn arrived at school before 7 a.m., left after 5:30 p.m. so she could provide informal child care to the students dropped off by their parents, and that she often dealt with police, children and family workers, and mental health agencies in addition to her daily tasks, she courageously tackled the barriers to an equitable and quality education for all.

Reflecting on Leadership

The stories of these principals (with the exception of the negative exemplar with which this chapter opened) demonstrate clearly that although transformative leadership may not be the norm, it is definitely possible. Moreover, they demonstrate that there are many ways to begin and many ways to proceed. In every case, though, there is clear evidence that many of the tenets of transformative leadership guide and ground the practice of these leaders.

Charles began with an activity with his small advisory committee; Carla tackled a culture of low expectations with consistent dialogue, focus groups, and opportunities for feedback; Leslie issued an open invitation to students and staff to form a committee she empowered to raise difficult questions and address controversial issues; Catherine insisted on free writing to encourage reflection and dialogue about difficult issues. The starting points and strategies were different, but each took a courageous stance where they were, to replace destructive assumptions and knowledge frameworks with positive approaches in which the teachers, collectively, took responsibility for the inclusion and success of all students.

These leaders were not satisfied with the status quo. They were not focused solely on "putting out fires" or on the day-to-day managerial issues (although in no way do they ignore them). They were not afraid of conflict or of taking on delicate or difficult issues. What they share is a firm sense of the moral purposes of education, the need for inclusive and equitable practices that call for a careful examination of dominant traditions, assumptions, and beliefs, and the need for extensive dialogue to build clarity and understanding about more liberatory and more optimistic ways forward.

In Chapter 8, I present the story of Sophie, a woman who grew up in poverty, who was ignored, neglected, and dismissed as never being able to amount to anything. Her story is one of transformation as we gain further insight into the forces that helped her change her circumstances and, ultimately, become a teacher. As we listen to her narrative, we will revisit, once again, the eight tenets of transformative leadership that I believe have permitted each of the leaders we have seen to successfully embark on a path of change.

For Further Reflection and Action

1. Compare and contrast the leadership of McGehee Secondary School and Rah-e-Amal school in Rawalpindi, Pakistan. What lessons for your own leadership practice can you take from each story?
2. Think about the "snowball writing" activity used by Charles. What are some prompts you might use in your school and with which groups?
3. How and where do you invite feedback about how well your school is meeting its goals? How might you use Carla Cox's strategy of dividing feedback into specific topics? How do you engage your staff in pedagogical conversations and with what goals? Is there a difficult dialogue you need to encourage in your school?
4. Leslie Thomas seems to succeed because of her strong belief in empowering every member of her staff and in permitting them to take responsibility for new and creative solutions. To what extent is it important for a transformative leader to "let go" and permit others to act according to shared goals? Is this a skill you have also acquired and, if not, is it desirable?
5. To which characteristics of a transformative leader do you attribute the success of Catherine Lake's school? Which characteristics do you exhibit and which might you need to work on to achieve more equity and inclusion in your school?
6. Are there policies and structural barriers to equity in your district that need to be challenged and, if so, how might you do so?

Chapter 8

Conclusion

My parents were on welfare. We moved a lot and teachers always thought I was stupid. Immediately whenever I entered a class I felt their prejudice. They told my father all they could do was baby-sit me because I would never amount to anything.
(Sophie)

I never had a toy when I was growing up. For Christmas we would get shoe boxes with about 10 nuts, an orange and an apple. That was our Christmas gift.
(Dr. Ruth Simmons, President, Brown University)

Throughout this book, we have focused on how the world in which we live is one of constant change that is volatile, uncertain, complex, and ambiguous (VUCA)—some wonderful, surprising, and awe-inspiring; others uncontrollable, disastrous, and resulting in heartbreak. We have noted that many changes, such as the increasingly volatile political situation of Middle Eastern Arabic nations, or natural disasters, are beyond our control and occur whether we long for them or not. Other changes, such as new policies related to school boundaries, literacy, or increased inclusion of special education students, are within our control but require moral courage and political will for change to occur. We have seen many instances of change that needs to happen—some would say that should have happened and that has not occurred—because it is still waiting for transformative educational leaders to take a courageous stand. The latter require courageous transformative leaders working together—sometimes in the face of political opposition, sometimes in the face of tradition to implement change that rectifies wrongs.

The focus on the need for change was, in fact, the central topic of Chapter 1. Then, in Chapter 2, we reflected on the ways in which some theories of educational leadership emphasize traits, some processes (many technical), and some specific educational goals or outcomes. There I argued the need for a theory that would combine all three—traits, processes, and goals—and posited transformative leadership as one approach that not only combines these aspects but that takes an explicitly moral stand in favor of inclusion, social justice, and both private and public good. Moreover, I argue for this normative stance because, as evidenced by Kymberly Wimberly (Chapter 7), Oakes and Rogers (2006) and others, we have seen how, without an explicit emphasis on issues of social justice, too little deep equity reform has truly occurred.

In Chapter 3, we began to focus on some of the ways educational leaders can implement meaningful reform—eliminating color-blind racism, rejecting deficit thinking, and opening up curricular processes to be inclusive of the lived experiences of all students. Each of these is a way of beginning to implement deep and equitable change by deconstructing and reconstructing knowledge frameworks and by focusing on equity, inclusion, and optimism for all children. Chapter 4 drew our attention to the need to pay careful attention to the ways in which power and privilege continue to play out in schools, marginalizing and excluding some and advantaging and benefiting others. Then, in Chapter 5, we reflected on the need for transformative educational leaders to focus on goals related to both private as well as public good—and to ensure that as we do so, we promote individual academic, social, and intellectual growth as well as an understanding of what it means to be a caring, engaged, and contributing citizen.

This discussion was extended, in Chapter 6, to include consideration of healthy identity construction as well as enhancement of our global curiosity and awareness of our global citizenship and responsibility. In Chapter 7, after giving one more example of the need for change, I provided examples of leaders who have demonstrated, in many ways, elements of transformative leadership. There we reflected on the fact that there is no prescription for being transformative in that we identified some leaders who confronted inappropriate pedagogies, some who identified the need for cultural change, and still others who focused on policies and structures. All however shared a clear sense of the multiple purposes of schooling, the need for equitable opportunities for all students, and the requisite moral courage in the face of opposition. We see evidence, in these exemplars, of some ways in which several transformative educational leaders combined tenets of transformative leadership with notions of critique, promise, and moral courage, and, hence, we are reminded that living positively and optimistically in a VUCA world requires that transformative leadership be undergirded by *vision, understanding, clarity,* and *agility* (Caron, 2009).

What should have become clear by now is that the eight characteristics I identified in Chapter 1 and again in Chapter 2 as fundamental to transformative educational leadership are so integrally related that it is difficult, if not impossible, to discuss or implement them discretely. The characteristics were listed as follows:

- the mandate to effect deep and equitable change;
- the need to deconstruct and reconstruct knowledge frameworks that perpetuate inequity and injustice;
- a focus on emancipation, democracy, equity, and justice;
- the need to address the inequitable distribution of power;
- an emphasis on both private and public (individual and collective) good;
- an emphasis on interdependence, interconnectedness, and global awareness;
- the necessity of balancing critique with promise; and
- the call to exhibit moral courage.

It must also be apparent that if one is driven by a sense of moral purpose and clarity about the multiple goals and purposes of education, one cannot identify the need for deep and equitable change without subsequently beginning to deconstruct the knowledge frameworks that perpetuate the structures and cultures that need to be changed, and trying to replace them with alternative ways of thinking and knowing. Moreover, until and unless we take these first steps, it is difficult to understand how we might reduce our emphasis on test scores and accountability to focus on emancipation, democracy, equity, and justice—issues that are, once again, necessarily interconnected to ways of thinking about promoting both public and private good, developing strong and healthy student identities, and fostering a global curiosity that leads to awareness and a sense of responsible global citizenship. Further, to do any of this successfully, and particularly to go beyond simple critique to introduce educational experiences that hold promise of a better future, requires a healthy dose of moral courage.

As a reminder about the need for each of these transformative elements, I begin here by sharing the story of Sophie's transformation from a young woman living in an impoverished and struggling family, to being herself, a mother on welfare, a successful and caring teacher. As we listen to her story (told primarily in her own words),[1] we will identify each of the eight tenets of transformative leadership. Although I will discuss them separately, the characteristics work hand in hand to fashion her transformative experience. It is important to acknowledge that Sophie's story does not need to be an isolated incident but simply a reminder of the power, potential, and possibilities of transformative leadership. It is important to indicate here, that it is not Sophie whom I believe to be a transformative leader (although she may well be in her current capacity as a teacher), but it is her situation, the barriers she faced, and the educators along her path who helped her transform her situation, her sense of self, and her capacity for learning and growth from whom we can learn. As indicated at the outset of this book, although many of these transformative leaders will (and must be) school principals or superintendents, some others will be teacher-leaders, community leaders, parents, and others interested in and involved in education who are simply informal leaders where they are.

I conclude this book by sharing briefly some of the insights of President Ruth Simmons of Brown University upon her appointment in 2001 as the first African American president of an Ivy League university. She is now a transformative leader and her story provides still further evidence of the importance, and the possibilities, of educating every child to a high level.

As these exemplars demonstrate vividly, success in education must never depend on the luck of the draw, on the family one is born into, the teacher one is assigned or the school one attends—and, yet, too often this is the case. For Sophie, the "bad luck" of her early experiences almost prevented her surmounting life's challenges and achieving her potential.

 ## Sophie's Story: An Exemplar

Sophie, as a child, grew up in poverty, and sometimes homelessness. She tells us that her parents were on welfare, her father had to work three jobs to feed the family, and her frequent absences from school affected her performance. She recounts how, from an early age, she could "feel the prejudice" as soon as she walked into a room, how she overheard teachers talking negatively about her parents and her absence on days when welfare checks were distributed. In fact, she recalls being "the little girl at the back of the classroom who was forgotten."

Sophie's story is not unique. As many of the incidents in this book remind us, it is repeated daily in classrooms and schools throughout the nation. It reminds us of the need for transformative tenet number one—the need for deep and equitable change.

The name-calling and assumptions made by educators about Sophie and her family are not simply evidence of isolated prejudice, but evidence of deep-seated, institutional discrimination that persists in our institutions and continues to marginalize those whose backgrounds and lifestyles—ethnicity, sexual orientation, social class, cultural practices—are not those of the mainstream. The distinction between prejudice and discrimination is significant. Such attitudes of deficit thinking and blame are not individual misperceptions or prejudices, but represent the entrenched and persistent *habitus* of schooling—beliefs about how things are. Therefore, they represent deeply ingrained discrimination that requires consistent and concerted effort if they are to be overcome.

The year she was 14, Sophie tells us, she was failing dismally and her family circumstances made it necessary for her to quit school. The following year, however, she registered once again in the same school and found herself in the same math class with the same teacher she had had the previous year—a teacher who had repeatedly made her feel incompetent and with whom she had repeatedly experienced failure. Recognizing that she had been dismally unsuccessful the previous year, her father made one of his rare visits to the school to meet with the principal and to request a change. There he was told, "It really doesn't matter who her teacher is—that one or another, because all we are really doing is baby-sitting that girl."

It is obvious that with an attitude like that, the principal of Sophie's school was not making an effort to deconstruct current knowledge frameworks; but instead was perpetuating the culture of blame, shame, and deficit thinking that existed in his school. Without leadership that helps teachers to create new, positive, and optimistic knowledge frameworks, even if teachers want to help students from less advantaged backgrounds, tenet number two is not implemented. Deeply rooted assumptions that persist in the wider society (as seen not only in Sophie's case, but that of Kymberly at the outset of Chapter 7) do not change simply with the passing of time. They must be explicitly addressed and challenged.

One way to address such assumptions is to ensure that all educators differentiate between what I often call "opportunity to learn" and what we know as "ability to learn." My favorite metaphoric example occurs in a kindergarten art class. Imagine one child whose parents have the time and money to buy her art materials, to paint with her at home, and to teach her to clean her brush or to use a new brush when she changes color. She enters kindergarten, is presented with paper and paints, produces a brightly colored masterpiece—and is immediately labeled a "gifted" artist and identified for enrichment activities. Now imagine her classmate, perhaps Sophie herself, whose father works three jobs simply to feed the family, and for whom there is no time or money for painting at home. She enters the class, is presented with the same art materials, and not knowing she needs to clean her brush between colors, produces a somewhat muddy, grayish work. Immediately, she is identified for "remediation" because her art is "inferior."

Recall that this is a metaphor. Although we rarely identify students for remedial or gifted art classes, from day one we do make assumptions about students' ability and potential future class placements. What we fail to understand is that we have no idea about Sophie's artistic *ability* because we have made assumptions based on her prior *opportunity* to learn. And so, instead of taking the few minutes necessary to teach her about cleaning her brush, we label her, stigmatize her, and relegate her to a lifetime of low level activities, leaving her forgotten in the back of the room. Changing our knowledge framework about opportunity and ability is one way to institute education that optimistically opens doors for all children.

Sophie grew up, married, had two children and the cycle repeated itself. She found herself illiterate, unable to help her children with their school-work, unable to provide any better for her family than her parents had for her and her siblings. However, when Sophie's husband abandoned the family, she made a decision. She was not going to be the parent who could not provide for her family. She was not going to be the parent who could not read the newsletters sent from school. She states, "I summoned my courage and registered in an evening class." There, she reported, "I encountered a French teacher who helped me tremendously, who taught with humor. We passed our evenings laughing and I learned so much. I said to myself, my goodness, that's what it is to learn. I felt so comfortable in her class that I couldn't do anything other than learn—and that was the first time in my life I was comfortable in a school."

The French teacher (we'll arbitrarily call her Madame Rivard) was the first transformative educator Sophie encountered. She had implemented tenet number three and, by focusing on emancipation, created a learning context that was democratic, and more equitable and just than any Sophie had previously encountered, one in which teacher and students could laugh and learn together. It was not a heavy-handed or oppressive atmosphere. She did not focus on deficiencies, but made learning fun. Hers was an inclusive classroom in which Sophie, for the first time, felt comfortable, respected, and able to learn. There (following tenet four) power was not wielded to keep students in their (subordinate) places but to empower, to encourage, and to build them up. There Sophie had the support to overcome the stigma and the prejudices that had negatively affected her identity as a learner.

Sophie, who saw herself as "not very quick intellectually" found herself explaining to herself and her teacher that she was not very good at math, that she was truly stupid, that she was stubborn and thick-headed and so forth. Then, she suddenly stopped, realizing that she was repeating exactly the negatives that had been constantly directed at her throughout her school years.

A lifetime of negatives, of being the recipient of deficit thinking, of being told one cannot do something, is hard to overcome. Sophie's self-concept had been formed in large part because of the negative attitudes and prejudices of those who saw her as stupid or lazy—a child who would never amount to anything. Fortunately, Sophie had the help of a caring and insightful teacher who told her that, in the future, she could "see her as a teacher," to which Sophie simply said, "Pardon? You're crazy!" Madame Rivard, seeing her potential, responded that she would be a wonderful teacher, exactly because of what she had lived and what she could feel—and insisted she "would be marvelous." Here the teacher saw beyond the assumptions, the fear, the previous lack of opportunity and failure to focus on the positives, and in so doing, she reached beyond the individual to the collective good—to the contributions Sophie could make as a teacher.

Although Sophie quickly responded, "You are crazy," her teacher persisted, "You need to go to university." So Sophie completed her three years of university, her three years of student teaching, and now, proudly says, "I am a teacher—a primary school and special education teacher." She explains that "when there are people who believe in you, who are there to help you, to encourage you, you can do anything." "Now I have choices," she proudly exclaims.

Here we see evidence of the positive and optimistic outcomes of a serendipitous relationship with a transformative educational leader. Once again, it is not "rocket science" although the explosion of accomplishments is certainly rewarding. Transformative leadership does not require extensive resources, or unusual skills or aptitudes. It requires having a vision of equity and justice, of the power of relationships, of rejecting deficit thinking, of offering encouragement, and of believing in people—even when they have been taught repeatedly not to believe in themselves. As Caron (2009) has advocated, helping those who are marginalized in our society requires the new VUCA skills—a *vision* of their potential and success; empathic *understanding* of their situation and solidarity with them as fellow human beings; *clarity* of purpose in terms of expecting excellence and equity, focusing on both private and public good; and *agility* in negotiating rules and systems to ensure that everyone has an opportunity to succeed (tenets five to eight).

Sophie's story is one that should be told and retold, taken to heart, and shared repeatedly. It is a story of liberation, of optimism, of success—and it must become just one of many similar tales told by every caring transformative educator as we work together to transform schools in this VUCA world.

Consistent Hope

Sophie's story, told in large part in her own words, is particularly powerful because it describes her transformation from an unsuccessful, apparently powerless, welfare mother, to a successful, contributing teacher. But it is not simply the story of one person. It is the story of a system that neglects, marginalizes, and casts off numerous individuals because they do not seem to "fit." It is the story of a system in which, too often, it is the luck of the draw—which teacher one has, which school one attends—that determines whether one is able to succeed or fail. Fortunately, it is also a story of transformation and hope, because finally, and still coincidentally, Sophie met a teacher who understood how to create equitable, engaging, and supportive learning communities.

Sophie's high school principal wrote her off and disrespected both her and her father. We cannot tolerate such principals in today's schools. This randomness must end. In every classroom, in every school, and in every community, each child who enters school must be able to count on having a teacher, and a school leader, who welcomes, respects, and supports him or her on a daily basis. Thus, transformative educational leaders must take steps to ensure that every disenfranchised student meets a teacher like Madame Rivard.

As further inspiration to aspiring transformative leaders, I conclude with the story of Ruth Simmons, eighteenth president of Brown University, whose life unfolded very differently from Sophie's, despite similar impoverished beginnings. Although I am in no way suggesting that had her early experience been different Sophie might have become a university president, in some ways, it is accurate to say that we do not and cannot know.

Ruth Simmons, President of Brown University[2]

Ruth Simmons, like Sophie, grew up in abject poverty, without any of the material advantages one can (unfortunately) usually attribute to highly successful students. As the youngest of 12 children, the daughter of a Texas sharecropper, she commented, "I would not have thought it possible for a person of my background to become president of Brown University." And yet, she describes her journey to the presidency as beginning on her first day of school:

> Remember, I'm . . . I'm in this dark house with a tin roof. That's my little world. And I go into this place that is bright and cheerful with this wonderful person called a teacher. And she's cheerful and she thinks I'm wonderful and she thinks I'm smart. So it was . . . it . . . it was like a veil lifting for me in a way.

One cannot help but wonder how Sophie's experience might have been different had she encountered a teacher who "thought she was smart" rather than one who made her "feel the prejudice" and who left her "forgotten at the back of the room." Ruth encountered a teacher who believed in her, encouraged her, and supported her—the kind of teacher every child is entitled to—and she began to feel a veil lifting (instead of closing in around her). Undoubtedly, Ruth's educational road was neither smooth nor consistent, but at least the early stages were positive, encouraging, and supportive (with her teachers even raising funds so she could attend Harvard). Her schooling experience, unlike Sophie's, enabled her to develop a positive academic self-concept and certain of her own abilities to stand up to the later prejudices she would face.

In graduate school, for example, she tells us she encountered a professor who would not speak to her because, in her words, "it just wasn't suitable to him that I should be African-American and be the best student in the class." Her account, reminiscent of Kymberly's tale in the previous chapter, again emphasizes the persistence of beliefs that both inhibit and fail to reward student success. And yet, Ruth did succeed—beyond almost everyone's wildest expectations to the point where, now,

> During her tenure at Brown University, Simmons has created an ambitious set of initiatives designed to expand and strengthen the faculty; increase financial support and resources for undergraduate, graduate, and medical students; improve facilities; renew a broad commitment to shared governance; and ensure that diversity informs every dimension of the university. These initiatives have led to a major investment of new resources in Brown's educational mission.
>
> (Brown University, 2011, ¶7)

Following this list of accomplishments, the Brown University website concludes, "As an academic leader, Simmons believes in the power of education to transform lives." Not only is she an embodiment of this principle, she has lived and proclaimed it throughout her career. As she said to Morley Safer a decade ago:

> Everything belongs to me. There is nothing—there is nothing that is withheld from me simply because I'm poor. That's what children have to understand . . . Education does not exist to provide you with a job. This is—this is where we've gone awry. Education is here to nourish your soul.

And this is not only what children have to understand, but every teacher, every citizen, every educational leader must understand it too. It is the message of hope and transformation I have tried to communicate in this book; and it is the message I am confident each educator—whomever and wherever they are—will take to heart.

Concluding Reflections

Each leader approaches transformation in his or her own way, attending to the characteristics of his or her context, and beginning where he or she is. In this book, we have examined numerous ways in which transformative leaders, at different stages of their journeys, have worked with their colleagues and communities to become more transformative and more attuned to issues of equity, inclusion, and social justice. We have seen the necessity to speak out, to challenge injustice, and to change the beliefs and attitudes that undergird the persistent prejudices and discrimination that still permeate American society. And we have heard stories of how leaders have made, can make, and are still making a difference in the lives of children. For the most part, the leaders described here are known only in the relatively small circle of their own school community; yet, they are making a difference where they are that has the potential to ripple to more distant shores. One never knows, however, when one might have the opportunity to teach a child who will one day become a university president, a great scientist, an influential politician. We do know that each teacher will encounter children who have the potential to live and act justly, and walk uprightly, happy, fulfilled, and contributing to the global community. Each child must have this opportunity.

Unfortunately, educational leaders like the ones Ruth Simmons encountered, like Zehra and the other leaders in this book, are still too rare. Too many leaders are still focused narrowly on managerial tasks. Too many are so concerned with the reputation or ranking of their school that they put testing and test scores ahead of students, inquiry, and learning. And yet, almost all would acknowledge, if pressed, that high test scores are not an adequate indication of preparation for a VUCA world and certainly not for global citizenship in a world that is begging for education and for justice for all.

The call is not for educational leaders to become politicians, social workers, humanitarians, or counselors—although we sometimes find ourselves engaged in an element of each of these. The call is for us to take seriously the fact that the playing field is still inequitable, the achievement gaps still unacceptable, the barriers for children from non-mainstream homes often untenable. We must start where we are, challenge and overturn the inequities where we find them, and engage daily in the tasks of transformative leadership as a matter of principle and conviction. The need is urgent, the task is daunting, but the rewards are enormous.

If we can enlarge the cadre of transformative leaders, then the mantra "all children can learn" will be transformed from words on a page to the lived reality of every child in every school. We owe our communities, our nation, and our world no less.

For Further Reflection and Action

1. Revisit each of the tenets of transformative leadership and discuss how your understanding of each may have changed over the course of this book. What reflections do they prompt now about your own leadership practice?

2. Does Sophie's story embody, for you, the tenets of transformative leadership—and act as a reminder of the pressing need for all of us to work together for the good of all children? If not, what messages do you take from it?

3. What inspiration do you take from Ruth Simmons' experiences? Which tenets of transformative leadership are illustrated by her story?

4. Does transformative leadership have the potential described and argued in this book? If not, what other aspects of leadership are missing that might affect inclusive, equitable, and democratic change? If so, what commitments are you willing to make to ensure your leadership is transformative as you move forward?

Appendix

In this section, you will find the description of a school that is in need of a new transformative approach to leadership to ensure that the learning environment is inclusive of all children and that its educational program is equitable, socially just, and of high quality. Imagine you are the school principal and as you read make a list of some of the changes that need to be implemented and the challenges you think you might face. As you finish, reflect on your goals for the school; then prioritize your list of challenges and needed changes. Then develop a plan including how you would proceed both immediately and in the longer term. (Who would be involved? How? What specific actions would you take? What data would you need? How would you know if you were successful?)

Jose Ferreira Elementary School

Jose Ferreira Elementary School is a large, urban kindergarten through eighth grade school with 698 students. It is a red-brick building, located in a low-middle-class area of town. During the day, the area is relatively deserted, but at night, it seems that a number of drug dealers congregate in the vacant lot around the corner, as needles and empty bottles are often found on the school's sidewalks and in the playground. Although the district has struggled to keep the school in good repair, two windows at the front are broken and the roof over the small library leaks, making some of the books damp and musty smelling. Unfortunately, the district says that the school must find money in its own budget for repairs—something that has proven to be impossible.

Mr. Bates is now entering his second year as principal of the school. During the first year, he developed collegial relations with staff members and with Ms. Cordeira, the assistant principal, who is entering her third year in this position. Mr. Bates and Ms. Cordeira have 32 years of combined experience in school administration. In general, "all the staff members get along" in part because teachers respect the autonomy and professional discretion of their colleagues, but in part because there has arisen a culture of avoidance of conflict.

Of the students, 54% come from very poor families and, hence, qualify for, and are provided with, free lunches. A large number of students (278) come from homes where the language of instruction is not the language spoken at home and very few of these children's parents are ever seen in the school. There is no coordinated parent volunteer program and only three occasions each year (parent–teacher conferences and the spring picnic) when parents are specifically invited into the school. The student attendance rate is 88%, with a 37% mobility rate. Last year, six students were asked to repeat their year, and 157 students qualified to receive special education services.

The two administrators rarely visit classrooms, except once a year, when they are required to conduct teacher observations, often saying that they respect the teachers' autonomy. Staff meetings are held once or twice a year and, for the most part, the teachers (who are all well qualified, with all but three having a bachelor's degree and over 15% having an advanced degree) work in isolation with their doors closed. The educators all know that the school has a reputation for not performing well, and many excellent teachers try to avoid being hired into Jose Ferreira Elementary School. In general, they believe it is because there are so many children from impoverished families as well as large groups of immigrant children attending the school. Often a teacher can be heard to say something like, "Well, what can they expect us to do when so many of the children come from homes that don't value education?" Although they have begun to offer after-school tutoring classes and some voluntary weekend sessions, achievement improved little over the results of the previous year.

Overall, curriculum and instruction are textbook driven. There are no examples of instructors encouraging students to process mathematics at a level beyond what might be expected on standardized tests. The reading program is fragmented and inconsistent, differs among teachers, and is reliant on a series of readers. There is one computer lab for the school that is seldom used. Assessment information comes solely from standardized tests given once a year. Discipline seems to be a growing concern.

How do you proceed?

Exercising Transformative Leadership

(Example Response)

The following are some points raised by one person who, having read this case, developed a response. Again, there are no right or wrong answers, although there are some points that must be considered if a leader wants to take a transformative approach to implementing change. In what follows, some of the key points from the case are identified, but again, different leaders will prioritize and address these issues differently. One assumption is that leaders will be asking the following questions about this case:

- Who is advantaged by this decision and who disadvantaged?
- Who is included in this decision and who will be excluded?
- Who is privileged and who will be marginalized?
- Whose voices have been heard and who has been silenced?

Challenges Faced

1. serious budgetary restrictions;
2. a school climate characterized by avoidance of conflict;
3. a hands-off administrative style on the part of the principal and a faculty completely isolated from each other;
4. extreme faculty attitude of deficit thinking toward students;
5. very low expectations by teachers;
6. textbook driven curriculum and instruction;
7. minimal use of technology by students or assessment of student performance;
8. high over-representation of students (22%) diagnosed for special education;
9. school in ill-repair and located in neighborhood of drug users;
10. few opportunities for dialogue with parents.

Note: although some may see the school's demographics as challenges (54% of students from very poor families; 37% mobility rate; nearly 40% from homes where the language is different from the language of instruction), transformative leaders are more inclined to simply see them as givens.

Changes Needed

1. create a warm and inclusive school climate where teachers feel valued and their voices are heard;
2. create a caring, inclusive, and equitable school climate where all students are held to (and attain) high standards;
3. create a caring and inclusive climate in which all parent voices are encouraged and parents are invited to become involved *on their terms*;
4. rejection and elimination of deficit thinking;
5. increase standards of academic excellence;
6. develop more engaging, culturally relevant, and interactive pedagogy;
7. cultivate more positive relations with the surrounding community.

Planning for Change

There are no right ways or places to begin, aside from knowing one's goals and what one hopes to accomplish.

Ways to accomplish the seven identified changes will definitely include the need for extensive dialogue, and the creation of an open, trusting, and inquiring community that respects, listens to, and includes all voices in order to eliminate deficit thinking and institute the required changes.

Below you will find a very comprehensive and ambitious plan developed by an educator who read this case and thought about leading Jose Ferreira Elementary School.

One Person's Plan

Step 1

As principal, the week before the beginning of the new school year, I would convene a one-day retreat of all faculty and staff to be held in a neighborhood community center. Volunteer parents would provide the lunch. The session would begin with the attendees watching a couple of videos featuring Margaret Wheatley and Parker Palmer that stress the imperative for teachers to restore identity and integrity to their professional lives, be authentically presented in the classroom, and deeply connected to their students.

Much of the retreat will involve break-out sessions in which pre-arranged groups of faculty and staff intensely discuss the following issues, before reporting their deliberations to the full assembly.

The groups are: a) school mission and organization; b) school culture; c) academic standards; d) curriculum/course content; e) instruction and pedagogy; f) meeting the needs of all students; g) parental involvement and communication networks; h) school safety and neighborhood clean-up; i) community connections for full service programs.

These groups will continue to meet and submit a final report that is shared with everyone, becoming the basis for an ongoing dialogue, "curriculum as dialogue."

Step 2

Within the first month of school, I will schedule 20-minute meetings with each faculty and staff member. In these meetings, I will stress the imperative that each teacher knows what their non-negotiable principles are and that they be committed to ensuring that every student, even the most disadvantaged, learns to their maximum ability.

I will ask each person to express his or her concerns, reservations, and needs. I will explain that I have an open-door policy in which I strongly encourage faculty and staff to make appointments to meet with me as frequently as they like.

Step 3

I will visit all classrooms regularly to observe teachers, engage them in conversation about strengths and weaknesses, and offer faculty mentoring for those who require it. If several faculty are experiencing similar issues, I will arrange for a professional development workshop on the topic.

Step 4

We will schedule regular monthly meetings of the entire school staff and faculty, during which the attendees engage in courageous conversations about our goals, including democratic schooling. We must eliminate deficit thinking and develop high expectations for all students. Teachers will brainstorm the reasons why students are performing poorly, using the free writing approach.

In subsequent sessions, we will focus on sub-groups of students to try to understand the reasons for their achievement gaps and what can be done to rectify the situation.

Step 5

Faculty and staff will also be organized to participate in weekly meetings on the basis of grade level and/or department to share best practices, develop collegiality, and break up the school culture of working in isolation, behind closed doors.

Step 6

I will strongly encourage teachers to make every effort to develop meaningful relationships with all of their students. Learning about each student's interests and activities outside of class can be helpful.

Step 7

In addition, teachers should develop relationships with the parents of their students. Teachers will be encouraged to make home visits as well.

Step 8

In an attempt to create a stronger bond between parents and the school, I will schedule weekly activities for parents. The first of these will be a breakfast at school. Depending on the results of a survey administered to parents, these activities will take place variously in the morning, afternoon, or evening, whichever best accommodates the parents' working schedules. To make families feel more welcome at school activities, notices will be circulated to parents prior to the activity in multiple languages spoken by the school community to provide explicit expectations, like appropriate dress.

Step 9

To repair the roof of the school library and also the broken windows, I will solicit from parents of the students any volunteers who possess the carpentry skills to do the work.

Step 10

I will develop networks with social service agencies in the community as well as parents, to attempt to provide more health services to students, as we move to becoming a full service community center. Parents who are nurses, dentists, eye doctors, or physicians may volunteer to help. Special attention will be given to transient students to make sure that they have proper housing, consulting with government authorities when appropriate. Local colleges and universities may have a service learning component in some courses through which students may volunteer to tutor our students. Services may be offered also to parents such as literacy and dropout prevention.

Step 11

In all of the above efforts, student participation in the decision-making process will be encouraged, when appropriate. A student-run newspaper and a robust Student Government Association will be developed, which will be given meaningful authority. When a committee is created, such as a Social Justice Committee, students will also serve as members.

Notes

Ultimately, student performance, however measured, is likely to improve only if I can create a vibrant learning community based on teachers who are authentic, who no longer display deficit thinking and low expectations, and who embrace rather than avoid conflict. To do this, I will need to create a more data-rich environment in which multiple sources of information provide a more complete picture of student performance and overall school life.

I will know that I am successful if students and parents are excited about learning and enthusiastically involved in extra-curricular activities. In addition, the objective data regarding test score improvement will reflect their passion. I will clearly see from the expressions on the faces of students and teachers alike when we have progressed to a genuine learning community.

Notes

1 Living in a World of Unfulfilled Promises: Examining the Context for Educational Leadership

1 See Caron (2009).
2 Some of these ideas are taken from a video, based on her 1994 book, *Leadership and the new science*, available at: www.trainingabc.com/Leadership-and-the-New-Science-p-16216.html.

3 Changing Knowledge Frameworks to Promote Equity

1 Minoritized, rather than "minority," is the term used throughout this book to emphasize how the traditional power of the White middle class has become normative and often marginalizes and excludes those outside this group, regardless of whether they are in the numerical majority or not.

5 Promoting Both Private and Public Good: Creating Inclusive School Communities

1 These data come from a colleague, Dr. Justine Kane, who was involved in a longitudinal study of these students, reported in Kane and Shields (2011).

6 Fostering Global Citizenship: Understanding Interconnectedness in Our Global Community

1 Some say that 35 times that number are unreported. See www.scienceinafrica.co.za/2002/april/virgin.htm.

7 Putting it Together: Transforming Schools

1 It is important to note that the allegations here are in dispute and the issue, as of December 2011, is before the courts; nevertheless, I repeat it here as told by a number of mainstream news outlets including *The Washington Post* (Hughes, 2011), CNN, CBC, and the Courthouse News Service.
2 The school, now in its thirteenth year, has expanded and moved several times. For more information on the school itself, please visit its website at http://rah-e-amal.org/rah_e_amal_school.php. (See also other stories such as http://raheamal.tripod.com/.) On this book's website, you will also find some of my personal pictures and video of my visit to the school (taken with permission).
3 An approach to literacy that includes: read to self, read to someone, listen to reading, word work, and work on writing (Boushey & Moser, 2006).
4 Her story is recounted in Waithman (2009).

5 Fraser (1995) argues that redistributive justice is necessary for material (including) financial injustices, but for injustices that are more abstract or cultural we also need what she calls recognitive justice that recognizes and legitimates struggles for socio-cultural equality as well as redistribution of material resources.

8 Conclusion

1 I met Sophie, and watched a video in which she was featured, at a conference in the spring of 2010. Subsequently I was given a copy of the video and permission to translate it from French and to use whatever portions I wished to help other educators understand how to educate students from backgrounds such as Sophie's (see Archambault, 2010). All data from Sophie are taken, with permission, from that video, prepared by Jean Archambault and others, original in French, translation mine, 2010. (Note that my brief video, with English subtitles, taken from this longer version, in which Sophie tells her own, powerful story, is posted on our website.)
2 The information about Ruth Simmons comes from the transcript of an interview televised in 2001 with CBS interviewer Morley Safer (see Safer, 2001).

References

Abel, W. (2011, July 25). Black student can't be valedictorian. *Courthouse News Service*. Retrieved August 2011 from www.courthousenews.com/2011/07/25/38410.htm.

Alexander, K. L., Entwisle, D. R., & Olson, L. S. (2007). Lasting consequences of the summer learning gap. *American Sociological Review*, 72(2), 176–180.

Altman, D. (2011). *Outrageous fortunes: Twelve surprising trends that will reshape the global economy*. New York: Henry Holt.

Apple, M. W. (1996). *Cultural politics and education*. New York: Teachers College Press.

Apple, M. (2001). *Educating the "right" way: Markets, standards, god, and inequality*. New York: RoutledgeFalmer.

Archambault, J. (director) (2010). *Supporting Montreal's Disadvantaged Schools Project* (movie). Funded by the Quebec Ministry of Education. Université de Montréal, Montréal, Quebec.

Bakhtin, M. (1984). *The problems of Dostoevsky's poetics*. Minneapolis, MN: University of Minnesota Press.

Bandura, A. (1997). Exercise of personal and collective efficacy in changing societies. In A. Bandura (Ed.), *Self-efficacy in changing societies* (pp. 1–45). Cambridge: Cambridge University Press.

Batsche, G., Elliott, J., Graden, J. L., Grimes, J., Kovaleski, J. F., Prasse, D., et al. (2006). *Response to intervention: Policy considerations and implementation*. Alexandria, VA: National Association of State Directors of Special Education, Inc.

Beane, J. A., & Apple, M. W. (1995). The case for democratic schools. In M. A. Apple & J. A. Beane (Eds.), *Democratic schools* (pp. 1–29). Alexandria, VA: Association for Supervision and Curriculum Development.

Bell, D. A. (1995). Who's afraid of critical race theory? *University of Illinois Law Review*, 4(Fall), 893–910.

Bellah, R. N., Madsen, R., Sullivan, W. M., Swidler, A., & Tipton, S. M. (1985). *Habits of the heart: Individualism and commitment in American life*. Los Angeles: University of California Press.

Bieneman, P. D. (2011). Transformative leadership: The exercise of agency in educational leadership. In C. M. Shields (Ed.), *Transformative leadership: A reader* (pp. 221–238). New York: Peter Lang.

Bieneman, P. (2012). *A study of collective efficacy in diverse award-winning elementary schools: An examination of tacit assumptions and underlying belief systems*. Doctoral dissertation, University of Illinois at Urbana-Champaign.

Bishop, R., & Berryman, M. (2006). *Culture speaks: Cultural relationships and classroom learning*. Wellington: Huia Publishing.

Bittman, M. (2008, January 27). The world: Rethinking the meat-guzzler. *New York Times Online*. Retrieved February 16, 2008 from www.nytimes.com/2008/01/27/weekinreview/27bittman.html.

Blackmore, J. (2010). "The Other within": Race/Gender disruptions to the professional learning of white educational leaders. *International Journal of Leadership in Education, 13*(1), 45–61.

Blackmore, J. (2011). Leadership in pursuit of purpose: Social, economic and political transformation. In C. M. Shields (Ed.), *Transformative leadership: A reader* (pp. 21–36). New York: Peter Lang.

Bogotch, I. E. (2000). *Educational leadership and social justice: Theory into practice.* Revised version of a paper presented at the annual conference of the University Council for Educational Administration, Albuquerque, NM. ED 452 585.

Bourdieu, P., with Passeron, J.-C. (1977). *Reproduction in education, society and culture.* London: Sage.

Boushey, G., & Moser, J. (2006). *The daily five.* Portland, ME: Stenhouse Publishers.

Brooks, D. (2011). *The social animal: The hidden sources of love, character, and achievement.* New York: Random House.

Brown University (2011). Website: President. Retrieved August 31, 2011 from www.brown.edu/about/administration/president/biography.

Buber, M. (1970). *I and thou.* New York: Charles Scribner's Sons. Retrieved February 2012 from http://courses.washington.edu/spcmu/buber/buber17.html.

Building a nation of learners (1995). The National Education Goals Panel Report, Washington, DC.

Burbules, N. C. (1993). *Dialogue in teaching.* New York: Teachers' College Press.

Burns, J. M. (1978). *Leadership.* New York: Harper & Row.

Cappiello, D. (2009). *Poll: US belief in global warming is cooling.* Physorg.com. Retrieved November 30, 2009 from www.physorg.com/news175502410.html.

Caron, D. (2009). *It's a vuca world!* Retrieved February 2012 from www.slideshare.net/dcaron/its-a-vuca-world-cips-cio-march-5-2009-draft.

Ciulla, J. (1996). Ethics, chaos, and the demand for good leaders. In P. S. Temes (Ed.), *Teaching leadership* (pp. 181–200). New York: Peter Lang.

Connolly, P. (2003). The development of young children's ethnic identities. In C. Vincent (Ed.), *Social justice, education, and identity* (pp. 166–184). New York: RoutledgeFalmer.

Cuban, L. (2003). *Why is it so hard to get good schools?* New York: Teachers College Press.

Cummins, J. (1989). Empowering minority students: A framework for intervention. In N. M. Hidalgo, C. L. McDowell, & E. V. Siddle (Eds.), *Facing racism in education* (pp. 50–68). Cambridge, MA: Harvard Educational Review.

Dahl, R. (2000). *On democracy.* New Haven, CT: Yale University Press.

David, M. J. S., Bowman, D. M., Balch, J., Artaxo, P., Bond, W. J., Cochrane, M. A., et al. (2011). The human dimension of fire regimes on earth. *Journal of Biogeography, 38*(12), 2223–2236 (see http://onlinelibrary.wiley.com/doi/10.1111/jbi.2011.38.issue-12/issuetoc).

De Tocqueville, A. (1835/2000). *Democracy in America.* Chicago: The University of Chicago Press.

Delpit, L. D. (1990). The silenced dialogue: Power and pedagogy in educating other people's children. In N. M. Hidalgo, C. L. McDowell, & E. V. Siddle (Eds.), *Facing racism in education* (pp. 84–102). Cambridge, MA: Harvard Educational Review.

Dryfoos, J. G. (1996). Full-service schools. *Educational Leadership, 53*(7), 18–23.

Eisenhart, M. (2006). Qualitative science in experimental time. *International Journal of Qualitative Studies in Education, 19*(6), 697–707.

Elert, G. (n.d.). *Income of the average person on earth.* Retrieved November 30, 2011 from http://hypertextbook.com/facts/2006/MateNagy.shtml.

Evans, R. (1996). *The human side of change.* San Francisco: Jossey-Bass.

Fennimore, B. S. (1997). When mediation and equity are at odds: Potential lessons in democracy. *Theory into Practice, 35*(1), 59–64.

Foster, W. (1986). *Paradigms and promises.* Buffalo, NY: Prometheus.

Fraser, N. (1995). From redistribution to recognition? Dilemmas of justice in a "Post-Socialist" age. *New Left Review, 212*, 68–93.

Freire, P. (1970). *Pedagogy of the oppressed.* New York: Continuum.

Freire, P. (2000). Pedagogy of hope: Reliving *Pedagogy of the oppressed.* In A. M. A. Freire & D. Macedo (Eds.), *The Paulo Freire reader* (pp. 237–264). New York: Continuum.

Friedman, T. L. (2005). *The world is flat: A brief history of the twenty-first century.* New York: Farrar, Straus, & Giroux.

Fullan, M. (1993). *Change forces.* New York: Falmer.

Furman, G. C. (1998). Postmodernism and community in schools: Unraveling the paradox. *Educational Administration Quarterly, 34*(3), 298–328.

Giroux, H. A. (1998). *Channel surfing, racism, the media, and the destruction of today's youth.* New York: St. Martin's Press.

Green, J. M. (1999). *Deep democracy: Diversity, community, and transformation.* Lanham, MD: Rowman & Littlefield.

Green, M. (1988). *The dialectic of freedom.* New York: Teachers College Press.

Green, P. (2001). Egalitarian solidarity. In S. J. Goodlad (Ed.), *The last best hope: A democracy reader* (pp. 176–193). San Francisco: Jossey-Bass.

Greene, M. (1998). Introduction: Teaching for social justice. In W. Ayers, J. A. Hunt, & T. Quinn (Eds.), *Teaching for social justice* (pp. xxvii–xlvi). New York: Teachers College Press.

Gruenewald, D. A. (2003). The best of both worlds: A critical pedagogy of place. *Educational Researcher, 32*(4), 3–12.

Grumet, M. R. (1995). The curriculum: What are the basics and are we teaching them? In J. L. Kincheloe & S. R. Steinberg (Eds.), *Thirteen questions* (2nd ed.) (pp. 15–21). New York: Peter Lang.

Gutmann, A. (2001). Democratic education in difficult times. In S. J. Goodlad (Ed.), *The last best hope: A democracy reader* (pp. 216–230). San Francisco: Jossey-Bass.

Hames-García, M. R. (2000). "Who are our own people?": Challenges for a theory of social identity. In P. M. L. Moya & M. R. Hames-García (Eds.), *Reclaiming identity: Realist theory and the predicament of postmodernism* (pp. 102–129). Berkeley: University of California Press.

Hollyer, B. (1999). *Wake up, world!: A day in the life of children around the world.* New York: Henry Holt.

Hughes, L. (1951). Harlem, *Poems.* Retrieved September 2011 from http://teachingamericanhistory. org/library/index.asp?document=640.

Hughes, S. A. (2011, July 28). Kymberly Wimberly, black valedictorian, claims school demoted her over race. *The Washington Post.* Retrieved August 30, 2011 from www.washingtonpost. com/blogs/blogpost/post/kymberly-wimberly-black-valedictorian-claims-school-demoted-her-over-race/2011/07/27/gIQAv5tkeI_blog.htm.

ISBE (Illinois State Board of Education) (2008). *Response to intervention plan.* Retrieved April 15, 2010 from www.isbe.net/pdf/rti_state_plan.pdf.

Kane, J. M., & Shields, C. M. (2011). You don't think we can be scientists . . .? Overcoming deficit approaches to students living in poverty. Unpublished case, submitted to the *Journal of Cases in Educational Leadership.*

Knapp, M. S., & Woolverton, S. (1995). Social class and schooling. In J. A. Banks & C. A. Banks (Eds.), *Handbook of research on multicultural education* (pp. 548–569). New York: Macmillan.

Labaree, D. F. (1997). Public goods, private goods: The American struggle over educational goals. *American Educational Research Journal, 34*(1), 39–81.

Ladson-Billings, G. (1996). "Your blues ain't like mine": Keeping issues of race and racism on the multicultural agenda. *Theory into Practice, 35*(4), 248–255.

Larson, C. L., & Ovando, C. J. (2001). *The color of bureaucracy: The politics of equity in multicultural school communities*. Belmont, CA: Wadsworth/Thomson Learning.

Leacock, S. B. (1911/2011). Gertrude the Governess. In *Nonsense novels*. Seattle, WA: CreateSpace Publisher. Retrieved February 2012 from http://en.wikipedia.org/wiki/Madly_Off_in_All_Directions.

Leithwood, K. (2010). Transformational school leadership. In E. Baker, B. McGaw, & P. Peterson (Eds.), *International encyclopedia of education* (3rd ed.). Oxford: Elsevier Ltd.

Leithwood, K., & Duke, D. L. (1998). Mapping the conceptual terrain of leadership: A critical point of departure for cross-cultural studies. *Peabody Journal of Education*, *73*(2), 31–50. Retrieved December 2011 from http://vnweb.hwwilsonweb.com.proxy.lib.wayne.edu/hww/results/results_single_fulltext.jhtml;hwwilsonid=HZRJQJCWKSDVVQA3DKDSFGGADUNGIIV0.

Leithwood, K., & Jantzi, D. (1990). Transformational leadership: How principals can help to reform school cultures. *School Effectiveness and School Improvement*, *1*(4), 249–280.

Leithwood, K., & Jantzi, D. (1999). The relative effects of principal and teacher sources of leadership on student engagement with school. *Educational Administration Quarterly*, *35*(supplemental), 679–706.

Loeb, M., & Kindel, S. (1999). *Leadership for dummies*. Foster City, CA: IDG Books.

Loewen, J. W. (2005). *Sundown towns: A hidden dimension of American racism*. New York: Simon & Schuster/Touchstone.

Lynn, M., Benigno, G., Williams, A. D., Park, G., & Mitchell, C. (2006). Critical theories of race, class and gender in urban education. *Encounter*, *19*(2), 17–25.

McKenzie, K. B., Christman, D. E., Hernandez, F., Fierro, E., Capper, C. A., Dantley, M., et al. (2008). From the field: A proposal for educating leaders for social justice. *Educational Administration Quarterly*, *44*(1), 111–138.

McKerrow, K. (1997). Ethical administration: An oxymoron? *Journal of School Leadership*, *7*(3), 210–225.

Menzel, P., & D'Aluisio, F. (2010). *What I eat: Around the world in 80 diets*. New York: Random House.

Menzel, P., Mann, C. C., & Kennedy, P. (1995). *Material world: A global family portrait*. San Francisco: Sierra Club Books.

Michigan Communities For Local Control (2011). *The Craig Fahle Show*, August 24, 2011, WDET. Retrieved August 2011 from http://wdetfm.org/shows/craig-fahle-show/episode/michigan-communities-for-local-control/.

Minister of Supply and Services Canada (1996). *Royal commission report on Aboriginal peoples*. Ottawa: Canada Communication Group.

Moya, P. M. L. (2000). Introduction: Reclaiming identity. In P. M. L. Moya & M. R. Hames-García (Eds.), *Reclaiming identity* (pp. 1–26). Los Angeles: University of California Press.

Nation at risk (1983). Report of the National Commission on Excellence in Education, Gardner, D. P. (chair). Retrieved February 2012 from www2.ed.gov/pubs/NatAtRisk/index.html.

No Child Left Behind (2002). Official U.S. Department of Education website. U.S. Department of Education, *Accountability*. Retrieved July 2007 from www.ed.gov/nclb/accountability/index.html?src=ov.

Oakes, J., & Rogers, J. (2006). *Learning power: Organizing for education and justice*. New York: Teachers College Press.

Ogbu, J. (1992). Understanding cultural diversity and learning. *Educational Researcher*, *21*(8), 5–14.

Palmer, P. J. (1998). *The courage to teach*. San Francisco: Jossey-Bass/Wiley.

Parker, L., & Villalpando, O. (2007). A racialized perspective on educational leadership: Critical race theory in educational administration. *Educational Administration Quarterly*, *43*(5), 519–524.

Paul (2009). *Canadian death panels*. Retrieved November 30, 2009 from http://cjunk.blogspot. com/2009/08/canadian-death-panels.html.

Perryman, J. (2009). Inspection and the fabrication of professional and performative processes. *Journal of Education Policy*, 24(5), 611–631.

Pillsbury, J., & Shields, C. M. (1999). When "they" becomes "we." *Journal for a Just and Caring Education*, 5(4), 410–429.

Pimm, S. L., & Lawton, J. H. (1998). Planning for biodiversity. *Science*, 279, 2068–2069.

Pinar, W. (2004). *What is curriculum theory?* Mahwah, NJ: Lawrence Erlbaum & Associates.

Quantz, R. A., Rogers, J., & Dantley, M. (1991). Rethinking transformative leadership: Toward democratic reform of schools. *Journal of Education*, 173(3), 96–118.

Reyes-Guerra, D., & Bogotch, I. (2011). Curriculum-inquiry as a transformative educational leadership skill. In C. M. Shields (Ed.), *Transformative leadership: A reader* (pp. 133–151). New York: Peter Lang.

Riehl, C. J. (2000). The principal's role in creating inclusive schools for diverse students: A review of normative, empirical, and critical literature on the practice of educational administration. *Review of Educational Research*, 70(1), 55–81.

Rio Declaration on Environment and Development (1992). Report of the United Nations Conference on Environment and Development. Retrieved September 2011 from www.unep. org/Documents.Multilingual/Default.Print.asp?documentid=78&articleid=1163.

Rudy, A. P., & Konefal, J. (2007). Nature, sociology, and social justice: Environmental sociology, pedagogy, and the curriculum. *American Behavioral Scientist*, 51, 495–515.

Safer, M. (2001). President Simmons, *60 Minutes*. Interview transcript, March 4, 2001, MMI, CBS Worldwide Inc.

Salinas, M. F., & Garr, J. (2009). Effect of learner-centered education on the academic outcomes of minority groups. *Journal of Instructional Psychology*, 36(3), 226–237.

Santana, S. (2009, November 14). Heckled at climate speech. *SunSentinel.com*. Retrieved November 30, 2009 from www.sun-sentinel.com/news/palm-beach/fl-al-gore-boca-2009 1114,0,5503886.story.

Sayani, A. (2010). *Pathologies and complicities: High school and the identities of disaffected South Asian "brown boys."* Unpublished dissertation, University of British Columbia, Vancouver, BC, Canada.

ScienceDaily. (2011, September 15). Scorched earth: The past, present and future of human influences on wildfires. Retrieved September 2011 from www.sciencedaily.com/releases/2011/ 09/110915113756.htm.

Selby, D. (2002). The firm and shaky ground of education for sustainable development. *Journal of Geography in Higher Education*, 30, 351–365.

Senge, P. M. (1990). *The fifth discipline: The art and practice of the learning organization*. New York: Doubleday/Currency.

Shah, A. (2008). *Immigration*, Global issues: Social, political, economic and environmental issues that affect us all. Retrieved November 30, 2009 from www.globalissues.org/article/537/ immigration#IntroductionWorldwideImmigrantsStatistics.

Shields, C. M. (2003a). *Good intentions are not enough: Transformative leadership for communities of difference*. Lanham, MD: Scarecrow.

Shields, C. M. (2003b). Dialogic leadership for social justice: Overcoming pathologies of silence. *Educational Administrative Quarterly*, XI(1), 111–134.

Shields, C. M. (2005). *Bakhtin*. New York: Peter Lang.

Shields, C. M. (2009). *Courageous leadership for transforming schools: Democratizing practice*. Norwood, MA: Christopher-Gordon.

Shields, C. M. (2010). Transformative leadership. In E. Baker, B. McGaw, & P. Peterson (Eds.), *International Encyclopedia of Education* (3rd ed.). Oxford: Elsevier Ltd.

Shields, C. M., Bishop, R., & Mazawi, A. E. (2005). *Pathologizing practices: Deficit thinking in education.* New York: Peter Lang.

Shields, C. M., & Edwards, M. M. (2005). *Dialogue is not just talk: A new ground for educational leadership.* New York: Peter Lang.

Shields, C. M., & Oberg, S. L. (2000). *Year-round schooling: Promises and pitfalls.* Lanham, MD: Technomics.

Shields, C. M., & Warke, A. (2010). The invisible crisis: Connecting schools with homeless families. *Journal of School Leadership, 20*(4), 789–819.

Sidorkin, A. M. (1999). *Beyond discourse: Education, the self, and dialogue.* Albany, NY: SUNY.

Singleton, G. E., & Curtis, W. (2005). *Courageous conversations about race: A field guide for achieving equity in schools.* Thousand Oaks, CA: Corwin.

Smith, D. (2004, February 7). Central Park Zoo's gay penguins ignite debate. *New York Times.* Retrieved April 2011 from http://articles.sfgate.com/2004-02-07/news/17414549_1_bruce-bagemihl-homosexual-gay-penguins.

Smith, D. M. (2000). Social justice revisited. *Environment and Planning, 32,* 1149–1162.

Smith, L. T. (1999). *Decolonising methodologies.* London: Zed Books.

Smith, W. J., Butler-Kisber, L., LaRocque, L. J., Portelli, J. P., Shields, C. M., Sparkes, C. S., et al. (1998). *Student engagement in learning and school life: National project report.* Office of Research on Educational Policy, McGill University.

Starratt, R. J. (1991). Building an ethical school: A theory for practice in educational leadership. *Educational Administration Quarterly, 27*(2), 155–202.

Starratt, R. J. (2005). The spirituality of presence for educational leaders. In C. M. Shields, M. M. Edwards, & A. Sayani (Eds.), *Inspiring practice: Spirituality and educational leadership* (pp. 131–136). Lancaster, PA: Pro Active.

Starratt, R. J. (2011). Preparing transformative educators for the work of leading schools in a multicultural, diverse, and democratic society. In C. M. Shields (Ed.), *Transformative leadership: A reader* (pp. 131–136). New York: Peter Lang.

Strike, K. A. (1999). Can schools be communities? The tension between shared values and inclusion. *Educational Administration Quarterly, 35,* 46–70.

Swartz, D. (1997). *Culture and power: The sociology of Pierre Bourdieu.* Chicago: Chicago University Press.

Taubman, P. (1993). Separate identities, separate lives: Diversity in the curriculum. In L. Castenall & W. Pinar (Eds.), *Understanding curriculum as a racial text: Representing identities and difference in education* (pp. 289–307). New York: SUNY.

Taylor, F. (1912/1990). Scientific management. In D. S. Pugh (Ed.), *Organization theory* (pp. 203–222). London: Penguin.

Taylor, M. E. (2002). *HIV/AIDS, the stats, the virgin cure and infant rape.* Retrieved November 30, 2009 from www.scienceinafrica.co.za/2002/april/virgin.htm.

Terry, R. W. (1993). *Authentic leadership: Courage in action.* San Francisco: Jossey-Bass/Wiley.

Thayer-Bacon, B. J. (2003). *Relational "(e)pistemologies."* New York: Peter Lang.

Theoharis, G. (2007). Social justice educational leaders and resistance: Toward a theory of social justice leadership. *Educational Administration Quarterly, 43*(2), 221–258.

Tienda, M., Alon, S., & Niu, S. X. (2008). *Affirmative action and the Texas top 10% percent admission law: Balancing equity and access to higher education.* Unpublished paper. Retrieved August 2011 from http://theop.princeton.edu/reports/wp/AffirmativeAction_TopTen.pdf.

Tooms, A. (2007). *"Is that a wedding ring?" A look at the panopticons of identity politics lived by gay school administrators serving homophobic communities.* Paper presented at the annual meeting of the American Educational Research Association, Chicago.

Valencia, R. R. (2010). *Dismantling contemporary deficit thinking: Educational thought and practice.* New York: Routledge.

Wagstaff, L., & Fusarelli, L. (1995). Establishing collaborative governance and leadership. In P. Reyes, J. Scribner, & A. Scribner (Eds.) (1999), *Lessons from high-performing Hispanic schools: Creating learning communities* (pp. 19–35). New York: Teachers College Press.

Waithman, M. (2009). *The politics of redistribution and recognition: A retrospective case study of one inner-city school.* Unpublished dissertation, The University of British Columbia.

Weick, K. E. (1996). Fighting fires in educational administration. *Educational Administration Quarterly, 32*(4), 565–578.

Weiner, E. J. (2003). Secretary Paulo Freire and the democratization of power: Toward a theory of transformative leadership. *Educational Philosophy and Theory, 35*(1), 89–106.

West, T. R. (2002). *Signs of struggle.* Albany, NY: SUNY Press.

Wheatley, M. J. (1994). *Leadership and the new science.* San Francisco: Berrett-Koehler.

Wheatley, M. J. (1999). *A simpler way.* San Francisco: Berrett-Koehler.

Wheatley, M. (2000). Good-bye command and control. In M. Fullan (Ed.), *The Jossey-Bass reader on educational leadership.* San Francisco: Jossey-Bass.

Whoriskey, P. (2011, July 26). Wealth gap widens between whites, minorities, report says. *Washington Post.* Retrieved August 26, 2011 from www.washingtonpost.com/business/economy/wealth-gap-widens-between-whites-minorities-report-says/2011/07/25/gIQAjeftZI_story.html.

World Bank (2005). *Income and poverty 2005.* World Bank, United Nations Development Programme. Retrieved November 30 from http://earthtrends.wri.org/pdf_library/da.

Index